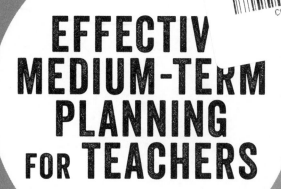

EFFECTIV
MEDIUM-TERM
PLANNING
FOR TEACHERS

SAGE was founded in 1965 by Sara Miller McCune to support the dissemination of usable knowledge by publishing innovative and high-quality research and teaching content. Today, we publish more than 750 journals, including those of more than 300 learned societies, more than 800 new books per year, and a growing range of library products including archives, data, case studies, reports, conference highlights, and video. SAGE remains majority-owned by our founder, and after Sara's lifetime will become owned by a charitable trust that secures our continued independence.

Los Angeles | London | Washington DC | New Delhi | Singapore

EFFECTIVE MEDIUM-TERM PLANNING
FOR TEACHERS

LEE JEROME AND MARCUS BHARGAVA

Los Angeles | London | New Delhi
Singapore | Washington DC

Los Angeles | London | New Delhi
Singapore | Washington DC

SAGE Publications Ltd
1 Oliver's Yard
55 City Road
London EC1Y 1SP

SAGE Publications Inc.
2455 Teller Road
Thousand Oaks, California 91320

SAGE Publications India Pvt Ltd
B 1/I 1 Mohan Cooperative Industrial Area
Mathura Road
New Delhi 110 044

SAGE Publications Asia-Pacific Pte Ltd
3 Church Street
#10-04 Samsung Hub
Singapore 049483

Editor: James Clark
Assistant editor: Rachael Plant
Production editor: Nicola Marshall
Copyeditor: Neil Dowden
Proofreader: Audrey Scriven
Indexer: Martin Hargreaves
Marketing manager: Dilhara Attygalle
Cover design: Naomi Robinson
Typeset by: C&M Digitals (P) Ltd, Chennai, India
Printed in India at Replika Press, Pvt Ltd

Library of Congress Control Number: 2014940523

British Library Cataloguing in Publication data

A catalogue record for this book is available from
the British Library

MIX
Paper from
responsible sources
FSC
www.fsc.org   FSC® C016779

ISBN 978-1-44627-370-8
ISBN 978-1-44627-371-5 (pbk)

At SAGE we take sustainability seriously. Most of our products are printed in the UK using FSC papers and boards.
When we print overseas we ensure sustainable papers are used as measured by the Egmont grading system.
We undertake an annual audit to monitor our sustainability.

CONTENTS

FIGURES

TABLES

ABOUT THE AUTHORS

Lee Jerome taught humanities in secondary schools in London for six years where he planned schemes of work on subjects as diverse as the regeneration of the neighbourhood in Lewisham, tourism in Italy, sociological theory, the history of medicine and a favourite – the life and times of Elvis Presley. He then went to work as Education Director at the Institute for Citizenship where he wrote and edited resources for teachers from Key Stage 1 up to Key Stage 4 and helped the QCA produce exemplar schemes of work and assessment guidance for citizenship teachers. In his work at universities he has planned and taught a variety of modules from first-year undergraduate through to doctoral level, including CPD, PGCE and Master's-level courses for teachers. His own doctoral research examined the journey of a curriculum subject from policy-making through to the pupil experience and reiterated the centrality of teachers in making decisions that shape the way pupils encounter the curriculum. Lee is Lecturer in the School of Education at Queen's University Belfast.

Marcus Bhargava taught history, citizenship, government and politics, and religious education in a central London comprehensive school for eight years. He developed schemes of work on a range of topics including medieval women, the contribution of Asian and Black citizens to post-World War 2 Britain, Nikita Khrushchev's USSR, democracy in the UK and nationalism. He also planned and delivered a major cross-curricular scheme of work with English, history and design and technology colleagues on the theme of crime and punishment. At a national level Marcus co-ordinated a major national curriculum project for the Qualifications and Curriculum Authority, exemplifying good practice in medium-term planning and assessment in citizenship. Marcus regularly lectures and advises on medium-term planning and assessment in universities, schools and to the DfE. Marcus has planned, taught and led a range of undergraduate and teacher education postgraduate programmes in universities and is currently Head of Initial Teacher Education at Goldsmiths, University of London.

PREFACE

Many books about learning and teaching are interesting because they challenge the current set-up of schools. Researchers or theorists develop novel diagnoses of the problems and devise more or less revolutionary prescriptions for how to make schools better – advising teachers on the need to teach emotional intelligence, address multiple intelligences, facilitate experiential learning, or devise community-based learning. We have some sympathy for the idea that schools are not always set up perfectly to promote learning for everyone, but we also wanted to write a book that was pragmatic enough to recognise that schools appear to be remarkably resilient social institutions, and the ways in which they operate are turning out to have some fairly persistent characteristics over time and across countries. Whatever the long-term future for schooling, we guess that for most teachers qualifying to teach now, schools will remain familiar places for the next few decades at least. This is not a book which seeks to realise any revolutionary change in schooling; rather we are seeking to maximise the potential of school-based teaching to secure consistently high-quality learning.

In the debate about how to raise attainment much attention is placed on the quality of individual teachers; thus the notion of 'the outstanding lesson' has emerged as a common discourse among teachers and their managers and inspectors. The characteristics of the outstanding lesson have been described, turned into checklists and teachers have been trained in these criteria and observed to ensure compliance. This is problematic for a number of reasons, but most obviously because teaching never has been, and never will be, the kind of activity where there is one fool-proof recipe for success. This is most obviously true because teachers and their pupils are quirky, individual people with different beliefs, interests, strengths and weaknesses. They also go about the business of teaching and learning in contexts which are vastly different due to the nature of schools, parents, resources, expectations, values, aspirations and economic conditions. We know the readers of this book will be striving to become excellent teachers with the skills to teach great lessons, but we also know that this is only part of the story. We cannot all be outstanding every day, not least because there will be nothing and no one to stand out from, but really because no one is perfect and we need to think about how to prepare teachers for a sustainable career in teaching, rather than a few furious years of frantic activity followed by burn-out and drop-out.

The answer we propose in this book may not be particularly new or revolutionary, but it is peculiarly absent from much discussion about contemporary teaching – the answer is planning. Perhaps because the effective medium-term plan is less evident than the show-stopping classroom performance, or because it is often collaborative rather than individual, the art of medium-term planning seems to have received much less attention than the individual outstanding lesson. And yet we will argue that effective medium-term planning is actually essential in securing consistently high outcomes. Planning helps you to achieve more than the sum of the individual lessons and is the only way to proactively manage your workload so that you can keep on top of the pressures of teaching, marking, reporting and administration.

At the same time as the importance of medium-term planning has become clearer to us, we have begun to worry that it may be a lost art in some departments and schools. Over recent years it has become increasingly possible to buy commercial schemes of work or to download schemes of work from other organisations (most notably in England from the Qualifications and Curriculum Authority until its closure in 2012). The availability of off-the-shelf schemes of work might help to speed up the planning process for teachers, but unless teachers grasp the full logic of those plans, they do not really fulfil the same purpose. On the surface they split up the time, sequence the activities, provide resources and suggest assessment tasks, but the plan is driven by assumptions and connections that may only be implicit, and unless the teacher using it can decipher these underlying ideas, understand them and relate them to their pupils, the teaching over time may lack responsiveness and therefore result in superficial teaching and learning. As Herbert Kohl pointed out a long time ago, in his reflections on teaching in an American 'ghetto' school, 'keeping one lesson ahead of the children is worthless. One must be more than one lesson ahead of the book to explain things to young children and help them understand that their doubts and questions, the things that take them beyond the textbook, are the very essence of learning' (1971: 59).

For student teachers, all this is challenging, not least because the individual lesson is a natural unit of time and activity to focus on. Indeed mastering the skills required to 'get through' a lesson takes a good deal of time and effort for many student teachers. In the early stages of initial teacher education it is not at all uncommon for a student teacher to have no idea what will happen next – teaching is simply one lesson followed by another, with the end of a topic arriving when they have run out of knowledge to teach, when the mentor tells them it's time for a new topic, or when a term finishes. Part of the student teacher's development is to begin to see how lessons and activities connect up to form a bigger, more coherent picture, but initially at least even this is seen as a simply linear, cumulative process, with lessons straightforwardly building one after the other, with each adding a different layer of knowledge. Most initial teacher education courses we have encountered encourage student teachers to undertake some form of medium-term planning to try to ensure they can engage with the notion of medium-term progression but, in our experience, many students struggle to grasp the full potential of planning.

As with most things in teaching, the source of our ideas comes from a number of areas. The first relates to our own practice as teachers and teacher educators. As former secondary school teachers and curriculum leaders, we enjoyed the process of medium-term planning because it simultaneously allowed us to think creatively about planning a learning journey for pupils that could deepen understanding, develop crucial skills and provide new and exciting ways for them to show what they had learned. As teachers we planned schemes of work across several humanities subjects, and we have also created some commercial medium-term plans through creating textbooks and collections of resources and activities for citizenship and history for primary and secondary schools.

Having made the move into university-based initial teacher education, where our focus was on training new teachers, we had to develop strategies to help our student teachers move from lesson by lesson planning towards planning for whole sequences of lessons. Over the years we have supervised, marked and moderated hundreds of student teachers' medium-term plans. As lecturers and external examiners we have spoken to student teachers about medium-term planning across eight institutions, and we have also worked with teachers enrolled on Master's courses to develop their planning. We have also provided school-based professional training for experienced teachers, encouraging them to think beyond narrow approaches to teaching and assessment. Our work at a national level with bodies such as the QCA and more latterly the DfE, where we have been involved in exemplifying good practice in medium-term planning and assessment, has provided us with wider experience of curriculum planning and interpretation.

This book represents our attempts to distil these experiences into a manageable account of what medium-term planning should be and how you can maximise its potential to enhance your practice. Drawing together our own reflections, interviews with experienced colleagues and ideas from the broader literature on learning, we suggest a model you can use to start medium-term planning and to review your practice.

ACKNOWLEDGEMENTS

Our experiences have helped us to develop the five As' model for medium-term planning that we explain in this book. But we also wanted to make sure that this didn't just reflect our own particular views on the issue, so we approached several colleagues to interview them about their perspective on planning. These interviews helped us to test out our ideas to make sure they made sense to experienced practitioners. They have also enabled us to exemplify the five As' processes, by providing us with detailed accounts of teachers' planning. These teachers' accounts are woven throughout Chapters 4–7 and we would like to thank our colleagues for contributing their schemes of work and giving up the time to be interviewed:

Suzanne Bhargava (secondary English). Suzanne has taught in secondary schools in London and is currently school librarian at The London Oratory School.

Dave Dennis (secondary science). Dave has been a science teacher and head of department in secondary schools and worked as an advisory teacher. He is now a lecturer in science education at Goldsmiths, University of London.

Vicky Harris (A level politics). Vicky is an A level politics teacher at City and Islington Sixth Form.

Anna Liddle. Anna is the education officer at the Campaign for Nuclear Disarmament (CND) and talked to us about planning the resource 'Truman on Trial'.

Michael Lowry (secondary history). Michael teaches history at Wallace High School and also contributes to the PGCE programme at Queen's University Belfast.

Andrew McCallum (secondary English). Andrew has taught English in secondary schools, worked as a literacy advisor, managed a PGCE course and is now Co-Director of the English and Media Centre.

Shiv Quinlan (primary). Shiv was a senior teacher in a primary school for several years before she joined London Metropolitan University as a primary PGCE lecturer.

Rubia Siddiqui (secondary maths). Rubia teaches maths in the Walthamstow School for Girls, where she has been a mentor to several maths student teachers.

Alasdair Smith (primary and secondary history). Alasdair has taught in both primary and secondary schools and taught a course for qualified teachers returning to teaching after a career break. He currently teaches at Connaught School for Girls in Leytonstone, East London.

Rebecca Smith (secondary modern languages). Rebecca taught modern languages in secondary schools before moving into initial teacher education. She works at the Institute of Education in London.

Rita White (early years). Rita taught and managed in early years provision for several years and is now a lecturer in early years at Kingston University.

We would also like to thank several of the PGCE student teachers from Queen's University Belfast who have contributed medium-term plans they developed in their university workshops. These are included in Chapter 8 and we are grateful for their permission to use these as they were still 'work in progress' from their five A's planning activities. Thanks to Gemma-Louise Bond, Andrew Chambers, Matthew Hunt, Reuben Johnston, Emma McDonald, Christina McGregor and Emma Mullan.

The idea for writing this book came to us during discussions when we worked together at London Metropolitan University. We wanted to be able to recommend a book to our students on just this topic, but conversations with our local SAGE sales representative confirmed that the book we wanted had yet to be written. We'd like to thank colleagues at SAGE for supporting us, and for providing thoughtful feedback on draft chapters, especially Rachael Plant and James Clark. We'd also like to thank our colleagues at London Met for the years of conversations and collaborative planning that helped us develop the ideas we talk about in this book. Working with them enabled us to try out different approaches for teaching student teachers about planning, but it also exemplified the experience of collaborative planning we recommend in this book. In addition to those we interviewed, we'd like to thank Alan Benson, Victoria Brook, Roussel de Carvalho and Greg Dyer.

We would also like to thank the authors who have agreed to let us reproduce some of their ideas in this book, including: Dale Banham (2000) for his King John learning journey (Figure 5.1); David Barlex (2005) for his design pentagon (Figure 4.2); and Jeffrey Wilhelm and his co-authors (2001) for their representation of scaffolded reading strategies (Figure 5.2).

Finally we have some personal thanks.

From Lee: thanks to Bhavini for being a great colleague with whom to start a career in teaching. We met on our PGCE and became firm friends and collaborators and such was our joint commitment to developing meaningful schemes of work that one of my fondest memories of collaborative planning remains the Key Stage 3 history planning we did on holiday in Spain at the end of our first year of teaching! I would also like to thank Robert, once again, for bearing with the writing process, especially as the deadline approached and encroached on time that could have been spent on other things. Thank you, as ever, for your patience and support.

From Marcus: Thank you to Suzanne for her multi-dimensional support for this book; from talking through ideas, proofreading, cups of tea, childcare through to her own professional contribution! To my boys Dhari, Ivo and Zeo, thank you for the smiles and hilarious distractions throughout the writing process. I've had the pleasure of working with some fantastic teachers over the last 16 years on medium-term planning who are sources of the ideas that appear here. Finally, thank you to my co-writer Lee for being an inspirational colleague, line-manager, mentor and friend. This book couldn't have happened without his hard work and dedication throughout the process.

SAGE would like to thank the following lecturers whose feedback helped shape the book proposal at an early stage:

- William Evans, Manchester Metropolitan University
- Alison Lesurf, Leeds Trinity University
- Elizabeth McCrum, University of Reading
- Carmen Mohamed, University of Nottingham
- Julia O'Kelly, University of Chichester
- Mary Watt, Middlesex University
- Nigel Zanker, Loughborough University

CHAPTER 1

MEDIUM-TERM PLANNING AS THE ROUTE TO OUTSTANDING LEARNING

By the end of this chapter you will be able to:

- define what is meant by medium-term planning and schemes of work;
- explain how medium-term planning embodies important concepts from learning theories;
- assess the argument about the importance of medium-term planning.

In this chapter we explain what we mean when we talk about medium-term planning and schemes of work and why this is connected to effective learning. We consider the relationship between learning theories and teachers' planning and argue that, while *outstanding lessons* are often the focus of initial teacher education and ongoing inspection and appraisal, these cannot offer a reliable or sustainable route to securing *outstanding learning* every day. What can help you to achieve this is high-quality medium-term planning.

What do we mean by medium-term planning?

It was interesting to us when we started researching this book to discover that our two main terms, which we had always understood to be everyday terms among teachers, did not appear in most educational databases. We found information listed under all sorts of other labels including instructional design, learning sequences or instructional sequences. Most of these terms were unfamiliar to us as teachers and so we became aware that there is a discrepancy between what writers and educational researchers say about the topic and how teachers in school talk about it. This is surprising because we are discussing one of the most fundamental building blocks of teaching, and a universal aspect of teachers' practice. It is also surprising because this really is not a very complex idea to grasp. Teachers plan in the short, medium and long term. We might quibble over where the line is drawn between each of these but the principle is fairly clear. Short-term planning is the practical daily planning that helps us to manage our time and the learning activities through the day. For most student teachers, short-term planning is usually described as lesson planning, although teachers in early years contexts may think about activity plans or day plans. When we talk about long-term planning, we mean the overall curriculum structure; typically this might be planned in terms of a whole Key Stage or exam course. The long-term plan chunks up the years ahead to make sure there is an agreed running order and that we can cover everything that needs to be covered in the time available to us. So a long-term plan for an A level course is simply the broad structure which sets out where each of the compulsory units will be taught over the two years of the typical A level course, and a Key Stage 3 plan in history might show how many weeks will be spent on each period of time or topic.

Medium-term planning is the process by which teachers set out the 'terrain maps of intellectual development to be visited when students progress from one level of capability to another' (Gagné and Briggs, 1974: 15). Simply put, the medium-term plan, or scheme of work, is the unit of planning where teachers describe their intended teaching and learning journey for a whole topic. The precise period of the medium term may well be a movable feast: for the early years teacher it might regularly be a fortnight block, where a topic provides the theme for the period; for a secondary history teacher the medium term may well be half a term with one lesson per week; while the English teacher, who may see their students three to four times a week, may plan in two- or three-week blocks. The length of time is less important than the attempt to provide some coherent account of how the teacher and students will tackle a chunk of learning, whether that chunk is transport, electricity or the causes of the First World War. The key assumption is that there is some conceptual coherence underpinning the decision to consider the content as a single entity – a scheme of work.

The idea of a map, introduced by Gagné and Briggs, is a useful one and helps to explain why simply writing a series of lesson plans is unlikely to be as effective as writing a medium-term plan. If we think about taking a group of children on a hike for an activity week, we would naturally think first about our start and end points, and these would be governed by what we know about the nature of the terrain, the fitness levels of the children, the weather forecast and other relevant factors. We wouldn't simply start at the starting point, walk as far as we could and then stop at 3.30 p.m. on the last day and see where we were. We wouldn't be allowed to do this on a hike because no headteacher would sign off a risk assessment that simply declared that as the journey plan. And yet some teachers, and some students teachers especially, set off in just this way on their regular learning journey in the classroom. They may start with a lesson on the topic in hand, plan the next lesson once the first one has finished, and continue like this until the time runs out and then set a test to check what the class learned along the way. The trouble with this is that the steps may or may not have led the pupils somewhere interesting, and that is too big a risk to take with someone else's learning. The medium-term plan therefore is the mechanism by which teachers attempt to plan a journey from where the learners are currently to where the teacher would like them to be. Once these two points are established the teacher can work out the details of the journey. There is no reason to plan every step as an equal stage, just as with a countryside hike we might accept that the going will be slower on some days than others depending on the weather, the terrain and who is travelling in our party. Similarly, with a scheme of work, the learning steps may be slower or faster, depending on the level of difficulty in the material, learners' prior level of attainment, or their familiarity with this kind of learning.

The challenge is to strike the right balance between planning in advance and responding to information as we proceed. On a walk if we discover that a bridge is down, or a road is flooded, we have to change our plans. Similarly, if we plan for a section of a scheme of work to take a lesson, but we do not complete that part of the learning journey successfully, we have to adapt our plan to accommodate that fact; we cannot just hope for the best and carry on, ignoring the fact that we have left some people behind. We may have to spend another lesson working through the same material, but in a slightly different way, or simply just take a bit longer to complete all the stages planned. Just as with a real journey, we may have to revise our planned ultimate destination if we encounter too many problems along the way, or we may have to plan to take a bit longer to get to the planned destination. But that's alright. We still get somewhere meaningful if we keep our plans sensibly under review.

So the scheme of work is always a best guess at a journey. It enables us to organise ourselves, our resources and our classes, and gives us a structure to make sure that the steps we take in individual lessons are likely to lead us somewhere worthwhile. A good scheme of work is powerful because it structures the teacher's and the learners' efforts so they can achieve something substantial. A good scheme of work is more than simply the sum of its parts, which is to say it is not simply a file into which teachers deposit a string of related lesson plans. Rather it is the document from which the teacher derives the lesson plans. Teachers should not plan lessons until they have planned their scheme of work. This is an axiom of effective planning. First, we define the overall learning journey, then we work out the individual steps along the way. It follows from this that a string of ten individually outstanding lessons might not add up to anything more than ten bits of learning. It requires forward planning to ensure that these ten experiences add up to one big coherent chunk of learning. Before we explore this thought in a little more detail, we want to say something about how this view of planning reflects our view of learning.

The link between planning and learning

This is not a book about learning theory – there are plenty of those aimed at student teachers. But it is a book about planning to enhance learning so it makes sense to say something about the ideas that underpin our approach to planning. Several of the contributors to Seels's (1995) book on instructional design note that almost everyone in the world of education now is a constructivist, and most of us are social-constructivists, although they also note that the practice in many classrooms is still recognisable from the era when people were happy to describe themselves as behaviourists. This is simply to point out that fashions in talking about education tend to change faster than the reality of teaching practice. Seels's book reveals a slightly angst-ridden debate between instructional designers (people who specialise in planning learning) about the extent to which their profession has kept up with these changes, but it seems to us that whether one reads the new material on instructional design, which explicitly discusses constructivist principles, or whether one focuses on the older material, which is more rooted in behaviourist models, the substance of what they advocate is largely the same. The rationale may change, but the advice on effective planning remains largely unchanged. Perhaps that just reflects the fact that teachers have always taught, and learners have always managed to learn, regardless of the dominant academic explanations. Good teachers, we suspect, have always adhered to the principles we outline in this book, regardless of the explanations they may have offered. Here, then, are a few principles related to our current understanding of how learning happens and what teachers should probably know about the process. (For a comprehensive and insightful discussion see Illeris, 2007.) For each of the principles we try to make some basic points about the implications for the planning process.

Principle 1: Intelligence is not fixed

There was a time when IQ was accepted by most people as a natural, heritable, unified and measurable characteristic of individuals. The history of IQ is bound up with attempts to divide people into categories, determine who can learn and who cannot, and therefore to make decisions about who should have access to learning opportunities and who should not. It is also bound up with some rather odious ideas about scientific racism and eugenics, as Kamin illustrated:

> The IQ test has served as an instrument of oppression against the poor – dressed in the trappings of science rather than politics ... The poor, the foreign-born and racial minorities were shown to be stupid. They were shown to have been born that way. The under-privileged are today demonstrated to be ineducable, a message as soothing to the public purse as to the public conscience. (1974: 15–16)

While most people working in schools would dismiss these implications, many still operate with some of the underlying concepts – that intelligence is a single, measurable, unchangeable thing. Except that we might not call it intelligence now, we might do as the headteacher in Gillborn and Youdell's study did, and talk about standardised tests as 'indicators of ability, whatever that means. And obviously indicators of some sort of general ability rather than just sort of subject-specific ability ... You can't give someone ability, can you?' (Gillborn and Youdell, 2000). In essence this is the old IQ belief with the terminology removed and replaced with the word 'ability'.

Meanwhile, the academic literature has blown several holes in the underpinning concept of IQ. Most famously, Howard Gardner (2011) has argued that intelligence is not just a single thing, but is actually a number of different things, and so he has described musical, visual, kinaesthetic, intrapersonal, interpersonal, naturalist and spiritual intelligence in addition to the more established logico-mathematical and linguistic intelligences that tend to be measured in IQ tests. Gardner's work has proved popular with many teachers because it opens up the possibility that everyone can be (differently) intelligent. However, in John White's (1998) critical discussion of IQ and of Gardner's response, he argues that once you have dismissed the notion that IQ is one thing, it is unnecessarily restrictive to settle for the idea that it is eight, nine or ten things. Instead he suggests that we could just accept the idea that intelligence is variable and multiple, or as White puts it (summarizing Ryle, 1949): 'Intelligent action has to do with the flexible adaptation of means in the pursuit of one's goals and there are as many types of human intelligence as there are types of human goal.' (White, 2008: 612)

We adopt this view not only because it seems to us a satisfactory intellectual response to the debate about intelligence but also because it resonates with our beliefs about teaching, which are ultimately based on an essential optimism about human nature and our capacity to learn and therefore be changed. As Sternberg argued: 'The fact that Billy and Jimmy have different IQs now tells us something about differences in what they now do. It does not tell us anything fixed about what ultimately they will be able to do' (1998: 11). That means for us as planners of learning for Billy and Jimmy, or whoever else happens to be in our class, if we can engage them in the material we prepare, find sufficient examples of interest to them, respond sensitively to their learning needs and plan smartly to give them chances to experience success as learners, they will stand every chance of progressing. Part of the solution lies in how we establish relationships with our pupils, our behaviour in class and our minute-by-minute responses to them, but part of the solution also lies in plotting a realistic journey for them from where they are to where we would like them to be. Part of the solution therefore lies in the construction of a good medium-term plan, which optimistically plots realistic progress rather than placing a false ceiling on expectations or unthinkingly setting unrealistic expectations which generate failure.

Principle 2: Learning is a process between what is known and what is to be known

Constructivist theory alerts us to the fact that individual learners are all busy building knowledge inside their own heads. It stands to reason that whatever new learning takes place builds upon existing foundations. Piaget described this construction as a series of schemas, in which learners process, code and store their representation of the world. Learning new facts and ideas involves a process of accommodation or assimilation in which learners take the new information and either fit it to their existing schemas, or adapt their schemas to accommodate the new information. In this way knowledge is being built and that building is constantly growing and sometimes even changing shape. Illeris (2007) captured this by adding a third type of learning, which he called transformational, holding out the prospect that it is possible for humans to undergo more or less complete changes in world-view by revising many schema simultaneously. We can think of this like a filing system: most of the time we simply drop new information into existing files, but every now and again we realise the old files don't really work anymore and have to re-label and re-organise the files, and occasionally someone might decide to completely change everything and go paperless, transforming the whole filing system. This clearly has implications for teaching in the moment, and for medium-term planning.

A good medium-term plan will operate at multiple levels, incorporating facts, concepts and skills because these relate to the complex ways in which we learn and construct the schemas which represent that learning. A medium-term plan should also embed opportunities for surfacing prior learning and prior mis-learning, such as common misconceptions, in relation to the topic so that teachers make time for learners to work through the processes of encountering, processing and relating new information to existing mental representations of the world. Otherwise, new learning may not connect securely to prior learning, misconceptions may persist alongside some contradictory book learning of facts and rules, and the deep structures of knowledge inside the learner's mind may remain flawed.

The gap between what the learner can do now, unaided, and what they can do with the help of a more knowledgeable other, was characterised by Vygotsky (1978) as the Zone of Proximal Development (ZPD). Teachers can do many things to help students to bridge that gap, and eventually, having practised a new skill or acquired a new level of understanding with help, the learner will be able to perform at this more advanced level independently. This again clearly requires some structured plans for the duration of the learning. The teacher might start with modelling an activity and collaborative work to replicate their demonstration, move on to providing some structure for pupils but withdraw themselves from the process, and eventually provide opportunities for pupils to practise their new learning independently. This process has been described by Bruner (1978) as scaffolding, for obvious reasons, as the teacher provides the scaffolding to support the learner, but then removes it gradually to encourage autonomy once the new knowledge has been built. The main point from the perspective of planning is that we would not normally expect to scaffold and cross the ZPD in a lesson; this generally takes place over a longer timescale, and so when we are designing a medium-term plan, these broad issues should underpin our planning. This will concern our changing role in the situation, the kind of resources required to support learners at different stages, and the kind of evaluative judgements we make along the way.

Principle 3: Learning is a social process

If we only think about how children construct knowledge in their minds this can lead us to an excessively individualistic view of children as independent learning units who achieve different levels of understanding at various stages of their life. In a nutshell, this is why people ultimately found Piaget's work a little limiting, because his focus was on how individuals build knowledge as a form of adaptation to their environments, but teachers were not really central to this process, which rather complicates the idea of a school (Shayer, 2003). Vygotsky's work, mentioned above, emphasised how learning takes place as a result of interactions between the learner and a 'more knowledge-able other' (MKO). This social dimension to learning is important because it emphasises the role of the teacher in the process, but it also emphasises how important it is to give learners opportunities to work with others, exploring different points of view, practising using new knowledge or skills in new contexts and gaining feedback on this process.

The social constructivist model of learning firmly drives the nail into the coffin of the old 'transmission' model of teaching, in which it is assumed that information can simply be decanted from expert heads into novice heads through the power of clear communication. This is sometimes characterised as the 'mugs and jugs' model of teaching, in which empty mugs represent children's empty heads and the full jug represents the teacher's full mind. With some careful aiming and preparation of the way, the contents of the jug can be dispensed in small portions to the waiting empty vessels. What the social constructivist model of learning makes clear is that there are no empty heads and there is no trouble-free method for decanting stuff into other people's minds. At every stage new information is being actively interpreted, translated and made sense of. A medium-term plan needs to reflect the reality of this process and build in opportunities for meaningful and focused social interactions. A teacher under pressure to cover an aspect of the curriculum cannot simply default to 'telling' the information rather than teaching it, because these are not the same thing.

Having said that, we do have to be careful not to overstate the point. Clearly learners *can* learn simply by listening (and individually processing) new information. Otherwise, lectures would not work, and clearly they do (sometimes for some people). The point we want to make is that we should not assume because the teacher has said something clearly and accessibly that it has been received in its entirety, understood completely, remembered accurately and is available for recall and subsequent use in a relevant situation. It may be, but the chances are that for most people in most situations it will not. Some teachers continue to relay a lot of information from the front of their classrooms, but we cannot safely assume that anyone has learned anything as a consequence. And so planning social interactions in which the new knowledge is used, remembered, re-used in different contexts, discussed, corrected and adapted is much more likely to result in meaningful learning. It is also much more likely to require careful thought over time and is exceedingly unlikely to emerge spontaneously, no matter how good an orator you are, or how erudite and entertaining a speaker you are when talking about your favourite topics.

Principle 4: Talk is powerful

This principle is really just a sub-section of the previous discussion. It follows that if social interaction is important, then talk is a potentially powerful strategy for teachers to harness in the classroom. Talk is simply the medium through which most of our social interaction is conducted. It is also the most accessible way we, as teachers, can understand what a student is thinking. In this sense, talk functions as externalised thought, and therefore teachers should treat talk very seriously in their planning. Teachers should not use group work or talk simply to add variety to a lesson (although that is certainly one benefit). Talk should be used deliberately when we are asking students to process difficult information, practise new skills or manipulate complex concepts, because it is the easiest way for us to be able to monitor what is happening and what sense students are making of the learning. It is also important because talking requires us to distil fuzzy and often inchoate thoughts into some concrete attempt to make sense. Talk is relatively low risk as a rehearsal strategy for new thinking, and it is much easier to adapt and refine one's thinking through conversation than it is to craft an essay, hand it in, get feedback, and then review what one thought and re-write the essay (Coultas, 2007). For this reason talk can be planned into medium-term plans at key strategic points to help explore complex higher-level thinking and to prepare for subsequent individual work.

Principle 5: Learning can be a metacognitive process

As Piaget pointed out, in many ways learning is just one natural part of how living creatures adapt to their environment. But one of the great features of human learning in particular is that we can also be aware of the process by which we learn. We can learn something and simultaneously think about how we are learning that thing and as a consequence of that thought process we can learn about learning. This is metacognition, and in many schools it is known simply as learning to learn. There are a variety of models to help us articulate the processes involved in learning, but the underlying idea is simply that teachers can both teach the topic at hand and teach how to learn more generally. In its most simple form, we might ask pupils when we are going to conduct a whole-class debate in PSHE to explain why a debate is a useful strategy for thinking about complex and controversial issues, or in history why it is helpful to prepare to write an interpretation of a historical event. In science we might ask pupils to remind themselves of a test that was useful to test gases collected during previous experiments. These are strategies we could employ (and re-deploy) within a particular subject discipline and revisiting these and talking about them is useful to help pupils understand the nature of the subject they are studying and the kinds of learning procedures employed within those subjects. Some models look for more general ways to characterise learning; for example Guy Claxton's very popular model focuses on the four Rs of resilience, resourcefulness, reflectiveness and reciprocity (Claxton et al., 2011). Teachers across the school can use these ideas to help pupils understand the underlying capacities they develop across all their learning, and therefore (hopefully) they can devise strategies to get over problems, be more confident in their capacity to learn and more successful as learners.

There is always an element of artifice about any model that purports to universally describe the valuable characteristics of learning for everyone in all situations in four words that all just happen to start with the letter 'r'. We are not seeking to advocate one model over another, but the principle for us in terms of medium-term planning is simply that if we want to harness this potential for pupils to learn about learning and be conscious of how learning does (and does not) take place, then this is only conceivable as a feature of medium-term planning. It is simply not feasible to imagine this arising spontaneously *and* in a coherent manner in off-the-cuff moments of reflection and discussion. The whole point of such an approach is that it forms a regular feature of the learning experience, and for this to happen, it has to be planned. And if you are going to plan it, then it has to be a feature of the medium-term plan.

Principle 6: People learn in different ways

On one level this is so obvious that we are almost embarrassed to point it out. We do so simply because this is not always so evident from observing how people teach, especially in the early stages of becoming a teacher. Although we all know as an abstract bit of knowledge that people must learn in different ways, it is very common at the beginning of a teaching career to default to a style of teaching which works for a limited range of learning styles or preferences. At a very basic level the medium-term plan is a useful mechanism for checking whether you are defaulting to a similar kind of lesson, or steering clear of certain types of learning activities. If the plan summarises the learning journey over 12 lessons, it will be evident whether there is a variety of activities across those lessons or whether the whole scheme of work is dominated by a narrow range.

As with our discussion of learning to learn models and multiple intelligences above, we are not going to advocate any particular model for thinking about learning styles and preferences. Some of these models are simple, such as the idea that learners are predominantly visual, auditory or kinaesthetic learners (VAK). Some of them are more complicated, such as Dunn and Dunn's (Dunn, 1990) exhaustive (and exhausting) classification which includes a whole variety of learning preferences across five domains of learning, including whether you prefer large or small spaces, hot or cold environments, whether you are impulsive or reflective, global or analytic and so on (our rough calculations estimate there may about 50,000 combinations across all their categories). Personally, when we worked together as PGCE tutors, we sought to eradicate all talk of VAK from our courses because this became a lazy shorthand way to simplify the complexity of learning and to label students. It is also simply mistaken to use these terms to describe learning preferences when they are actually just modes of communication. Almost all the children you teach in a mainstream school can happily process information provided to them through talking, looking or doing and they will do this naturally throughout the day. To believe that a child cannot learn easily via one or more of these modes of communication is problematic to say the least, as the following quotation from a pupil illustrates: 'I learned that I was a low auditory, kinaesthetic learner. So there's no point in me reading a book or listening to anyone for more than a few minutes' (Abrams, 2005). We have always assumed that this student was being ironic, but either way, it shows what a dangerous over-simplification such models can be – either a waste of time, or a waste of potential. Frank Coffield has produced a comprehensive critique of many popular learning style models and shows them all to be flawed (Coffield et al., 2004). The point is really just to acknowledge, as we have already mentioned above, that a teacher should not assume that the way they prefer to learn about a topic is necessarily going to be the optimal way for all their pupils to learn, and therefore employing a range of types of learning activity across a sequence of lessons is likely to be better than sticking with a very limited repertoire.

Principle 7: Learning is often related to experience

There is a whole branch of learning theory which is concerned with the relationship between learning and experience. Following on from the discussion about the need for variety across a scheme of work, one might say that learning through the experience of actually doing something is just one of the learning strategies teachers should be incorporating into their medium-term plans. We would endorse this view, but we also want to point out that there are some broad ideas in the literature about experiential learning that might help clarify how this could be planned. The first point to make is that while the learning and the experience are related we must also remember that they are separate. Just because a group of children has planned and participated in a trip to the zoo, there is no guarantee about what they have learned from this experience. Some will have learned that giraffes are taller than lions, others that you need to conduct a risk analysis ahead of a school trip and others that you should not sit next a child on the coach who is prone to travel sickness. This might all be genuine learning and some of it may be more or less relevant to the curriculum their teacher is following or the aims of the project they have planned. In order to make sense of this mass of possibilities, advocates of experiential learning have considered how to move from the experience itself to the learning that may be derived from it. This need not be difficult, but is worth spending time on, and it may consist of nothing more than providing time and a structure for learners to reflect on the experience, interrogate it for meaning, discuss it and draw some conclusions about it. If we want the learning to be linked to a theme in our planning, then we need to incorporate reflection on that link in our preparation for the experience itself and the follow-up activities.

The famous experiential learning cycle (Kolb and Fry, 1975) summarises this in four phases, which we simplify as: (1) have an experience, (2) reflect on that experience, (3) identify what you learned from the experience, (4) plan to use the learning and then (1) engage in another experience. This seems to us a fairly accurate characterisation of how most teacher education programmes work, with student teachers planning learning activities, teaching them, evaluating their effectiveness, target setting and using these targets in the next plan, and then teaching again. Clearly the whole process, if it is going to be used to its full potential, needs to be planned over time, to build in opportunities for these stages to be worked through and re-visited if possible.

Conclusion

In this chapter we have explained why medium-term planning is important as the framework in which you work out the planned learning journey for your class. Deep, significant learning takes time, it does not generally happen in minutes, but builds over hours, weeks and months. It seems odd then that so much of a student teacher's initial experience of planning for learning should be focused at the level of the lesson plan, where the unit of time is seconds and minutes. Clearly we need to plan for lessons to be organised, coherent and purposeful, but it is equally clear that teachers must also have a bigger picture in place which describes how the learning will unfold over the longer timescale. Having set out our case for why medium-term planning should be an integral part of teachers' work, we outline some of the principles of effective medium-term planning in Chapter 3. Before we get there though, we take a slight diversion to spell out some of the reasons why medium-term planning doesn't always get the attention it deserves in schools and why it is more difficult than it may at first appear.

Further reading

Illeris, K. (2007) *How We Learn: Learning and Non-Learning in School and Beyond*, Abingdon: Routledge.
This is a very good introductory text which synthesises a variety of explanations of learning into a coherent model. Unusually for such a book, it addresses the vexed question of why learning doesn't happen, as well as how we learn when things go smoothly.

Shayer, M. (2003) Not just Piaget; not just Vygotsky, and certainly not Vygotsky as *alternative* to Piaget, *Learning and Instruction*, 13(5), 465–485.
This article illustrates the valuable contributions of both influential theorists, and discourages a simple 'one or the other' approach.

CHAPTER 2

THE CHALLENGES OF MEDIUM-TERM PLANNING

By the end of this chapter you will be able to:

- understand the importance of *subject knowledge for teaching* for effective planning;
- understand the different conceptual levels of subject knowledge that teachers must use to plan effectively;
- identify obstacles to effective medium-term planning in the contexts where you are teaching;
- review a medium-term plan to identify specific learning intentions.

In this chapter we consider some of the reasons why effective medium-term planning is difficult and why teachers, especially student teachers, sometimes fail to plan effectively. We start by considering subject knowledge as a key area that causes problems for many, and discuss this in relation to the concept of *subject knowledge for teaching*. We also discuss some of the problems of planning for deep learning in a context where there is often pressure to 'cover' substantial areas of subject content. Here we discuss the perceived tension between breadth and depth. Finally we discuss the 'audit culture' that has had an effect on teachers and in some cases can encourage a superficial approach to planning.

Why medium-term planning is more difficult than it may appear

Subject knowledge and behaviour management often loom large in the minds of student teachers. Phillips (2002) discusses this as a part of the early 'myth making' of teaching, where your sense of the challenges of teaching is informed by an incomplete understanding of the nature of learning and teaching. When visiting schools and sitting in on classes, if you have not taught extensively, you may observe two main things to make you worry. First, you might see the myriad forms of poor behaviour children and adolescents are capable of, including low-level non-compliance with tasks, off-task chatter, poor punctuality, incomplete equipment, missing homework, arguments, failure to listen, failure to follow instructions, shouting out, moving around, answering back, making silly responses to raise a laugh, asking silly questions and occasionally worse. Not surprisingly you might start to worry about how you will cope under this deluge of distractions and challenges to your authority. Second, you will probably witness the class teacher displaying mastery of the subject being taught, delivering clear summaries of potentially complex content, adjusting the language to suit the needs of the children, and of course responding to questions throughout the lesson, sometimes answering questions directly, at other times asking subtle questions of the pupils to elicit their understanding, and also correcting misunderstandings where they arise. It wouldn't be surprising if you, as a relative newcomer unfamiliar with the syllabus or curriculum, should find that you are unable to respond to those questions, miss the errors and have no idea what relevant questions will help the learners to make progress. As a consequence the myth develops that good teachers are simply good at controlling behaviour sufficiently so that they can effectively communicate their voluminous subject knowledge to pupils.

Given what we had to say about our view of teaching and learning in Chapter 1, you will not be surprised to hear that this myth quickly gives way to a more nuanced set of worries, covering a whole host of areas of which you may be unaware. Hence, as new teachers observe, plan, teach and spend more time with children and young people, those two big worries dissipate, or at least become less significant against the more realistic backdrop of other concerns such as those relating to inclusion, assessment, progression, whole school initiatives, collegial working, accountability mechanisms, report writing, parental expectations, pastoral issues, exhaustion and time management. New teachers are often overheard comforting themselves with the fact that behaviour is usually better than they feared, and as long as they keep one step ahead of the students, they can learn the content as they proceed. In English, perhaps the teachers will aim to be one chapter ahead of the students as they read a play, while in science, perhaps just a couple of pages of the textbook will be enough to cope with the subject knowledge demands of a lesson and plan some links between lessons.

This may work as a coping strategy but it is insufficient to inform effective medium-term planning. While new teachers may be able to 'get by' with a just-in-time approach to reading around the subject, this is inevitably disempowering in the medium term because it means you can only teach within frameworks that have been established by others. As Sam Wineburg put it:

> As teachers, we often cede the responsibility for thinking through these questions to others – textbook writers, district personnel, test directors, or any other group designated as experts. In doing so, we become spectators to the knowledge creation process, outsiders who bob up and down in response to others' actions. Unless teachers take up these questions and begin to wrestle with issues of knowledge, students will smell passivity and feel small in their own ability to create new knowledge. The discussion of what knowledge matters most is one in which all of us must take a part ... Each domain – math, history, literature, geography, physics – has its own conceptual structure and its own distinctive way of knowing. (1997: 255)

The person who designed a scheme of work, or textbook, may well have used their deep subject knowledge to make important links between lessons and to embed a subtle model of progression within a sequence of lessons, but if, as the class teacher, you do not share this knowledge or fail to understand the reasoning that informed the sequence of lessons, you will be at a disadvantage when it comes to teaching it. While the lessons may proceed more or less smoothly and the children may complete the work, you may not be able to draw out the deeper conceptual understanding that should underpin progression across the whole plan, and therefore connections and challenges are likely to be missed. A teacher may survive in the classroom by keeping one step ahead of the children but they and their pupils will not flourish.

The real problem with subject knowledge

The early career myth of subject knowledge is that teachers know everything about their subject. In fact that is far from true; what they do know is a lot of stuff that non-teachers do not know, which is a very different thing. A model of *subject knowledge for teaching* from the Training and Development Agency for Schools (TDA, 2007) helps to clarify what we mean by this by dividing subject knowledge into three categories: (i) subject knowledge per se, (ii) subject pedagogy and (iii) knowledge about pupils' development in the subject (see Figure 2.1). Subject knowledge per se is probably what most entrants to the profession are worried about and simply means one's level of knowledge about the content being taught, whether that be *Macbeth*, quadratic equations or the formation of fjords. There is a wealth of knowledge out there in the world about these topics and teachers need to know at least some of it in order to teach accurately. Subject pedagogy refers to the traditions within their subject/age phase that help teachers to teach that content effectively; this might include the judicious use of film and drama when teaching *Macbeth* in English, the appropriate way to present the method for solving simultaneous equations in maths, or the appropriate comparisons to draw between fjords and other natural features in geography. The third area is pupils' development and whilst part of this includes knowledge about how children learn in general, it also includes the teacher's informed ideas about how children make progress in relation to particular concepts within their subject and what common misconceptions arise. It does not matter how much time a teacher spends learning the first type of knowledge, their teaching will always be of limited success unless they also nurture the other forms of subject knowledge. This view of subject knowledge represents a challenge to all teachers, but especially primary school teachers, where they are commonly teaching across all subjects.

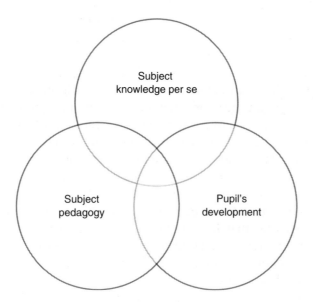

Figure 2.1 TDA's model of subject knowledge for teaching

In our information age, which is marked by ready internet access to most of the knowledge children are likely to need, one sometimes hears calls for teachers to reconceptualise their work to focus on general thinking skills instead of building foundational knowledge. In his book *What's the Point of School?* Guy

Claxton plays with this notion by arguing that: 'Being adept at gaining and using knowledge is what counts; not having a vast store of "general knowledge", just in case. (It's better and easier to google it these days.) "Knowledge" is not what's true; it's what helps. Knowledge is what you use to get things done' (2008: 77). We will return to Claxton shortly, but at this stage we want to argue that the debate about subject knowledge per se cannot simply be left there. As Michael Gove, then Secretary of State for Education, pointed out:

> Unless you have knowledge – historical, cultural, scientific, mathematic – all you will find on Google is babble. And unless that knowledge is imparted at school, in a structured way, by gifted professionals, through subject disciplines – then many children will never, ever, find it. No matter how long they search across the borderless lands of the internet. (Gove, 2013)

This commitment to subjects and to the structure of knowledge can lead you one of two ways. In one direction E. D. Hirsch has attempted to codify subject knowledge by listing all the important knowledge children are deemed to need. Hirsch (1987) provides a list of thousands of concepts, which he takes to constitute what every literate American should know (it starts: Aaron, Hank; Abandon hope, all ye who enter here; abbreviation; Aberdeen; abolitionism; abominable snowman; abortion …). There is a debate about whether this Core Knowledge Curriculum constitutes a Gradgrindian trudge through self-evidently important facts, or whether 'it is about acquiring knowledge to make analysis and critical thinking possible' (Green, 2013). David Green, for example, claims the Core Knowledge Curriculum is misunderstood and misrepresented in England and that learning this essential core will be particularly empowering for those children who lack the cultural literacy others take for granted. However, there is a distinction to be made here between the general proposition that knowledge is important, and the specific assertion that one can describe that knowledge as a list of facts to be learned. The second response avoids the charge of being overly simplistic and instead of listing what constitutes essential knowledge, it seeks to analyse subject knowledge more thoroughly.

In this second tradition, Shulman (1986) established an influential model for thinking about teachers' subject knowledge. There are some similarities between his three-part model and the TDA one discussed above – he also wrote about (i) subject content knowledge (subject knowledge per se), (ii) pedagogical content knowledge and (iii) curricular knowledge. But, in relation to subject matter per se, he argued that teachers need to move beyond simply knowing about the facts and concepts in a subject area and understand the structures of the subject in terms of:

(1) the substantive structures, the principles and concepts which organise the knowledge in this domain;
(2) the syntactic structures, the rules by which knowledge is established, the procedures for establishing validity, what we might call the epistemological foundations for the domain.

While he does not make the connection himself, this resonates with Bruner's arguments in *The Process of Education* in which he argued that 'the continuity of learning that is produced by the ... transfer of principles, is dependent upon mastery of the structure of the subject matter' (1960/1977: 18). In this tradition, then, the real intellectual demand for teachers in terms of subject knowledge is not the relatively superficial knowledge we gain to deal with the content of lessons (or that kind of knowledge we tend to come across through an internet search); it relates to a deep knowledge of the subject. In our experience working with postgraduate students on teacher education courses, the extent to which university courses prepare undergraduates with this deep subject knowledge is often limited. It is common to meet science or history graduates with good degrees, who may well have lots of subject knowledge per se but who do not have much knowledge about their subject. The scientist with an impressive grasp of genetics may be unable to articulate how science works as a form of knowledge; the historian with an in-depth knowledge about the Cold War may not know what distinguishes history as an endeavour from other subjects. This is important according to Shulman because this syntactic structural knowledge is one of the dimensions we should know well enough to teach. It is also important because one of the reasons for maintaining a curriculum divided into subjects is that these subjects represent established ways of encountering, explaining and coming to know the world. Thinking about the genetic modification of crops scientifically is different from thinking about it economically; just as approaching the analysis of a building aesthetically is different from approaching it as an engineering problem. While a full understanding might require an individual to balance these perspectives, we need to understand the distinctive contribution offered by each of them.

For Bruner, the deep structure of a taught subject is important for several practical reasons:

(1) Understanding the fundamentals makes a subject more comprehensible.
(2) Placing new knowledge into a structured pattern helps to secure memorisation.
(3) Understanding the fundamentals helps learners to identify the relevance of existing knowledge to new situations.
(4) Revisiting core concepts and subject structure helps to ensure learning is progressive over time, and minimises the risk that new learning simply replaces earlier learning.

Ultimately Bruner argued that teachers must strive to make learning motivating and significant and one of the most effective ways to achieve this is to render it 'worth learning'. This is partly about making it relevant, but is also about showing how individual lessons contribute to the broader task of engaging with the world, making generalisations and interpreting complexity in order to achieve understanding. It is this commitment to helping young people to understand the structure of knowledge that leads him to proclaim: 'The foundations of any subject may be taught to anybody at any age in some form ... To be in command of these basic ideas, to use them effectively, requires a continual deepening of one's understanding of them that comes from learning to use them in progressively more complex forms' (Bruner, 1960/1977: 12–13). And this in turn leads to the concept of the 'spiral curriculum' in which learners return not to the same content repeatedly, but to the same concepts and principles with new facts and cases, to ensure progression and consolidation and to train the mind in the nature of the subject.

The work of Shulman and Bruner helps us to articulate a different curricular response from that promoted in the Core Knowledge Curriculum model. One can accept the general proposition that knowledge is important without being condemned to teach endless Hirsch-style lists of facts and memorisation tests. As Bruner argued, setting out to teach all the ideas and concepts you might ever need to use in adult life is likely to be the most difficult route to teaching and learning, not least because the lack of structure will limit learning and motivation. Young people could not be realistically expected to learn lists year after year without some coherent system for making sense of the information. Consequently, according to Shulman, teaching about knowledge requires teachers to move beyond the substantive and into the syntactic nature of subject domains. We would argue that Bruner and Shulman may actually provide the route to Hirsch's desired outcomes (cultural literacy) and also give us reason to doubt that Hirsch can provide both the outcome and the means to achieve it. Knowledge is sometimes represented as though it were one single thing, but it is not.

An example of *subject knowledge for teaching*

An illustration of how this might work in the classroom will probably help at this point. We draw on our experience of teaching history in this example and provide a case study from the literature of science teaching below. Imagine you have been asked to teach a short sequence of history lessons on the subject of 1066, the Norman invasion of England and the victory of William the Conqueror. The background, preparations and conduct of the Battle of Hastings will involve you in some detailed reading – there are important facts to know about the events, including the main characters, their motivations and rival claims to the throne, logistical issues for each side relating to weaponry, supplies and manpower, and also contextual information such as the geography of the battle and the weather. There are also a number of substantive concepts such as invasion and monarchy, with which you will need to familiarise yourself. These may build on previous study when these concepts may have been considered (for example the Viking invasions in the North) and may well be discussed again later (for example by considering how the style of monarchic rule changes over time). While it is factually correct to say that Harold and William were kings, if we are to claim that students have understood the substantive concept of the monarchy we would require them to do more than merely list its incumbents. You might also plan to tackle syntactic concepts, which are specific to the nature of history as a discipline. In this example you might choose to focus on causation and consequence, placing the events in an explanatory framework, and establishing some of the implications of the Norman Conquest. In Bruner's terms it would make sense to use the concepts rather than the facts to help to organise the curriculum, because in many ways these are the deep structures that define the subject, and it is an understanding of these which is likely to make the learning feel useful and relevant. It is unlikely that a detailed knowledge of 1066 will prove useful to anyone, other than in a pub quiz, whereas an understanding of the tradition of monarchy will be potentially both interesting and useful in understanding aspects of British politics today. Similarly if your history teaching can impart a sense of how complex events unfold, how they can be understood in the historical context and how others construct arguments to convince us about causation, this constitutes powerful knowledge that can be used in a wide range of contexts.

None of this is common sense. It has to be learned by the teacher and incorporated into planning so that learners have access to it. If we are teaching three forms of knowledge – facts, substantive concepts and procedural concepts – then that is what we must plan for. And, unlike the fact that William became king as a consequence of the Battle of Hastings, which can be learned quickly and easily, the longer-term learning that forms the powerful bedrock of a genuine understanding of the contribution of history (or any other subject we happen to be teaching) has to be planned consistently over time to ensure learners have sufficient opportunity to engage, understand and incorporate this knowledge into their own understanding of the world. It is not necessarily difficult, it is just different. In this case we might decide to really emphasise our procedural concepts by framing the whole scheme of work around just two questions: 'How was William of Normandy able to become King of England?' and 'What difference did it make?' By focusing our selection of resources and activities on these apparently simple questions we ensure that by the end of the sequence of lessons the children will be able to engage with the underlying concepts of cause and consequence. Later on, they may use their knowledge when they come to similar questions on different topics, such as 'Why did the English Civil War start?' or 'What were the effects of industrialisation?' As students return to the notion of causation they will be able to develop an increasingly sophisticated sense of what kind of subject history is, and how they can use it to inform their understanding of the world, for example by thinking deeply about how to answer questions such as 'Why is there a continuing North/South divide in England?' or 'Why are some countries in the world so poor?' In order to answer these questions we need to have moved beyond the kinds of explanations young children spontaneously offer, which usually focus on the role on individuals or single factors in causing any change, and understand that to some extent all explanations of complex situations are provisional interpretations (Lee et al., 2001). These are the lessons that can be learned through a well-planned course in history if the teacher is sufficiently attuned to the nature of their subject. The same can be said for most subjects, so the unit of work on holidays in French may also be about mastery of the subjunctive; the science scheme of work on rocks may be essentially about classification systems; and the primary project on counting and the abacus may be about establishing the fundamental concept of place value.

 Case Study   A philosophically informed teaching proposal on the topic of energy for students aged 11–14

Papadouris and Constantinou's (2011) article seeks to establish a new view of teaching about energy because in their view secondary school teaching often simplifies the concept so much that it becomes inaccurate. They want to develop 'teaching simplifications that are both developmentally appropriate for students ... and also epistemologically coherent and conceptually valid' (p. 962). They also argue that if we want children to develop an understanding of the Nature of Science (NOS) we have to teach it more explicitly. They identify the following learning objectives in NOS:

(1) the role of observational data in science;
(2) aspects of the nature of scientific theories;
(3) the dependency of science on social factors;
(4) the role of subjectivity in scientific progress;
(5) the distinction between observations and inferences or interpretations.

They also note that NOS should help to tackle naive and fallacious ideas about science, such as that it 'relies on a certain stepwise scientific method that is uniformly and invariably applied' (p. 963).

They argue that one of the reasons why it is so difficult to teach about energy is that the concept is an abstract and 'transphenomenological' construct that 'provides a unifying framework enabling the analysis of a very diverse range of phenomena across many domains' (p. 965). They further argue that traditional teaching approaches ignore both these dimensions and treat energy in a simplified form in specific contexts and therefore end up missing the key point about energy and crucially side-stepping the reasonable child's question 'What is energy?' The result is that children often lack any specific definition of energy and confuse it with other concepts such as force, momentum or electric current.

They propose that any teacher tackling this area should start with the question, 'What is energy and why is it useful in science?' (p. 966), although by the end of the scheme they also add a third question, 'How do we use [the concept of energy] in science?' (p. 976). They argue that the appropriate teaching response should explain energy as 'a theoretical framework that has been invented in science, so as to facilitate the analysis of changes occurring in physical systems regardless of the domain they are drawn from' (p. 966).

In their proposed scheme of work they make the following decisions:

- Work is primarily computer based to enable them to embed the use of models and illustrations.
- The *Physics by Inquiry* approach is adopted which promotes students' collaborative group work in order to encourage them to discuss, predict and reason. The teacher acts as a facilitator, for example by using Socratic dialogue to encourage students to articulate their thinking clearly.
- Activities are sequenced to guide students through three inter-related ideas: first relating to the *nature of energy*, second the *value of energy* in science and third the *elaboration of energy as a theoretical framework* for analysing changes in physical systems.

The scheme of work starts with activities which present the students with observations and encourage them to devise their own interpretations. These examples clearly relate to the first and fifth NOS principles and some of them relate to the concept of energy. The second phase presents students with a range of models demonstrating how the concept of energy is used in a variety of contexts. The third section focuses on constructing 'energy chains' to encourage students to think about how energy is stored and transferred.

By the end of the scheme of work, the authors argue that students have been guided to understand both aspects of the NOS and energy and that students will be able to:

(Continued)

(Continued)

- draw the distinction between observations and interpretations;
- recognise the role of creativity and invention in formulating theoretical frameworks;
- appreciate that in science we sometimes build theories to interpret observations;
- appreciate energy as a theoretical framework that has been invented to facilitate the analysis of changes in physical systems.

The case study illustrates the need for teachers to think very clearly about the nature of the learning to be achieved and to have a deep understanding of the subject knowledge in hand. Papadouris and Constantinou demonstrate how their planning operates at the level of facts (data to handle), substantive concepts (energy) and procedural or syntactic concepts (the nature of science). They also demonstrate their pedagogical commitment that if you want students to understand that scientific theories are creative inventions to account for data, then you need to plan opportunities for them to experience how to respond to the data and construct their own interpretations.

Source: Papadouris, N. and Constantinou, C. (2011) 'A philosophically informed teaching proposal on the topic of energy for students aged 11–14', *Science and Education*, 20 (10), 961–976.

Knowledge about learning

This brings us back to Claxton, who we quoted earlier, apparently arguing against knowledge. In fact, he posed his views in this dramatic way to make sure readers were paying attention to his next point. His more complete view on the matter is that: 'Simply studying these approved canons of knowledge and greatness does not help you learn to live your life. However, all is not lost, for it turns out that the way that you study them can make all the difference' (Claxton, 2008: 81). This makes much more sense but it also adds yet another level of planning complexity. By way of example, he argues that two classes can learn exactly the same content in maths and even go on to get exactly the same grades in their exams, but that the way the teachers approach their teaching can mean that one group is completely incapable of using this knowledge outside of the exam situation, whilst the other group can use it in numerous situations and have gained such confidence in their ability as numerate people that they can tackle new problems creatively. While the second group has been properly educated, the other has simply been schooled. The difference, according to Claxton, is that the educated group have received an 'epistemic apprenticeship' (2008: 82). We would argue that what we have said above about procedural knowledge is part of an epistemic apprenticeship because the teacher not only teaches the learner about some new subject knowledge but also helps them understand why that knowledge is important, what kind of knowledge it is, how it fits into the bigger picture and how they are learning it. For Claxton, the apprenticeship also inducts learners into a more general model for thinking about 'learning to learn'.

Whilst his models are thoroughly theoretically grounded, Claxton also tries to capture what 'learning to learn' means in ways that are accessible to young people. Many schools adopting Claxton's models will also incorporate into their medium-term plans core ideas such as reciprocity, resourcefulness, reflectiveness and resilience (Claxton et al., 2011). Claxton's idea is that by being explicit about what constitutes a good learner teachers can help children to develop these characteristics. This harnesses the potential we discussed in Chapter 1 for people to learn and reflect on their learning, or metacognition as it is also known. Sometimes these ideas will be used within lessons to help children to think about how their learning is progressing; at other times teachers might build in opportunities across lessons, for example building in extended opportunities for collaboration in order to focus on reciprocity. So, sitting above the planning for subject knowledge we may also place additional layers of planning, which are commonly adopted across the school as a whole. This common approach helps children develop a shared language for thinking about themselves as learners and for discussing their learning with others.

There are other models available to schools to help them achieve what is essentially the same thing but described in different language (Glevey, 2006). It is also fairly common to see Bloom's taxonomy of skills being used across the curriculum for similar purposes, ranging through knowledge, comprehension, application, analysis, synthesis and evaluation (Bloom et al., 1956). As we noted in Chapter 1, the point here is not to prescribe which model to adopt; this must ultimately depend on the decisions made at whole-school level (and not all schools adopt clear models for learning to learn across the curriculum). The point here is to simply note that for us as teachers, this represents another level of professional knowledge about learning that has to be acquired in order to inform medium-term planning.

So far then we have set out to illustrate where the first set of subject knowledge problems may arise for teachers who are new to medium-term planning. To borrow from Donald Rumsfeld's inspired account of the nature of knowledge: (1) 'There are known knowns. These are things we know that we know.' For novice teachers this will include what you can remember from your degree subject knowledge. (2) 'There are known unknowns. That is to say, there are things that we know we don't know.' For novice teachers, this list is likely to be long and will cover all the topics in the curriculum you haven't studied, or have forgotten. (3) 'But there are also unknown unknowns. There are things we don't know we don't know.' We hope that we have begun to bring some of these out of the shadows and to explain what it is that is lurking below the surface when you observe a teacher and what constitutes deep professional knowledge. Inevitably, most readers of this book will be focusing on their own subject or age phase and so our examples in this chapter can only really start you on the process of further reading. Our hope is that we might help you convert some 'unknown unknowns' into 'known unknowns' which is at least the start of an important process.

 Activity

Next time you are observing an experienced teacher ask them about the different levels of subject knowledge. You might want to use the following prompts, although you may need to adapt them to suit your subject and age phase:

- What is this lesson about?
- If, in a month's time, the children have forgotten a lot of the facts from today's lesson, what do you hope they will remember?
- Does today's lesson build on anything the children have already learned? What and how?
- Will the children use today's learning in any later lessons?
- Thinking about the end point of this sequence of lessons, what is the main contribution of today's lesson? In other words, what function does this lesson serve in the whole sequence?
- Does this lesson cover aspects of the subject that will be covered again, perhaps later in the year or Key Stage? When and why?
- How did you select these activities for today's lesson? How will they help the children to learn the subject better?
- How did you decide what would constitute a reasonable expectation of the children today?
- If you taught this lesson to children three years older/younger, how would you approach it differently?

Not all the levels of planning in the preceding section will be written formally into plans, but you should hopefully find that teachers' responses give you some indication of the different levels at which they are planning.

Subject pedagogy

If we return to the TDA model (Figure 2.1) we also need to think about the subject pedagogical traditions that established teachers will understand and draw upon as planning resources. By this we simply mean that experienced teachers within a subject or age phase will have learned that there are recognisable patterns and traditions in what teachers do. In a primary class this might involve the use of number lines to build young pupils' confidence and competence in maths, or in an early years setting, it could include a tried and tested routine for learning outdoors when the first ice of winter forms on the playground. In science it may involve ways of setting up and reporting on experiments, while in English it may involve ways of scaffolding writing in different genres. These go beyond mere subject knowledge and move more firmly into the kind of professional knowledge teachers have about teaching in their specialist areas.

In part you can get access to this knowledge by observing lessons but a significant part of it will also emerge from discussions with colleagues and reading the literature, in particular the professional journals for the subject and age phase in which you are specialising. The numerous textbooks designed for student teachers are also useful introductions to this area and the debates that go on within the different traditions, for example within the science community there are ongoing debates about the value and role of practical work; in languages teachers debate the appropriate role of target language and the best approach to grammar; in early years the debate rages between those who favour a play-based approach and those who reproduce 'schooling' patterns in the foundation stage. You can only really make full sense of your placement or school context by interpreting it within these debates. It may be your secondary subject department or primary school is split between rival pedagogical traditions or it may be that everyone has come to share a particular approach. As a newcomer it is important to position yourself in relation to established practice, but also to appreciate the range of alternative positions available. In a typical teacher training course, with two school placements, it may be that the pedagogical approach you adopt in one context is out of place in another. This represents a significant intellectual challenge, and of course also requires a different approach to planning in each context. If you arrive in an early years setting which is committed to play-based learning and set up your classroom with tables in rows and try to teach from the front, this will be seen as provocative and subversive. Similarly if you arrive in a languages department committed to maximising the use of the target language and learning language in context, you will experience problems if you plan chunks of time learning disconnected grammar rules.

Learning about learners

It is also worth pointing out that the one area where teachers become undisputed experts is knowledge about their class. This varies depending on how often teachers see their classes; for example the RE teacher in secondary school may see 22 classes a week (up to 660 students) and is frankly doing well if they remember everyone's name, but most teachers see more of their pupils and many primary teachers get to spend most of their day with the same group of pupils for at least a year. The point is that this is knowledge where there are no real shortcuts and yet, as your knowledge about a group of students grows, you can fine tune the medium-term planning to ensure a better fit between the learners and the teaching. Knowing a group, their strengths, weaknesses, interests and friendships, is vital in devising a plan that will be suitable, or at least interpreting a plan and adapting it to fit each class.

Many teachers, and we include ourselves, are guilty of sometimes thinking that a lesson they planned was fine, but the children spoiled it. When the sense of frustration subsides and we re-evaluate the experience we have to admit that the lesson may well have been fine for a different situation, but it was ultimately our failure to read the situation and respond which was the source of the problem. This mismatch between teacher expectations and pupil readiness may simply arise spontaneously on the day (a strong wind or unexpected snowfall can be enough) but it can also arise because we have misjudged the scheme of work entirely, and so the learners never really connect to the learning.

Schön's (1983) influential book on the reflective practitioner argues that our ability to reflect on a situation and design effective responses is at the heart of the definition of professionalism. Schön explains that a professional's claim to professional status is not really based on their technical knowledge, but actually on the way they draw on experience to frame a problem and develop effective solutions. Most medical problems presented to doctors are not textbook cases that can simply be traced back to a medical dictionary. Instead the doctor listens, draws on their technical knowledge, their prior experience, their knowledge of the local area and the patient's medical history, and begins to identify likely diagnoses. In their book *Instructional Design* Smith and Ragan make the same point in relation to designing learning sequences:

> Novice designers sometimes have the impression that doing design work is a 'cut and dried' activity. This is not the case. For example, if one were to give several architects the same conditions – site, materials and purpose – the plans for the structures that they would create would vary radically ... All of the designs may 'work' in the sense that, when executed, the buildings would remain standing and serve their purposes. However, some imaginative and ingenious structures may inspire awe, while more mundane structures may be totally forgettable. (1999: 4)

Smith and Ragan's argument calls into question some of the literature we have already discussed, for example in the case study above on energy, which seeks to establish a model for teaching energy that will work for everyone.

They remind us that the teacher must plan responsively and that this requires the planning to take account of the teacher's knowledge, the students' knowledge and interests, the inherent learning demands of the topic being taught, the curriculum and exam syllabus restrictions, the resources available, the time available and the nature of the school or department context.

This is why we argue that planning is often more complicated than it may at first appear. However, if we do not seriously attempt to manage these competing factors and impose some kind of order through a coherent medium-term plan, we are effectively rejecting a key tenet of professionalism. Butcher et al. (2006) discuss a range of perspectives on planning:

- Engineering approach emphasises aims and outcomes.
- Mechanic's approach emphasises the method of instruction.
- Cookbook approach focuses on the content (ingredients) of the curriculum.
- Railway approach focuses on timetables and sequencing.
- Detective approach evaluates the curriculum to identify and put right problematic areas.
- Religious approach places a particular belief at the heart of the planning, for example a belief in a particular teaching technique.
- Bureaucratic approach focuses on interpreting the rules, norms and regulations.

These are all useful reminders that the planning process may become distorted if we excessively focus on one element over another and forget to keep bringing the planning decisions back into some form of coherent overall picture. The discussion so far has sought to explain why this is difficult, but this difficulty also provides a fascinating intellectual challenge to the teacher and ultimately the ability to create coherence from these competing demands is one of our main claims to professional status. Politicians may argue that teaching needs ex-soldiers because of their expertise in discipline, or ex-scientists because of their subject knowledge expertise, but this mistakes one form of valuable knowledge for another. The teacher's claim to expertise is at least partly based on this ability to pick a path through infinite possibilities to maximise the learning for a specific group of children in a specific context. If we do not rise to that challenge, or even worse, if we think it is acceptable to abdicate responsibility for planning to someone else, we have to question what specific claim to professional expertise remains.

Content overload

In addition to the challenges inherent in the planning process, there are a number of additional problems which emerge out of the way schools tend to work today. Teachers have always had a tendency to worry about content coverage and one of the effects of the national curriculum and exam syllabi is that they can be seen as a restrictive list of content to get through. In this case planning can descend into the crude process of simply dividing up the year into prescribed chunks. If the A level syllabus is built around four units then there is an understandable temptation simply to divide up the year so that one unit is taught in the autumn, the second unit in the spring, and the summer focuses on revision and assessment. The syllabus then specifies what must be taught; for example one A level English Literature unit covers poetry and prose 1800–1945 and the teacher must select one poet (each with 15 poems selected for study) and one novel. Clearly this could break down to half a term of poetry and half a term of prose. It might also be tempting to cover one poem each lesson. This is the 'railway' approach to planning described above and it also means that if the teacher loses a lesson in the first half term because of school closure or illness, they will feel they are playing catch-up to get through the content required before the end of the unit. This is a common problem and most teachers worry about the content, either because their curriculum requirements are particularly onerous, or because their departmental schemes of work put pressure on them.

This is exacerbated by the fact that schools are under pressure to perform well in public league tables, and this pervades the whole ethos of most schools. Teaching to the test is a perennial problem which Torrance (2007) has argued has gradually transformed much teaching practice so that, rather than securing learning and then assessing it, we have moved through assessment for learning and are now in a situation where we are so constantly fixated on the final grade that we see assessment as learning. In other words, every lesson is so thoroughly focused on the learning objectives that we are always under pressure to generate evidence of achievement, so we can move on the next objective. This fuels the tendency of teachers who feel they must simply get through so much content that there is little room for flexibility.

Sipress and Voelker have explored the history of this way of thinking and the countervailing educational arguments and conclude:

> Proponents of the coverage model have good intentions, but over the past century their preferred pedagogy has come up short again and again. If we truly wish our students to engage in critical thinking and discussion … it is not enough to ask them to simply consume our expert knowledge. (2011: 1066)

This echoes much of what we have discussed above, that while subject knowledge is important it must be seen in the wider context of learning the subject and learning to learn. Like Claxton, they argue that all teachers should place a common concept at the heart of their teaching, so that learners are empowered to learn. Sipress and Voelker explore this issue in the context of introductory units in university courses, and they simply state that 'argument' should take that central position and drive the selection of content and pedagogical strategies. They argue that lecturers, when faced with one single course to 'introduce' their discipline, tend to create the pressure of content coverage by assuming that the best way they can maximize their time is to fill it with as much as possible. Sipress and Voelker argue that the best approach is simply to help students appreciate the kinds of perspectives each area offers, the contribution it makes to understanding and the way in which knowledge is contentious and debated within the discipline.

This is relatively easy to resolve in a university context, where the lecturer can simply re-write their course to specify less coverage and more depth. It is more difficult for teachers in school where the need to 'cover' content is non-negotiable. The only response is for teachers to assert their professional judgement and seek to bring the unwieldy content under control. In the case of the English course we took as our example above, rather than trudge through a poem per lesson, the teacher will have to bring some order to bear, perhaps chunking up the content according to some principles which emerge either from their understanding of the exam, or from their deep understanding of the poems themselves. For example, they may choose to start with several poems which they think will provide a particularly accessible starting point for their students. They may then cluster poems together into themes so that lessons hang together more coherently as sequences and build upon one another to achieve depth rather than simply add knowledge of another poem with each lesson that passes. On this approach whilst the same 15 poems may be covered in five weeks, they may be incorporated within three significant themes; for example perhaps a selection of Hardy's poetry could be studied on the themes of satires of circumstance, war and patriotism, love and loss. This would certainly make more sense than simply listing poems by number and interpreting them one by one. The teacher who wants to encourage deep learning and avoid the slavery of content coverage should select from the specification (and actually select the specification in the first place) with an eye to the extent to which such an organising scheme is possible.

If teachers do not wrestle endless content into some comprehensible shape then they are left feeling powerless and out of control. If this is a teacher's starting point, what message does that send out to their pupils? The aim is to achieve some sense of mastery over the content not to be cowed into submission by it. The only possible route to a solution is through forcing the content into a meaningfully structured medium-term plan.

Activity

Find a scheme of work from a school where you are working or from the internet.

- Write out all the content covered on post-it notes, so each item is on a separate sheet.
- If the scheme of work already organises the content into themes or chunks, re-create this by clustering the post-it notes around these organising themes.
- Now try to work out an alternative way to structure the content, making new connections and developing new conceptual themes.
- Identify meaningful titles for each cluster.
- Now think about the relationship between these clusters. How are they linked to one another? Is there a logical sequence in which they could be taught?
- Produce a draft of how you could teach this content in the time available. Then think about how you would approach this if you only had half the time. Which examples or themes would you skip over or drop in order to ensure that the main concepts were taught?

Initiative overload

As with content overload, the issue of initiative overload is also exacerbated by the way that schools work now. Schools are seen as part of the solution to many social problems and so the list of things they should achieve grows. The Every Child Matters (ECM) policy is a good example of how this impacts on planning. ECM represented a serious attempt to align children's services around five key outcomes – to ensure children are safe, healthy, enjoy and achieve, make a positive contribution and achieve economic well-being. This is clearly a serious agenda for all schools and has serious implications, most obviously for the pastoral system, for monitoring children identified as being at-risk and for safeguarding procedures. It was also picked up in many schools as a curriculum issue and so when the policy was being implemented we met primary headteachers who had mapped the five outcomes against the whole curriculum and heads of department in secondary schools who had done the same against all their departmental schemes of work. We also met colleagues who had painstakingly mapped their whole PGCE course against all the sub-themes beneath these five headings (there are 25 objectives in total). In one university where new courses were being planned and approved we asked the team presenting their course to explain how they could have mapped the objective for children to 'live in decent homes and sustainable communities' as a learning outcome on their teacher education course because it seemed outside of their remit to prepare teachers to somehow take action on pupils' housing conditions. The answer came back that because all providers had to incorporate ECM in their courses, all these outcomes must feature in the plans. The planning grid remained in the documentation and the course was validated but no one had any realistic plans to teach student teachers about housing policy. This illustrates how none of us are immune from the pressure to be seen to be doing something, even if in our hearts we know we can't do anything. As a sop to this constant call for action we can always produce a mapping document to demonstrate where things seem to fit.

This makes a mockery of planning. If we produce plans that we have no intention of implementing, then planning becomes an exercise in covering one's back, rather than a serious attempt to think about how to strike the right balance between the development of different skills and concepts and the coherent synthesis of different agendas. If we are not careful we end up paying lip service to these competing agendas and this serves no one's interests. ECM is not the only policy where this kind of curriculum mapping becomes the solution. Most schools have mapped literacy and numeracy across the curriculum, and others we have worked with have mapped Gardner's eight intelligences, or sought to avoid teaching citizenship properly by dispersing it across the curriculum and mapping it against pre-existing schemes of work. What all this means is that a series of lessons, let's say on the growth of cities in geography, might simultaneously claim to develop an appreciation of rights and responsibilities, the conventions of persuasive writing, the interpretation of descriptive statistics, the use of ICT to display data, prepare children for economic well-being, and develop their interpersonal intelligence and capacity for reflection. We have to differentiate here between deliberate teaching designed to move a student on in some significant way, as opposed to simply re-using existing skills or knowledge. We can be sure that the geography teacher is clear about how the pupils' understanding of the growth of cities will be enhanced during these lessons, but will they actually take time to teach the skills required to engage thoroughly with reflection on group-work experiences – identifying learning, providing feedback to peers, thinking about targets for future work? Will they also have time to teach students how to use Excel software to make graphs, or will they rely on the fact that the children can already use the software? It is easy to map things we are doing or skills we are planning to re-use, but this is different from seriously planning to teach these areas. The problem for the novice teacher examining these plans is that they need to interpret these overwhelming schemes of work and exclude all the stuff that is essentially there for a different purpose – as a response to policy rather than a serious teaching purpose.

Geoffrey Howson wrote of the maths curriculum that it was a pious cliché to justify the subject's place in the curriculum through claiming that it promoted 'spiritual development through … helping pupils gain an insight into the infinite' or 'moral development through … helping them learn the value of mathematical truth' (quoted in Bangs et al., 2011: 78), but it is likely that someone somewhere has mapped this against their maths schemes of work. It is possible that a teacher has actually sought to kindle a sense of wonder at the concept of infinity, but it is more likely that the box was ticked and children's sense of wonderment left untroubled.

The impact of this cross-referencing tick box culture was evident in one of the interviews we conducted for this book. Andrew, a secondary English teacher, was reflecting on the National Literacy Strategy (NLS) which was a hugely detailed document for English teachers. Whilst we have already illustrated the situation where multiple objectives are listed without any real intention to actually teach them, Andrew illustrates the opposite problem, that so many objectives can be added in, this obscures the overall purpose. The NLS included detailed lists of grammar points that were expected at specific phases in each key stage and in hindsight he felt this had a hugely distorting effect on his planning and teaching:

> *Looking back at the dozens of schemes of work I wrote between 2002 and 2008 the entire focus was on a lesson by lesson approach. They may have had an interesting topic – I designed one around the animated children's film* The Iron Giant *which is based on Ted Hughes's book* The Iron Man. *When I look back on that it is very much designed along the lines, here's an interesting film that you can do lots of things with, let's do lots of interesting things with it, some of which are integral to studying animation and film, many of which actually are quite tangential to that … [Looking back] it struck me how incoherent as a whole the unit was, that actually there were so many objectives in the National Literacy Strategy that you would make a scheme of work out of interesting ideas and then randomly attach the objectives it met to the lessons. It seemed that was what Ofsted wanted, they wanted all these itemised lesson plans. It was so complex that no one would ever be able to cross-reference or check … Because there were so many objectives, and because the smaller objectives are easier to demonstrate in a lesson (like the use of complex sentences, you get endless lessons about complex sentences, about connectives, about ways to start paragraphs which had nothing to do with the subject matter of the lessons) you just suddenly get a*

disconnect ... Teachers start to feel like I've got to have this objective for this lesson and then I've got to demonstrate it at the end, and then I've got to start again, instead of the more logical way I personally plan to [now], and encourage teachers to plan to, which is that you don't have to have endless objectives, you've got these to work with over the term, continue with them.

Part of Andrew's current job is designing resources for teachers to use as the basis of their own planning in schools and his approach now is more aligned with the one we discuss in the subsequent chapters of this book. It is significant though that for years he felt he had to respond to policy documents in a given way, and that this was deeply flawed and actually prevented deep learning across a scheme of work. For him, a large part of the medium-term planning task was focused on cross-referencing the externally imposed literacy objectives, but this distorted the planning and masked (or promoted) a lack of coherence.

This final point then is a warning that not all the plans that exist in schools are good, in part because they can become vehicles for other agendas, which are not really about planning teaching and learning. We do not want to be misunderstood here though. We do think that running some themes across the curriculum can be powerful, and we think literacy is a very reasonable area for every teacher to focus on. We just want to note that in some schools the response in planning documents is the response in total and the teaching is largely unaffected. What we would much rather see is teachers being more selective about what they are going to achieve, integrating it genuinely into their medium-term plans and then teaching it rigorously.

Activity

(1) Take a scheme of work from a subject other than English and identify all the different uses of language and the opportunities to address specific issues related to language, communication and grammar.
(2) Now identify a strong literacy/language theme which could make a useful theme across the whole sequence of lessons and which would be complementary to the subject focus of the scheme of work.
(3) Look for opportunities to incorporate genuine literacy learning alongside the subject learning, so that pupils' knowledge and skills will be developed rather than simply re-used in a new context.
(4) Finally revise the plan so that literacy is genuinely embedded.

Conclusion

In this chapter we have explained some of the challenges that confront teachers setting out to plan learning over the medium term. Some of these challenges are simply inherent features of the nature of planning and our discussion of subject knowledge and the wider idea of *subject knowledge for teaching* was intended to demonstrate the multifaceted nature of this area. There is no way to avoid this and so we simply urge teachers to understand this area of their professional knowledge base and seek to develop it and articulate it consciously. Other challenges arise from the school context, and content and initiative overload provide examples of this. In saying something about these areas we have sought to highlight the problem and indicate that there can be sensible and proportionate ways forward. We hope this discussion has helped first by explaining why every teacher is not a good planner, and second by helping you to appreciate the scale and nature of the obstacles that need to be overcome in order to plan effectively. In the next chapter we start to explore the answer to these problems and suggest some principles that should inform effective medium-term planning.

Further reading

Schön, D. A. (1983) *The Reflective Practitioner*, Aldershot: Ashgate.
People still talk about the role of reflection and the model of the reflective practitioner in teaching, but we recommend returning to the source of many of these ideas. This book says some important things about the nature of professional knowledge and practice.

Shulman, L. S. (1986) Those who understand: knowledge growth in teaching, *Educational Researcher*, 15(2), 4–14.
This is a thought-provoking discussion of what we really mean when we talk about subject knowledge in the teaching profession.

CHAPTER 3

PRINCIPLES OF MEDIUM-TERM PLANNING

By the end of this chapter you will be able to:

- understand the key concepts from the educational literature that inform medium-term planning, focusing on constructive alignment and assessment;
- understand the importance of teachers as active agents in interpreting curricula and creating learning opportunities;
- appreciate that our model of the five As operates as a way of organising your planning and implementing these principles.

In our first two chapters we outlined why we believe medium-term planning is a central element in effective teaching and learning, as well as considering the challenges of doing it well. The remainder of the book will focus on how to develop medium-term plans that deliver high-quality learning and feedback for pupils. This will be based upon existing research, our interviews with teachers drawn from primary, secondary and post-16 contexts and naturally our own teaching experience. Before we get to that point we want to provide you with an overview of the key principles underpinning our approach alongside some of the sources of our ideas. The three principles we discuss below are:

- constructive alignment;
- formative assessment pedagogy;
- a belief in the power of critical, reflective and collaborative professional practice.

Constructive alignment

As outlined in Chapter 1, we hold a social constructivist view of education and have utilised social constructivist approaches to organising learning throughout our teaching careers. At the heart of social constructivist learning approaches is the belief that learning is always maximised when learners are able to construct meaning themselves. This happens through effective learning opportunities that facilitate the active engagement of learners in analysing and using concepts, hypothesising, identifying additional questions and strategies for answering these, and testing the reliability and provenance of information and evidence. As Piaget summed it up: '… the principal goal of education in the schools should be creating men and women who are capable of doing new things, not simply repeating what other generations have done' (Piaget, quoted in Jervis and Tobier, 1988).

In social constructivism, learning is promoted and constructed through effective dialogue, negotiation and review. This has impacted on how we have personally approached teaching, particularly the emphasis placed on collaborative, discursive and active forms of learning. Table 3.1 may help to give you a sense of what some of the key features of a constructivist classroom look like, versus more traditional forms of schooling, though we are aware that such comparisons may oversimplify. It's common to find classrooms where some elements of social constructivism sit alongside more didactic or 'traditional' forms of teaching and learning.

Table 3.1 Traditional versus social constructivist classrooms

Some features of 'traditional' classrooms:	Some features of 'social constructivist' classrooms:
Curriculum seen as fixed, with planning based on breaking down the curriculum into its constituent parts	Curriculum seen as dynamic, with planning focused on varying interpretations of the major concepts that make up a learning area
Learning is seen as largely the acquisition of 'factual' knowledge	Learning is seen as a process of constructing meaning, building on the developing knowledge and experiences of the learner

Some features of 'traditional' classrooms:	Some features of 'social constructivist' classrooms:
Emphasis on formalised forms of teaching resources, e.g. textbooks	Emphasis on using a range of learning materials including primary sources of evidence derived from investigations by learners
Emphasis on the primacy of the teacher as the sole authority on learning in the classroom	Emphasis on the ever-changing nature of knowledge and understanding; learning intentions may be negotiated and modified in the light of learners' development
Focus on learning activities that are directed and assessed by the teacher	Focus on flexible approaches to achieving learning intentions and the assessment of those intentions being shared by teachers and learners alike
Learners tend to work on learning activities on their own and with limited involvement with others	Learning is collaborative, with many opportunities for learners to work together
Assessment takes summative forms, focused on fixed conceptions of success and often based on testing	Assessment takes formative forms, with learners at the heart of the process and based upon a wide evidence base

Teaching in a way that promotes social constructivism requires careful planning including a clear focus on what you are trying to achieve. As Shuell suggests:

> If students are to learn desired outcomes in a reasonably effective manner, then the teacher's fundamental task is to get students to engage in learning activities that are likely to result in their achieving those outcomes ... It is helpful to remember that what the student does is actually more important in determining what is learned than what the teacher does. (1986: 429)

If what goes on in classrooms is not held together by the glue of the short- and medium-term learning intentions, learning is likely to happen in a vacuum; pupils will be unclear about why they are doing things and the gains in knowledge and skills are likely to be short-lived, or even non-existent.

This highlights one of the most important ideas we have taken from the existing literature on medium-term planning, the principle of *constructive alignment*. This means that learning is best promoted when constructivist approaches to learning are blended with clearly defined learning intentions, learning opportunities that deliver these intentions and assessment approaches that check the extent to which these intentions have been realised.

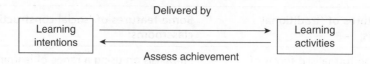

Figure 3.1 Constructive alignment of learning

There are four steps involved in constructively aligning learning:

1. Identifying learning intentions.
2. Selecting learning activities (tasks, questioning, process elicitation) that deliver these intentions.
3. Using evidence from these activities to assess the extent to which intentions are being realised, making adjustments where necessary.
4. Assessing the overall achievement of learning intentions, providing formative feedback and where necessary a measure of the standard achieved (such as a grade).

This list probably seems quite obvious and logical to you, but aligning learning in this way is not as easy as it seems. It requires careful work at the planning stages and a commitment to achieving these learning intentions at the delivery stage. It relies on the teacher having sufficient subject knowledge to identify the intentions; the ability of the teacher to tap into the learning being achieved at different points; and their willingness to make necessary adaptations, even though this might significantly alter what they were planning to do initially. It may be hard to do the latter when there is a need to cover lots of content for an exam, or where the teacher has limited time. We have designed this book to take you through these steps in some detail, providing you with both a framework and the benefit of experienced teachers' reflections.

Clarifying your learning intentions is always going to need to be your first step in any learning cycle. This is because the learning intentions:

• help the teacher to focus their teaching and select appropriate activities and resources;
• provide a framework for assessment and evaluation;
• guide the learner as to the ultimate direction.

If a sequence of lessons tackles a single theme there may be no need to separate out different learning intentions for every lesson in order to meet all these criteria.

Morrison and his colleagues suggest that learning intentions can be framed in some routine ways and suggest an essential and optional element. The essential elements include:

(a) an action verb;
(b) a subject content reference.

For example:

Name the parts of speech used in a sentence.

Make a mobile-phone case.

The optional elements include possible additional statements to further clarify the learning:

(c) level of achievement;
(d) conditions of performance e.g. time/resources.

For example:

Name the parts of speech used in a sentence, using technical vocabulary in the target language, instantly and without reference to notes or dictionaries.

Make a mobile-phone case, which is complete and works, using resources available in the D&T room which cost less than £5 in total.

Gagné and Briggs (1974) and Morrison et al. (2007) offer suggested typologies to help teachers and planners to frame their learning objectives so that they are clear (summarised in Table 3.2). However, learning objectives are not entirely straightforward as they tend to focus on the observable characteristics of learning, and are thus sometimes thought of as being overly influenced by the behaviourist approach to learning. We think this is particularly obvious when we get to the affective dimension, where the suggestions tend to describe the behaviours that would follow from the feeling, rather than focus on the feeling itself. It is perfectly possible to adopt learning intentions like this, which may not be directly measurable or easily assessable, because at the initial stage the purpose of devising these statements is to indicate what we hope the pupils will learn.

Useful though hierarchical schemes such as Bloom's taxonomy are, Butcher et al. (2006) point out that we use these skills all the time and that we should not fall into the trap of assuming that all 'evaluation' is necessarily more demanding than all 'comprehension'. Evaluating a recipe in a cookery class is not inherently more challenging than simply explaining the general theory of relativity. The usefulness of the taxonomy might be better seen in planning sequences within a medium-term plan, for example, it probably makes sense

Table 3.2 Classifying learning objectives (adapted from Gagné and Briggs (1974) and Morrison at al. (2007))

Morrison et al.	Gagné and Briggs	Learning objectives
Cognitive based on Bloom's taxonomy	Intellectual skills *individual competence* Cognitive strategies *own learning/thinking* Verbal information *facts/recall*	Bloom's taxonomy and related verbs: • Knowledge *Arrange, define, duplicate, label, list, match, memorise, name, order, recall, relate, repeat, reproduce* • Comprehension *Classify, describe, discuss, explain, express, identify, indicate, locate, report, restate, review, select, sort, tell, translate* • Application *Apply, choose, demonstrate, dramatise, employ, illustrate, interpret, operate, practise, prepare, schedule, sketch, solve, use* • Analysis *Analyse, appraise, calculate, categorise, compare, contrast, criticise, differentiate, distinguish, examine, experiment, question, test* • Synthesis *Arrange, assemble, collect, compose, construct, create, design, formulate, manage, organise, plan, prepare, propose, set up, synthesise, write* • Evaluation *Argue, assess, attack, compare, defend, estimate, evaluate, judge, predict, rate, score, select, support, value*

Morrison et al.	Gagné and Briggs	Learning objectives
Psychomotor	Motor skills	Can be considered hierarchically: *Imitation, manipulation, precision, articulation* Or grouped: *Gross-bodily movement, finely co-ordinated movement, non-verbal communication, speech*
Affective *Based on Krathwohl's taxonomy*	Attitudes	Krathwohl's hierarchy is as follows: • Receiving • Responding • Valuing • Organising • Adopting Morrison's suggested verbs relating to this area include: *Acclaims, agrees, argues, assumes, attempts, avoids, challenges, co-operates, defends, disagrees, disputes, engages in, helps, is attentive to, joins, offers, participates in, praises, resists, shares, volunteers.*

to understand new content before you try to apply it or critique it; although of course, having made a critique of an idea, we might then return to lower levels of the taxonomy to explore it in more subtle ways.

In Chapter 2, we explored the debates and challenges around subject knowledge. These challenges inevitably have an impact on the planning of learning intentions. Biggs (1996) has argued that teachers can find it difficult to develop the knowledge and understanding they want to promote because 'they do not know how to descend from the rhetoric of their aims to the specific objectives of a given course or unit'. He suggests that in order to make this transition, 'they need a framework of some kind to help them operationalise what "understanding" might mean in their particular case' (Biggs, 1996: 351).

This difficulty arises because teachers often define learning intentions in relation to 'declarative' or second-hand knowledge about that which has been 'discovered' in the world, but such knowledge can only take you so far; it needs to be 'put to work' for it to mean anything. The suggestion for teachers is they need to frame learning intentions and activities in ways that develop 'functioning knowledge' that pupils can use and that they can spot during the process of learning (Biggs, 2003). Similarly, Hattie argues that teachers and their pupils need to understand the surface, deep and conceptual knowledge involved in meeting learning intentions. Hattie describes surface knowledge as the knowledge needed to understand and contextualise a concept; deep learning as being concerned with the relationships between ideas; and he argues that conceptual thinking emerges when 'surface and deep knowledge turn … into conjectures and concepts upon which to build new surface and deep understandings' (Hattie, 2012: 77).

So far we have explored the importance of establishing clear and deliberate learning intentions to inform your planning. Hussey and Smith (2003) have also highlighted the need for teachers to recognise and appropriately deal with *emerging* learning outcomes. In any learning situation, other forms of learning are likely. Some of these may be predicted by the teacher (for example a lesson in which the process of voting is being analysed might lead to an interesting discussion about candidates in an up-and-coming election), while at other times they might be completely unexpected. The teacher has to make both immediate and longer-term decisions about this; in our election example allowing the pupils to discuss the candidates might add interest and context to the discussion, but letting the discussion go on without structure and focus could prevent the planned learning intentions being realised. If the pupils are very interested, it would be worth the teacher making future adaptations to the medium-term plan to capitalise on this properly.

Chapters 4 and 5 explore the issues raised above in more depth and provide a workable framework for you to identify relevant learning intentions and relate these to lessons and learning episodes across your sequence. In Chapter 6 we explore ways that teachers align intentions with activities that bring the learning alive.

Formative assessment pedagogy

A second theme emerging from the literature about planning concerns formative assessment, or assessment for learning (AfL). This has been one of the most significant ideas to emerge within education in recent decades and it has continued to have a substantial impact on teaching into the 2000s. In many ways AfL was not really concerned with assessment, and much of the discussion involved the principles of effective teaching and learning we outlined above and in Chapter 1. But what it did do was reshape the debate around assessment so that, rather than focus on the summative judgement at the end of a course or unit, teachers became much more focused on the ways they could use their judgements of learners' attainment to feed back into the learning process and secure further progress. The Assessment Reform Group (ARG, 1999) trawled through a huge range of research literature on factors that had an impact on learning and distilled their message into five key factors that influence learning:

1. The extent to which pupils get effective feedback.
2. The extent to which pupils are actively involved in their learning.
3. The extent to which teaching is adjusted to take account of assessment.
4. The extent to which teachers recognise that assessment has an impact on self-esteem.
5. The extent to which pupils understand themselves and how to improve.

Their follow-up field work, which followed groups of teachers trying to implement these ideas, demonstrated that although these factors seem like common sense and are readily comprehensible, they are in fact fairly difficult to develop meaningfully in everyday practice (Black et al., 2003). The ARG noted that there are several countervailing forces in schools such as the pressure to 'cover' the curriculum, the perceived need to ensure lessons have a brisk 'pace' and the fear that bored children will misbehave if they are not constantly occupied by new things. In fact, after some difficulties, their implementation project showed that teachers could change their practice to improve these five areas. This might involve slowing down a bit to develop depth, asking fewer but more open-ended questions, and developing alternative thinking activities to help ensure there are no prolonged awkward silences. Improved practice also included children being involved much more (and much more productively) in regulating the classroom and the learning through self and peer assessment and the shared development and review of learning objectives.

It has been impressive how teachers have engaged with AfL, how policy-makers have attempted to promote it, and generally how long the idea has sustained interest in a field where fashions come and go almost as fast as education ministers. It is notable, however, that much of the focus of the AfL movement was on how teachers could make slight changes in their classroom teaching. Teachers were encouraged to think about how they asked ques-tions and facilitated pupils to develop good answers; how they used learning objectives; and how self-assessment could be used. As a result we have seen a proliferation of classroom props such as lolly sticks (with pupils' names on to pick out of a bag for no-hands up questioning), traffic lights (in some cases actual traffic lights, but in most classes just red, amber and green cards to indi-cate how well pupils feel they have understood something) and mini-white boards (to give the teacher a quick indication of what sense pupils are making of a problem). We have also seen, in almost every classroom we have visited over the last decade, a box on the board or front wall of the classroom for the teacher to write today's lesson intention, and we have also seen that the vast majority of lessons start with pupils copying down the intentions.

Clearly, some of the performance of AfL techniques has become divorced from the principles that underpinned the ARG's original work. The principle that pupils should understand what they are doing and what they are learning so they can take more active responsibility for their own learning has been forgotten in some classrooms, where pupils copy learning intentions as pas-sively as they copy the date and title. While we see student teachers drilled into the 'learning intentions on the board and in their books' routine, we rarely see them being drilled into good habits of explaining how this lessons fits into a planned learning sequence. In order for learners to really understand the learning, it makes sense that teachers should be explaining how this les-son builds on prior learning (what are we re-using from before?); where we should get to by the end of this lesson (what are we learning today?); and why this is important in the big picture (what are we doing next and why do we need today's learning to be successful?). If we return to the principle that underpinned the suggestion that teachers should make greater use of learning intentions, it was really to ensure that there is a sharper focus on learning and that learners should be drawn more actively into the process and encouraged to take more responsibility for their own learning. They can then undertake an activity in the full knowledge of what the purpose is, and what they are striv-ing for. They could also review their own performance, help others to do the same and think about how to improve. It is absolutely crucial that this learning journey has been worked out in advance by the teacher, and that the teacher uses this to help the pupils locate themselves in the overall plan. If we return to our initial metaphor at the start of this book, where we argued a medium-term plan could be likened to a map, we need to ask ourselves why, having worked out the route, we would then hide the map from the rest of our hiking party? Surely everyone would benefit from knowing where we are heading, why we are going there and what our route is. This seems useful not least because then everyone can look out for obstacles ahead, flag up interesting features we might focus our attention on and also share difficulties they might have with parts of the journey. In the classroom, if everyone knows where the learning is heading, not only can they make sense of their own personal journey as they piece together parts of their learning into a coherent whole, but they can also think about alternative strategies to get around difficulties and make more connections to the big picture as they progress, rather than waiting for it all (hopefully) to make sense in the final lesson. Quite simply, we do not believe that it is possible to implement AfL unless the teacher has developed a sound medium-term plan, and uses this as part of their everyday teaching. In this way pupils at least have the choice about joining in the learning with a full commitment and an enquiring mind. Otherwise the best we can hope for is that children simply comply with the tasks we set, when we set them, but are still essentially passive learners.

The other feature of AfL that has changed a lot of school practice is the notion that marking and feedback should be seen as mechanisms for feeding forward into the next steps in a learner's journey. It has become relatively common to see comment-only marking, or at least marking comments which really focus on the precise objective of a task or lesson. It is now less common just to see the kind of marking that praises a pupil for effort, or comments on minor points of presentation. Some schools have pasted in grids at the back of exercise books for teachers and pupils to engage in a dialogue about comments and targets, and many schools have regular target-setting events throughout the academic year, where pupils are set individual targets for the forthcoming period. But, as with the learning objectives at the start of the lesson, this sometimes ossifies into another ritual where genuine engagement is limited. It is unusual in our visits to schools to see student teachers being inducted into how to use this feedback so that it becomes feed-forward. Rather it seems that the effort and time involved in providing quality marking are seen as a separate task and then the next lesson is so full that there is no time to 'waste' going over old stuff; the pressure is on again to cover some more material, to move on, and be seen to be moving on. The trouble with this is that the lessons, which are ultimately just arbitrary divisions of time imposed on learning for the purposes of managing the school day and resources, become the defining features. They can appear to be discrete entities, whereas the pupils should be encouraged to see each lesson, each homework and each marking comment as part of the overall learning journey for that scheme of work. If teachers take that approach, the medium-term plan becomes even more important and replaces the lesson plan as the main unit of attention. That seems to us to be the best way to proceed. Marking then has a real urgency and real purpose, because it is integrally linked to the collective endeavour to move on and progress. Unless teachers see their marking in this way, we cannot expect learners to use it in this way. And if teachers do expect pupils to use it, then they should build it into their plans. The medium-term plan is as much a plan for formative assessment as it is for teaching and learning, indeed these are all ultimately aspects of the same process.

In Chapter 7 we explore the principles of effective formative assessment in relation to planning for assessment across a sequence of lessons. We move from considering some of the skills that teachers bring to the act of assessing, to exploring the role of learning intentions, success criteria and feedback in helping to move learning forward. A key principle we explore is that learners need to develop an understanding of the *processes* by which they can demonstrate their knowledge and skills and that assessment practices should be as concerned with process as end products. Timely feedback on these processes will not only help with the improved quality of end products, but will also help to provide a greater transfer in knowledge and skills, because pupils are more likely to be able to apply this knowledge in a new context.

A focus on the process of learning also includes recognition of the role of making mistakes and errors in helping people to get better at anything (see the case study in Chapter 6). Hattie (2012: 124) provides an enthusiastic justification for a classroom culture in which error is welcomed:

> Errors invite opportunities. They should not be seen as embarrassments, signs of failure or something to be avoided. They are exciting, because they indicate a tension between what we *now* know and what we *could* know; they are signs for opportunities to learn and they are to be embraced.

Such an approach relates to the work of Dweck (2006) and her suggestion that effective learning comes about when children develop a 'growth mindset'. She is critical of classroom environments where there is insufficient cognitive challenge for pupil and where feedback messages are blurred by convoluting feedback on learning with motivating messages that can detract from the key feedback (such as what knowledge errors and learning processes need to change). However, Dweck believes that teachers can create a classroom culture and systems that will help pupils to respond to the learning challenges they might face at the point of learning (process level) and in response to their work (product level). Planning at the medium-term level requires a careful consideration not only of how learning is sequenced in a way that increases the challenge over the course of the lessons, but also of how assessment processes and feedback can help pupils to work through these challenges, rather than run away from these.

A belief in the power of critical, reflective and collaborative professional practice

The third theme we want to discuss relates to the role of the teacher as an active curriculum interpreter and creator of learning opportunities. The literature about the role of the teacher leads us to understand medium-term planning as more than just a practical way to plan sequences of lessons. Creating medium-term plans also provides teachers with the opportunity to promote important values, develop wider skills and ensure that the curriculum is turned into a meaningful and valuable learning experience for children. It is also a professional learning process, in which knowledge of subject, pedagogy and learners blends to create a learning journey for pupils and teachers alike. While learners make progress against learning intentions teachers are able to progress in a variety of other ways, including developing an awareness of how knowledge and processes can be taught and learned; developing their understanding of the strengths and weaknesses of their learners; and developing their pedagogical expertise as they explore adaptations they can make in the here and now, in the next few lessons or when delivering the plan again. Because it is often the case that other teachers will use the same medium-term plans too, it is also potentially a collaborative process in that it opens up a dialogue between teachers about clarifying intentions and activities, comparing evidence of attainment in terms of pupil work and so on.

   Teachers have often told us that they feel constrained by the context in which they work. The pressure (and often the ever-changing nature) of national education policy, the interpretation of these by schools and then the systems that schools create as part of this interpretation, not only put pressure on teachers but can also have a de-motivating and de-professionalising impact. In Chapter 1, we made the point that ten 'outstanding' lessons do not necessarily mean that outstanding learning has been achieved because the focus is on the individual bits of learning rather than coherent whole. However, the pressure of inspection has led schools to often focus on getting teachers to deliver outstanding lessons (that include features that can be ticked off) rather than develop outstanding learning over the medium term. Collaborative medium-term planning can be a process through which teachers re-assert their agency as creative agents of the curriculum, rather than the passive curriculum deliverers which policy sometimes envisages.

Critical reflective practice requires teachers to develop their own model of professionalism, which, while being flexible and responsive to the context they are working in, is rooted in their own principles, experience and research. Goodson (2000: 32) has outlined a model of 'principled professionalism' in which teachers are engaged in 'a self-directed search and struggle for *continuous learning* related to one's own expertise and standards of practice rather than compliance with the ... *endless change* demanded by others'. Such a process involves the development of 'collaborative cultures' of support within and beyond the school and 'increased opportunity and responsibility for exercising *discretionary judgement* concerning the issues of teaching, curriculum and care'. This model has strong links to Fullan's own model of teachers as change agents (Fullan, 1993). For him teaching is a moral profession, with teachers guided by a moral purpose such as the desire to make a difference and improve children's life chances. Teachers can affect change through developing their own practice in relation to four capacities.

Personal vision building

This involves identifying why teachers want to teach and using that vision to underpin their practice. Revisiting this regularly gives teachers an ultimate focus and Fullan also claims that building this sense of personal purpose is the route to organisational change. Such visioning may well influence, either implicitly or explicitly, your learning intentions and the skills and knowledge you seek to build, because you are more likely to put your medium-term plans into a broader framework that guides how you teach over the longer term. In Chapter 4, where we discuss the process of defining a clear focus and making the difficult decision about which content not to include, it is likely that your values will inform this process and help you impose a shape on the planned learning.

Inquiry

Teachers are career-long learners and need to be engaged in an ongoing quest to develop their practice and to consider other ways of approaching issues in teaching and learning. This involves blending broader principles of learning, educational research and subject and phase pedagogy in order to develop ways of approaching their teaching. Planning at the medium-term level provides a framework for active teacher research: trialling and testing some of these ideas over an extended period of time and making use of the findings in order to further influence their practice.

Mastery

Mastery refers to the technical skills teachers develop over time that enable them to teach well-organised and effective lessons. This obviously goes hand in hand with inquiry. If the inquiry aspect is concerned with researching effective teaching and learning approaches, mastery is using what you have learned from that process to underpin your future practice. Medium-term planning will always combine elements which teachers feel comfortable with, because they have prior experience of making such approaches work. These can also be developed to provide teachers with new opportunities to extend their teaching repertoire and deepen their mastery of teaching skills.

Collaboration

For Fullan, collaboration is an essential capacity because it avoids the 'ceiling effect' of working on one's own; we learn from our colleagues' valuable knowledge and experience too and this presents us with ways of thinking about learning. International research has shown how highly effective school systems such as those of Japan and Finland have a culture where 'collaborative planning, reflection on instruction and peer coaching are the norm and constant features of school life' (Barber and Mourshed, 2007). Similarly, Hattie (2011) argues that there needs to be ongoing collaborative dialogue between teachers that analyses the impact of teaching based upon evidence of progress and co-planning next steps. The planning of a medium-term sequence of lessons can sometimes be a sole endeavour by one teacher, while at other times it might be shared out. Sometimes the only collaboration is in the practical aspects, such as sharing resources. While we are not trying to suggest that all medium-term planning must be collaborative in terms of its realisation, we do believe it is important for teaching teams to be able to come together to discuss the learning intentions, key activities and assessment opportunities before teaching from the plan, and then to have regular conversations about how well it is working in practice and any adaptations that might help.

As we discussed above, all teachers need to be able to respond to the context in which they work and certainly the teachers we interviewed for this book had to factor in a number of practical and institutional factors when conceptualising their plans. As a teacher you will be expected to use the systems and follow the procedures that exist in your school. As such, we do not present any one way as *the way* to do medium-term planning. To do this would be pointless in the sense that it is impossible to provide a template or a rubric that could be adapted across all phases, subjects and contexts. It would also fly in the face of what we have said about the importance of teachers using their own critical judgements and professional reflections.

What we do believe, however, is that our five As approach can act as the basis of planning in any phase, subject or context because the five As mirror how teachers already approach teaching and learning over the medium term. We have interviewed teachers who have worked in very different educational settings, who had to bear in mind a range of factors when planning their sequences of lessons, including meeting the needs of very diverse classes, developing wider social skills, fulfilling the demands of examination specifications and using end of unit summative assessment tasks. What struck us was their clarity in what they wanted to achieve, their willingness to use a range of approaches to help pupils achieve this, and the way in which they went about identifying the extent to which their pupils had learned.

The five As of effective medium-term planning

The principles discussed in this chapter are fairly well established in the literature but our experience with student teachers has shown us that it is not always easy to implement them in practice. Over the next four chapters, we will be explaining our five As model of effective medium-term planning. This is intended to provide a clear, accessible framework in which you can start to implement these broader principles.

Table 3.3   The five As of medium-term planning

Articulation	You should have a clear idea of what you want your students to learn and why this is important and appropriate
Alignment	You should structure the learning so that the order in which students engage with new material enables them to progress to higher levels of understanding and skills.
Activation	You should provide activities that support this learning.
Assessment	You should know how you are going to assess the important things you want your students to learn.
Adaptation	Along the way you should monitor the students' progress against your intentions and update your plans to ensure they learn effectively.

We want you to consider these as both principles and steps. Principles, because research and experience show that effective teaching and learning require these elements to be in place, and steps, because they provide a practical set of things to do when approaching your planning. All the steps take place at the planning level, but some such as activation and assessment will also happen at the point of learning. In turn, the adaptation step is one in which you respond to the actual learning on the ground – reconsidering how you are articulating, aligning, activating and assessing your pupils both in the short and longer term.

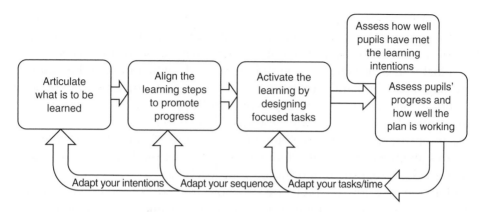

Figure 3.2 The five As as a learning cycle

The need to reflect and adjust means you are left with a cycle of teaching and learning, where planning becomes fluid and dynamic, responding to what learners are revealing to you in terms of their knowledge, understanding and skills.

Getting started with the five As

The five As may seem simple, but as Chambers points out, 'skills of planning come easily to some trainee teachers … Other trainees can be given exactly the same guidance, and yet find it extremely difficult to produce plans that look coherent and pay sufficient attention to detail' (2008: 46). So, what seems simple to some will be less obvious to others, and while a lucky few will instinctively understand how to construct plans that embody these five principles, many others will find particular aspects of the process difficult.

In order to help you overcome the obstacles you encounter we have tried to break the process down into a series of separate stages. This approach applies some principles of time management, drawn from outside of the educational world. For instance, the time-management system popularly known as 'Getting Things Done' (GTD) turns things that you want to achieve into projects that can be divided further into next-step actions to achieving a successful completion of the project. Allen (2001) suggests there are several stages involved in effective project planning, including mind-mapping to open up numerous ways forward, refining what you actually intend to do based upon your underpinning values and vision and only then devising a sequence of actions. He uses a quote from the writer Alvin Toffler to make a key point: 'You've got to think about the big things while you're doing small things, so that all the small things go in the right direction' (Allen, 2001: 93). This is a key theme we have discussed earlier in relation to aligning learning with intentions.

However, there is always a tension in dividing up a complicated task into separate steps. While this is helpful in explaining what is going on beneath the surface, it is wrong to give the impression that these stages are only encoun-tered in a linear form. In reality the next four chapters are all inter-related. Decisions you make later about assessment may cause you to come back to the initial stages and change your focus. Similarly, when looking for resources you may find a brilliant activity you really want your students to experience, or find an organisation offering a wonderful opportunity for a visit that you cannot turn down. In such cases you would need to review your overall inten-tions to ensure that the various dimensions to your plan come into alignment. It is this alignment that is the ultimate goal so that the final plan is coherent and provides a realistic blueprint for your teaching.

While the next few chapters are therefore framed as though we were talk-ing you through the planning process from the blank-page beginning to the final plan, we also want to emphasise that the actual process you follow in any given situation might be different as you jump between stages. The key thing is to remember to use these principles to ensure the final plan is coherent and all the elements are aligned with your overall learning intentions.

Conclusion

This chapter has explored constructivist ideas of learning and the relevance they have for medium-term planning. In particular we have considered two important themes from the education literature, constructive alignment and formative assessment. These provide the foundation of our approach to plan-ning, but we have also discussed the nature of the planner in this chapter and argued that all teachers should engage in critical, reflective and collaborative professional practice when interpreting curricula and creating opportunities for learning. Finally we briefly introduced our five As model of effective medium-term planning, which is our way of translating these influential ideas into a workable process. In the rest of the book we will look at this model in greater detail, exploring how it can be implemented in your professional practice.

Further reading

Biggs, J. (1996) 'Enhancing teaching through constructive alignment', *Higher Education*, 32, 347–364.
This is a classic statement of one of the most commonly used principles to inform planning.

Fullan, M. (1993) 'Why teachers must become change agents', *Educational Leadership*, 50 (6): 12–17.
Fullan provides a succinct argument for a profession which combines practical exper-tise with values and collegiality. It provides an antidote to some narrower, individualist and technicist models of teacher professionalism.

CHAPTER 4

ARTICULATING LEARNING

By the end of the chapter you will be able to:

- understand how to develop a clear purpose about what to include in your medium-term plan;
- identify appropriate knowledge, concepts, skills and attitudes to frame a plan;
- use curriculum frameworks to help you develop a focus for the learning;
- analyse the content in order to identify key organising themes.

Introduction

Being articulate means being precise and clear in your communication. The first stage in planning is to achieve precision and clarity about the nature and purpose of the medium-term plan. This is ultimately about finding a focus for your efforts for the duration of the plan. With a clear focus, everything else becomes easier – you know exactly what you are assessing, you can make decisions about the kinds of activities required and you can also make strong connections between lessons. Without a clear focus, lessons can meander along, and while they may be pleasant diversions, they may not get the students to a significant destination. In this chapter we will set out five steps to help you think about how to achieve that clarity and precision. We illustrate these steps with extracts from interviews with experienced practitioners.

In the next chapter we talk about ordering the content into some form of logical sequence and clearly the two processes of articulation and alignment may often take place simultaneously. If you are familiar with a topic, you will start to sequence ideas in your head as soon as you start to identify the kinds of content you want to include. We have split these chapters just to focus on one thing at a time and to provide a fail-proof recipe for the reader who is feeling overwhelmed by all the decisions they have to make. The following sequence is designed to enable anyone to work from the infinite range of possibilities about what *could* be included in a medium-term plan to a specific statement about what *will* be taught. We have tried not to assume that anything is immediately obvious to anyone and to make teachers' implicit knowledge explicit. Inevitably some of this may seem obvious to many readers, but equally we know from our work with student teachers over the years that some of this will not be obvious to all. In this chapter, then, we focus on five steps to get started. By the end of this stage you should be able to make a clear statement about what your medium-term plan is for – you should be able to articulate its purpose and scope.

Step 1: A world of possibilities

A student once told a colleague that while she was enjoying her history lectures she was feeling slightly overwhelmed because 'there is just so much of it'. This is true for every subject in the school curriculum – we are always battling with the notion that there is simply so much we want our pupils to know. A teacher might simply say they are teaching about natural selection in biology, democracy in citizenship or poetry in English, but these are all such broad areas they could keep people busy for years if they really wanted to explore them fully. If teachers embark on teaching these broad areas with the aim 'to do justice to the topic', it is easy to get bogged down in fact after fact, without thinking about what it all means. Inevitably teachers who plan like this don't have enough time to teach all the content they want to cover. As we explored in Chapter 2, this word in particular, 'coverage', is often the enemy of clear medium-term planning, and a teacher who feels they need to 'cover' everything is likely to feel they are always rushing and is more likely to teach a lot of content rather superficially. This first step, then, can have an almost therapeutic feel to it as the purpose is to brainstorm everything you know about the topic. It is the only time when you can be free to go on and on.

In this first step we are advising you to let rip, writing down everything you can think of, everything that is in the textbooks, everything your colleagues recommend as important content. Practically speaking, this will benefit from a very large sheet of paper, or even several stuck together. This is a kind of unburdening process, because this brainstorm will provide you with the raw material which will ultimately be worked up into the structure for your medium-term plan. There is some similarity here with Anne Lamott's advice to aspiring writers that the first step to perfection is to get on with the 'shitty first draft' (Lamott, 1995). She explains that a quality piece of writing can only emerge from some form of raw material, a first rough draft. Waiting for the perfect piece of writing to form in your head before starting to type is unrealistic. Once that first draft is out there in the world, you have something to work on, critique, amend or reject. And out of that a process of re-working emerges the thing we are aiming for. Perfection can only really emerge from such a process; we cannot expect it to emerge from our minds fully formed. That is what we would advise for getting started on a scheme of work. It does not really matter at this stage how accurate your recollection of subject knowledge is, that can all be checked out in the future, the point is to get every possibility out there so you can start to work with it. This can be done alone but is much more interesting if you can get a couple of colleagues involved in the process.

In our interviews, Rita, an early years teacher, provides the best demonstration of how this process can be collaborative and also form part of the teaching cycle for children:

We planned as a team – all the reception teachers and the nursery officers and nursery nurses – all planned together, everyone came up with ideas. They had resources, including some books related to transport, but aside from that we also looked at the children we had in the class ... We started a discussion about transport, so we had a thought shower about exciting ideas we could do, you know, get the fire brigade in, go for a walk in the local area, do some data handling, use the ICT board to go and count cars; there was also a walk to school scheme, so we introduced that as well. The third element was starting with the children's interests, so we did a mind map with the children. Whatever the topic, we always asked the children, 'What do you know about the topic?' We would generally do this one to two weeks before a half-term break, using carpet sessions to get discussions going. Then we would ask them, 'What don't you know?' This is hard because if you don't know something you don't know you don't know it, but they do know what they are confused about. So that will tell us already where they are starting from and bits of knowledge they are unsure about, but we're not really trying to just fill gaps, we are trying to build on what they know, so if they know that cars go fast, we might bring in the science of the ramps, at a basic level, to explore different surfaces and friction, to explore how fast a car can go and whether it goes faster on carpet or wood. At the same time, knowing what they want to know helps us to develop knowledge. And we also ask them, 'What do you want to do?' That way you give the ownership back to the children. They may come up with fantastic things they can't possibly do, but as much as possible you want to engage them and come up with solutions, so if they want to fly, we can't do that, but we can fly kites and look at how aeroplanes fly.

Early years practice is often very different from teaching and planning practices in the rest of the school system because it is so personalised and so focused on holistic child development. Therefore, as Rita states, the topic themes in this context really just provide a framework for a range of linked experiences, as opposed to a pre-determined statement of knowledge to be acquired. Nevertheless, this collaborative process does not have to be limited to working with very young children, and this is a good example of how the rest of the sector can learn from the good practice that has emerged in many early years settings. Rita's interview also illustrates how this first phase ideally starts with what children already understand and can do in the area you are planning – this can be a learning activity in its own right, an issue we return to in Chapter 6. We will say more about assessment in Chapter 7, but it is worth bearing in mind as this is a recurrent theme which runs under the surface of every step in this chapter.

Looking at the rather different context of the secondary maths department, Tanner and Jones (2000) recommend this initial brainstorm phase should identify the main mathematical concepts which will underpin the topic and they also note this is a good time to use the research literature and conversations with experienced colleagues to think about common misconceptions that might be associated with this topic. This is echoed in Chambers' chapter on planning in which he quotes a maths teacher as saying, '… in my planning, I think hard about where problems are going to come up. I identify what the key ideas are, and where there are going to be stumbling blocks' (2008: 60). Identifying the controversial or particularly problematic aspects of a subject is an important element to this initial step. Writing about science, Arriassecq and Greca argue that a 'deep epistemological analysis of the intrinsic problems of a given theory is the starting point' for any teacher's planning of a scheme of work (2012: 838). In their example, they argue that teaching Special Relativity Theory is particularly difficult because it requires a scientific understanding of the concepts of space and time, which does not sit easily with the everyday understanding children are likely to have learned thus far. Therefore, the scheme of work has to incorporate strategies for surfacing these beliefs and ideas and dealing with them explicitly. They stress the need for 'not regarding the obstacles as a negative aspect of learning, which could lead to a block preventing students from achieving the desired objective, but as a dynamic and motivating aspect' (Arriassecq and Greca, 2012: 839). In other words, teachers should select which obstacles will be overcome and treat these as the learning objectives in a scheme of work, not set learning objectives which pay little regard to the obstacles.

By contrast, Ellis's (2007) work with English teachers discusses a more subjective approach to thinking about what is to be taught. He quotes Hillocks's argument that:

> 'Pedagogical content knowledge appears not to be some body of pre-existing knowledge that teachers dip into, but knowledge constructed by the teacher in light of the teachers' epistemological stance and conceptions of knowledge to be taught … learning theory, and students.' (Hillocks, 1999, quoted in Ellis, 2007: 45)

It follows that a teacher's initial beliefs about their subject influence the teaching decisions they make and Ellis speculates that one of the differences between novice and expert teachers is that novices cannot yet use their values to transform subject knowledge into pedagogical knowledge effectively. For us this is relevant because it reinforces the notion that the production of a scheme of work is always a creative and subjective process. Getting others to look at your initial brainstorm can also be useful in helping you to identify where your own interpretation is already shaping the planning. Others may bring different perspectives, which can help you to broaden out your view of the topic beyond your own preconceptions.

The following extract from Andrew's interview demonstrates how he draws on a clear idea about the nature of English teaching in framing a scheme of work on debating. Andrew's background is in secondary English teaching and at the time of the interview he was in the middle of planning a unit of resources and was beginning to identify the key areas to focus on:

> *At the moment I am looking at some work to develop formal debating in English lessons because it's part of the new national curriculum Key Stage 3 [11–14-year-olds] requirement. My starting point now is what we want the children to learn in this unit that is to do with formal debating, not what they can tangentially learn whilst doing formal debating. So there are some very clear things that are to do with formal debating, such as rhetoric, rhetorical techniques in the speech aspect of formal debating. There are also very clear objectives to do with listening and responding to stimulus from other speakers; within that you would also have opportunities to work on*

structure and planning and delivery of your speech within a debate. But there would also be room for a wider remit of what is debating, and this links to some work I did editing a special edition of a magazine on different kinds of debates. I think given where this has come from there is very much an expectation of formal parliamentary-style debates taking place in the classroom, as they do in many extra-curricular areas of schools now, but actually the unit I have got in mind would allow students to experiment with different forms of formal debate, both parliamentary ones but also things that happen in non-parliamentary forums, which I only know a little bit about at the minute, such as the Occupy Movement where people can indicate their approval or disapproval of what has been said by hand gestures for example, which I think happens in lots of those new organisations that are attempting to do democracy in a new way. So I want children to be able to explore that and because it has an English focus it would always be doing that by exploring the possibilities for meaning that are generated in those different forums. So, how is language used there, compared to there? How does the modality of what you are doing factor in? So, gesture, whether it's filmed or on the radio or scripted, all those kind of issues.

Andrew is actively interpreting the curriculum through his understanding of English in the broad sense of 'generating meaning in different forums' and is consciously extending the range of examples he will be using to include extra-parliamentary debates. While providing him with opportunities to explore the English-specific issues of modality and gesture, it also ensures he can present students with a wide range of political examples where debate

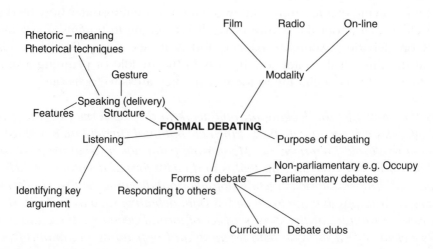

Figure 4.1   Andrew's brainstorm

is important, which in itself represents a particular political perspective. The start of his brainstorm might be represented in Figure 4.1. This is already an interpretation of the field. Discussing this developing brainstorm would help to add detail to the areas that are less well developed, for example on the purposes of debating.

 Activity

Start your own brainstorm on a topic you will be teaching.

1. Start with your own knowledge about the topic.
2. Add other ideas from resources available in the school/library/internet.
3. Share your brainstorm with others to complete it with additional detail.
4. Discuss this with experienced teacher colleagues and add in any other content ideas they suggest, paying special attention to problem areas they anticipate.
5. Make sure you identify obstacles, difficulties, challenging concepts, common misconceptions and controversial issues as well as the relatively settled knowledge in this area.

Step 2: Curriculum constraints

In addition to defining the subject knowledge relevant to teaching the topic under consideration we also have to take account of the curriculum. In England this is an increasingly difficult area to speak about as more and more schools are being granted the freedom not to adhere to the national curriculum; however, most schools will be working within some kind of curriculum framework, national or otherwise. For every examined course, there will be a detailed specification that will help you to shape the scheme of work. This step is about being aware of the overarching framework within which you are interpreting the topic. Practically this is likely to require you to expand or underline important aspects of your initial brainstorm with all the requirements specified in whatever curriculum documents you are working towards. We think it is probably best to consider the topic area in its own right first, and then to think about the curriculum, although one could equally start with this step and subsequently limit the brainstorm within these parameters. We prefer opening up possibilities before closing them down, because this process may actually enable you to make new connections and interpretations which help make the teaching more creative from the learners' perspective.

Rita, whose early years planning we have already discussed, shows a clear example of this in her planning:

> *On the one hand, in early years everything starts from assessment. So, you've observed children and everything you do with them is based on what you know they can do, what stage they are at, what their interests are. Every member of staff is also a key person for a group of about 15, who they get to know really well, as well as working with the whole 75. So we had assessed them in the six areas of learning – it covers language, personal and social development, maths, there was a knowledge element, knowledge about the world, and we had a checklist, and we could see for example that these children might avoid being out in the mud with mini-beasts, or hadn't really done anything with computers, so we'd have an idea about where groups of children were at, and what experiences they could do with being introduced to.*

Rita is working with the areas of learning identified in the early years framework, but she is also operating with her own checklists to keep track of the kinds of experiences the children have participated in. This was especially important for her because the curriculum in her setting was predominantly defined by the kinds of experiences planned for the children. In her setting children had some freedom to choose the activities they engaged with and so it was important that the staff developed their own way of describing and recording the kinds of activities the children experienced. This would help them to plan further activities and perhaps encourage children to broaden their range over time.

At the other end of the age range Vicky described how she used the Edexcel GCE A level Government and Politics Specification as the context in which she developed a scheme of work on pressure groups. The following summary presents some text from the specification and also some of Vicky's summary of the overall structure. You can see how important it is to refer to such documents very early in any planning process and to ensure that the required content is included.

Overall purpose

'This unit introduces students to the key channels of communication between government and the people and encourages them to evaluate the adequacy of existing arrangements for ensuring representative democracy and participation.'

Assessment

'Students are required to complete two structured questions from a choice of four. Each question will have a mark tariff of 5, 10, and 25 marks.

The 5-mark questions will require students to demonstrate their knowledge and understanding.

The 10-mark questions will require students to demonstrate their knowledge and understanding, as well as analyse and evaluate political information, arguments and explanations.

The 25-mark questions will require students to demonstrate knowledge and understanding, analyse and evaluate political information and construct and communicate coherent arguments.'

There are three overarching assessment objectives for the course:

1. Demonstrate knowledge and understanding of relevant institutions, processes, political concepts, theories and debates.
2. Analyse and evaluate political information, arguments and explanations, and identify parallels, connections, similarities and differences between aspects of the political systems studied.
3. Construct and communicate coherent arguments making use of a range of appropriate political vocabulary.

Module outline

The whole A level programme includes four modules. This scheme of work forms part of a larger module called *People and Politics* and is taught in the first year of the two-year programme; it forms half of the AS qualification, alongside the *Governing the UK* unit. The second year, which leads to a full A level, includes two additional modules which explore themes in political analysis. This module is divided into four units:

- Democracy and Political Participation
- Party Policies and Ideas
- Elections
- Pressure Groups

Required content for the pressure groups unit

Key concepts

- pressure group
- sectional/promotional groups
- insider/outsider groups

(Continued)

(Continued)

- pluralism
- elitism
- functional representation
- pluralist democracy

Content explanation

- Nature of pressure groups – a knowledge and understanding of the features and functions of pressure groups; of how and the extent to which they differ from political parties; and an awareness of the different kinds of pressure groups.
- Pressure group power – a knowledge and understanding of how pressure groups exert influence and of the extent of their influence, and an awareness of the distribution of power amongst pressure groups, including the factors that influence this.
- Pressure groups and democracy – a knowledge and understanding of the relationship between pressure groups and democracy and, in particular, of the extent to which they promote political participation and responsive government.

(Adapted from Edexcel, 2013 and interview with Vicky)

On one level this is so specific that there may seem little room for teacher individuality. But as Vicky's interview made clear, she was actively interpreting this all the way through, even at the level of the title of the module:

> *Although the overall module is called* People and Politics *I tend to think of it as 'How do people make change?' In the first college where I taught, this would been the first module in the year and the running order of the units was to start with democracy, then do elections, then pressure groups and then finally consider policies and ideas. This means this unit would have taken place before Christmas towards the end of the first term of A level. In the college where I am teaching this year, the order is different and so students have already studied the module on* Governing the UK. *This means the kids have had a lot more academic engagement and so I have had to re-plan it completely.*

Not only is Vicky actively interpreting the specification, she is doing this very specifically for the context in which she is teaching. For her, the most significant issue in re-planning this unit was not the change of college, but actually the change of sequencing between units. Rather than use pressure groups as a way to introduce British politics, she can now use that prior knowledge in her teaching about pressure groups. Clearly this would open up different possible ways of teaching and in fact would require her to change her expectations as this unit of work would also serve as an opportunity to consolidate and extend prior learning. At the brainstorming phase the content from the specification and the expectations of the 25-mark question would have to be included, as would any specific content to be revisited from earlier modules.

 Activity

1. Return to your brainstorm and add in any specific content required by the curriculum/specification you are using.
2. You could also highlight any areas of your brainstorm that are particularly important in the curriculum you are using.
3. Make sure you have some notes relating to the level of expectation in relation to key concepts as well.

Step 3: An even broader view of what to include

This focus on the precise nature of the knowledge to be taught is characteristic of much of the planning literature. However, while this provides an invaluable starting point, teachers are also doing much more in a medium-term plan than developing subject knowledge and understanding. They must also pay attention to developing several other areas:

- skills – generic study skills, subject specific skills, exam skills and so on;
- values and attitudes – those related to learning, for example, respect for evidence, willingness to reflect on performance and those related to broader social objectives such as a willingness to work together, valuing others' opinions and contributions;
- they will also be alert to responding to pupils' needs and interests, and therefore will be thinking about making relevant connections in their teaching in order to secure motivation and engagement.

Sometimes these broader elements are included explicitly in the curriculum structure, but this is not always the case; for example the 2014 National Curriculum for England focuses more on subject requirements than its immediate predecessor. This change in presentation style does not mean teachers teach less, it just means they have to exercise a bit more thought to identify what those overarching elements might be. Many of these elements, such as overarching values, may also be identified through statements about the school values and ethos. In practical terms this step requires you to add even more content to your initial brainstorm, building out from the specific issues of content coverage to the broader kinds of learning intentions you want to promote. The following examples illustrate some of the models teachers draw on in order to broaden out their view of what they are planning to achieve.

This broader picture requires us to think about our ultimate goal and what we can do to get children to achieve it. There are tensions between the need to help pupils achieve the highest grades possible and the concomitant temptation to 'spoon-feed' them, and the broader goal to help children become independent and critical thinkers. Most teachers want to promote pupils' independence but not all teachers plan explicitly to achieve this. Writing about this tension in the context of modern languages, Hurd warned that if we genuinely aspire to helping young people to achieve this latter goal we have to recognise that: '[If] learners are not trained for autonomy, no amount of surrounding them with resources will foster in them that capacity for active involvement and conscious choice, although it might appear to do so' (1998: 72). This is a particularly acute issue for A level teachers, and Meiring and Norman (1999a: 122) have developed a framework to underpin all their A level teaching which puts this goal at the heart of their planning. Their three key principles for A level planning are referred to as the STAR model:

- Structure – knowledge of concepts and terminology.
- Autonomy – choice and responsibility.
- Reflection – independence, analysis, inference and reasoning.

These three principles are not lifted from a specific curriculum document, but would inform the initial stages of the planning process. At this stage we should be aware of the skills required for reflection, and we might be identifying areas in the scheme of work where such skills could be developed. Partly this informs the choices we make when deciding on activities (Chapter 6), but it is worth being alert to these issues at this early stage because we might want to spend longer on a particular piece of content because it offers opportunities to engage with this area of skills development. As a very basic example we might want to plan in an opportunity to teach some vocabulary that would enable pupils to reflect on their performance in the target language and revisit this to consolidate and extend this aspect of the work in subsequent units.

The same principle holds with children before they get to A level; for example, Rubin provides a similar piece of advice for modern languages teachers working with younger and less successful language learners: 'Often poorer learners don't have a clue as to how good learners arrive at their answers and feel that they can never perform as good learners do. By revealing the process, this myth can be exposed' (Rubin, 1990: 282). In exploring the implications of this insight in relation to a plan for promoting reading strategies, Grenfell and Harris point out:

> It is unrealistic to assume that simply telling students about possible fruitful strategies will ensure that these pass into their repertoire and can be drawn on automatically. Explicit reminders to use the … strategies will be necessary alongside a number of tasks and materials likely to promote them. (1999: 77).

In addition they point out that different strategies may be more suitable for different texts or purposes and so initially the teacher may have to help the pupils to identify the most appropriate strategy for their purpose. Again, while this might only be developed fully when we select activities, it is useful to have these themes identified at this stage; for example, when thinking about this initial brainstorm, we might specify some reading strategies, perhaps even consider types of texts. One scheme of work might focus on *bandes dessinées* texts, whilst another might focus on sport websites. Thinking about the conventions of each form would be helpful at this early stage to enable you to think about exactly what you will need to teach to make such texts accessible.

As an A level teacher Vicky is used to dealing with the tensions identified by Meiring and Norman, and in this extract she talks about how she tries to bring together her knowledge of the specification and her understanding of how the students engage with politics:

> *Obviously for the students to be successful in their AS they have to pass their exam so the exam content has dictated what needs to be taught. There are three assessment objectives for the specification and the second one is the intellectual skills and in A2 that turns into synoptic thinking, and so really what we want to do as AS teachers is really scaffolding the idea that kids can start seeing the real questions … the nuances in political themes and apply political concepts. The synoptic theme for the pressure groups unit is really, 'Do pressure groups contribute to democracy or elitism?', i.e. 'Are they democratic, do they promote pluralism or do they promote elitism?', so really my whole idea of planning is taking them to that point, that's what we want them to be able to answer … 'Do pressure groups disperse power or concentrate it?' That is the synoptic theme of the*

25-mark exam questions and that kind of dictates what is going to hap-pen over the three weeks.

Politics is really dependent on concepts ... these concepts like power, authority, representation need to be mainstreamed into the students' awareness so whenever they are talking or writing a politics essay for an exam, these are the kinds of thematic they are picking up on – how does the topic I am looking at apply to these concepts? In this unit we will start with wider concepts like democracy and representation and then move on to the more specific concepts that relate to pressure groups, like they have certain statuses, they can be insider or outsider pressure groups, sectional, promotional etc. ... So we are obviously starting with wider concepts and big learning questions, like 'How do people make change in a democracy?' and that would be our thematic question for the week, and then we scaffold the concepts, re-using previous concepts and introducing new ones on top of that.

I will give historical examples of people who made a change, you know either the Suffragettes or the anti-Apartheid movement, you know big movements for progressive change – change that gives rights and empowers people. It's not strictly necessary to put the historical dimen-sion in, that's a personal choice that I have made. I feel that an honest interpretation of the themes that the specification brings up requires the students to understand that politics is about progressive relationships in society, and that if you want to understand these themes of democracy and representation you have to understand that women didn't have representation before the Suffragette movement in the UK and that working-class people couldn't vote before 1867 and there has been a progressive movement of people making change using democratic sys-tems to acquire rights, and that's why pressure groups ultimately feed into that idea of pluralism and democracy which is the kids' 25-mark question.

You do not need to fully understand the terms Vicky is using to describe pressure groups to appreciate what is happening here in terms of her active interpretation of the specification in order to develop the wider picture. The content is there, but so also is a pragmatic approach to teaching exam tech-nique. This is aligned with an appreciation of the higher-level thinking skill of synthesis in the synoptic-style question. And yet with all this jostling for attention she is also ensuring that her interpretation includes some historical material to help the students appreciate change over time, and also help them understand that their experiences are defined by a particular time and place, and cannot be seen as universal starting points. At this stage of the planning it is her addition of the historical dimension and her selection of specific examples that would find their way into the planning brainstorm. Even with such a specific and extensive exam specification Vicky is still adding in more material to include in her plan.

Chris Husbands (1996) provides another example of how this broader dimension can also relate to the broader purpose of teaching a specific subject. Writing about history he argues that teachers' planning needs to reflect three principles, which he derives from the subject pedagogy research literature, and not from any specific curricular framework. He argues schemes of work should aim to consistently revisit three core ideas:

- Extend, enrich or refine children's mini-theories about the events they are studying such as understanding international rivalry in order to understand the beginning of the First World War.
- Restructure their understanding of causation, for example to avoid the assumption that proximate cause may be most significant.
- Provide interpretive statements about the past in which they make their own assumptions and reasoning explicit.

Here Husbands develops cross-cutting principles based on his understanding of what it means to learn history, and the kinds of historical reasoning he wants pupils to demonstrate. He wants his pupils to get used to explaining how they come to know something, or what their reasons are for coming to a specific judgement about an event or person. It is also based on research into common misconceptions, or conceptual problems; for example young children are not very good at identifying complicated causal reasoning and instead tend to pick the nearest related event as the main cause. As Wineburg argues,

> ... to know how to construct a historical argument, to know how to evaluate and question sources, to know when analogies to other events are appropriate and when they are misleading is not a generic "thinking skill," a "process," or a disembodied system of "metaknowledge." It is content knowledge in the richest sense. (2008: 126)

Barlex (2005) provides another example of this kind of overarching planning template, this time from the perspective of design and technology. His framework for planning addresses five important questions that teachers should use to structure their medium-term planning (Figure 4.2). There is little here that most design and technology teachers would question, and in some ways these models really just set out to summarise the professional knowledge that teachers develop over time. Often this knowledge remains implicit for the teachers themselves who more or less unconsciously draw on these ideas to inform their planning choices. For the novice teacher there are two routes to getting to know what these principles are: first, by referring to the literature where practitioners such as Barlex and Husbands have taken the time to try to distil these complex issues into workable models; and second, by asking carefully focused questions of the teachers with whom you are working.

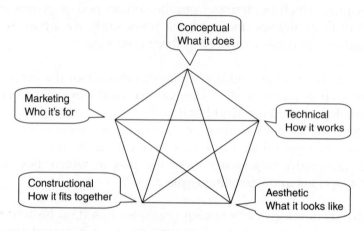

Figure 4.2 The design pentagon (Barlex, 2005)

In the next interview extract Shiv's explanation of how she came to find a focus for her year 2 (six to seven-year-olds) science scheme of work is helpful in thinking about what the overarching aims are and how she came to identify them.

> *This was designed for a specific year 2 class. I was doing PPA [planning, preparation and assessment] cover and I was teaching them science for this cover. I had taught the group when they were in year 1 so I knew them and although the topics were set up on termly themes already, how I approached the topic was up to me. I had strong feelings about what that group needed and so I used the plan to look more at their Sc1 skills rather than knowledge about the human body. I knew they had a lot of that from last year, and I also knew what was going to follow this, which was a topic on Keeping Healthy, and so I thought we can hit all that body stuff again. I thought they needed more science organisation skills, so I planned it that way.*
>
> *They were a broad range of ability, and so there were some children who were very able to be articulate when talking about their ideas but they couldn't write them down. That's why I wanted to take that group and get*

them more organised in their science skills because there are a lot of children in there who had a lot to offer in science if they could organise themselves. Not even just in terms of writing ability but that they would be able to give their findings through talking or drawing – they just needed to organise the process of finding things out. That's what I was particularly concerned with, with that group.

The school has a six-stage investigation process that is used from year 1 to year 6:

1. Raising a question – what are we trying to find out?

2. Thinking of a method – how are we going to find out?

3. Prediction – what do I think we are going to find out?

4. Investigation – finding out.

5. Presenting your evidence.

6. Analysing your evidence.

This has been around in science textbooks and theory for a long time and it's quite a common model. What might be different in this school is that we broke it down to use with year 1 and year 2.

Here Shiv is clear that she was de-emphasising the development of new knowledge about the science of the body and instead focusing on developing the children's ability to engage with the school's science investigation process. This is important because it means her initial brainstorm would be almost entirely about concepts and processes rather than knowledge.

Anna provides another interesting illustration of how one might think about the broader picture at this stage of planning. Anna is education officer at the Campaign for Nuclear Disarmament (CND) and we interviewed her about a teaching resource she had produced for secondary teachers which looked at the American bombing of Hiroshima and Nagasaki. She had developed the resource to be used in four different subjects and so had to be very clear about the overarching goals and the different specific subject lenses that could be used to explore the topic.

The idea of writing Truman on Trial *was to get kids thinking about what happened in Hiroshima and Nagasaki but also to plug into four main subject areas so that the issues weren't just seen as something you could tuck away somewhere, but it could be looked at in citizenship, RE, history and English. I wrote it so that all four subject areas were covered and there are follow-on activities for each of the areas. I think quite often Hiroshima and Nagasaki are taught quite badly. I've been in to schools before, picked up a textbook, turned to a page and it says 'Why it was necessary to drop the bombs on Hiroshima and Nagasaki?' but as citizenship educators – educators of any sort – we should be saying, 'Was it necessary to drop the bombs?' and let the kids work it out for themselves. What I think of as moral is giving the kids all the information and empowering them to make up their own minds on the issue. So if a class did this and everyone came out against the bombing of Hiroshima and Nagasaki I wouldn't consider that as a win, because some kids will think it was right, and I'd be happy with that if they got to that point through informed thought, discussion and being empowered to be in control of their own learning. I want to make sure that they understand what happened to people when these bombs were dropped and sometimes the story is just, 'Oh, these bombs were dropped and these towns were destroyed and then the war ended ...' Students need to know that it wasn't like that, people suffered and people are still suffering, but if students weigh that up and think that was a sacrifice that was worth it, then that is an informed decision.*

I did it across four subjects for various reasons. Partly I wanted to make sure this was as usable as possible to as many people as possible. So in the citizenship route, I am focusing on the process and the subject matter. The act of doing the trial, collecting data, doing a news report are all part of citizenship. In history they look at the changing nature of conflict and the origins of the Cold War, and it's about exploring a historical issue through primary and secondary data, analysing where the data come from, and thinking about the reliability of sources; for example, we think about whether an eye-witness testimony is reliable. In English, the thing that's fantastic is speaking and listening (in the old curriculum) and spoken English (in the new curriculum) and getting kids to explore ideas, have debates and look at different points of view. The trial gives them the chance to do some performance and get a drama element in and the follow-up activity suggests doing some poetry, including a haiku for or against, which gets persuasive language in alongside a creative element. In religious studies in Key Stage 4 and GCSE students often study war and peace, the morality of war and the notion of a 'just war', and their follow-up lesson is about getting kids to develop their own 'just war' theory and applying their theory to the bombings of Hiroshima and Nagasaki.

As well as showing how the subject area shapes the teacher's take on the topic, this also illustrates how the core, independent moral reasoning, remains constant, whatever subject route is adopted. As with the other examples in this section Anna adds in more objectives than are strictly required by the curriculum. The teachers discussed in this section avoid this becoming overwhelming because these additional concepts, knowledge and skills are actually central to the content and the approach they want to take. These additional layers of planning will serve to make the medium-term plan simpler and more coherent in the long run and should help to avoid the problem of 'coverage' or 'overload' we discussed in Chapter 2. They can be seen as serving an integrative function, binding together the other elements into a coherent overview (as with the concepts of 'science investigations' or 'moral reasoning'), or providing significant themes running through the plan (as with the explicit preparation of exam technique).

 Activity

1. Revisit your brainstorm and add in any cross-curricular skills you feel could be developed in this topic.
2. What kinds of values work could be developed through this unit?
3. Are there any integrative themes or concepts that will help to bind this plan together?
4. Make sure you have identified additional perspectives that would help you to engage the pupils and develop their understanding and skills within a meaningful broader context.

Step 4: Chunking and junking

So far in this chapter we have been advising you to expand your brainstorm with more and more possible areas to cover and it may now be looking rather unwieldy. That is fine, because this is now your raw material for the actual planning process. The next stage is to wrestle this huge list of possibilities into some coherent shape and this will require some higher-level critical thinking and some ruthless cutting. This is another example of a planning decision that teachers may often make unconsciously; for example, Chambers, whose book is full of excellent advice on planning and teaching, states in this regard, 'it is clearly desirable to split up the work on algebra in a given year into separate units of work, each lasting perhaps three weeks, and to place the different algebra units at different times within the year, rather than do them all in one go' (2008: 49). But he does not share why this is the case. Why is it better to chunk up topics into three-week units? Why wouldn't you want to teach algebra in one go? And how would you chunk up the whole of algebra into several smaller units – what would go where? We start this section by explaining why these themes and chunks are important and then illustrate some strategies you could use to start this process yourself.

Ollerton provides part of the answer when he argues that creating a modular structure is the first principle of planning. He says a module is 'a collection of ideas and tasks connected by a common theme or broad concept ... For students to access concepts in depth they need time to learn, develop and construct their understanding of concepts and structures' (2006: 144). For Reigeluth (1999) this means configuring large amounts of information into smaller units in order to accommodate memory and learning limitations. This connects with 'cognitive load theory', which emphasises the constraints of working memory on learning (Sweller at al., 1998). Working memory is generally thought to be fairly limited, with the capacity for holding about seven items or elements at a time, and given that it is most commonly used to process information (and this often involves comparison or organization of some kind), then we are probably only able to process two or three items simultaneously.

> The implications of working memory limitations on instructional design can hardly be overestimated ... Anything beyond the simplest cognitive activities appears to overwhelm working memory ... [but] despite these apparent restrictions, the intellectual heights to which humans are capable indicate that structures other than working memory must play a critical role in human cognition. (Sweller at al., 1998: 252–253)

The explanation for this apparent contradiction lies in our long-term memory. We store processed information in our long-term memory, and this is called up to work on in our short-term memory as needed.

As an example Sweller at al. discuss chess players. The experienced chess player is better able to understand what is happening on the board because they have a vast knowledge base in their long-term memory, which records thousands of patterns of play and possible sequences associated with them. By contrast the novice is likely to be working harder in their working memory, but is unlikely to succeed as a consequence. The secret for experienced chess players is that they remember patterns of pieces and moves, rather than trying to remember each piece individually. According to constructivist learning, which we discussed briefly in Chapter 1, knowledge more generally is also stored in patterns or sequences, which are called schemas, or sometimes 'mental models' (Smith and Ragan, 1999: 21). Schemas organise facts according to how we will use the information. While schemas function as mechanisms for the storage and organisation of knowledge, they also reduce the working memory load, because the working memory can deal with an entire schema as a single unit, even though that schema may include huge amounts of information.

Sweller et al. use the example of 'restaurant' as a schema which we can call to mind to use. If we think about all the experiences, knowledge and understanding we bring to bear to grasp this concept it is quite huge. We know about menus, staff roles, etiquette, pricing, types of food, types of restaurant, furniture layout and so on but it is all organised in one schema. This becomes very obvious if you observe a modern languages class in which the teacher is using a menu as a resource. It becomes evident in some contexts that many young children have very little direct knowledge of how a restaurant works, and confusion arises where the teacher cannot understand that they are drawing on a complex schema which is relatively undeveloped in some children. Sweller at al. point out that if we engage with an area frequently the schema may also become automated. Hence we can read a page of information quickly without having to recall what each letter is and how it combines with others. Once we have automated reading we have working memory free to think about the meaning of the text, whereas the novice reader may find their working memory overwhelmed with the process of reading and fail to extract meaning from the text. The same is the case for successful mathematicians, who come to read maths problems in such a way that they automatically know what to do, while others may have to consciously work through the possibilities or try to recall and compare similar problems from the past.

It follows from their analysis of the nature of constructivist learning that teaching should therefore aim to help learners construct and automate schemas. This proposition is shared by Ivie who argues that 'strengthening cognitive structures helps students retain information longer, and subsumptions provide students with basic structures on which to build new concepts' (1998). Subsumption is the term used to explain how concepts become integrated into higher concepts as one develops increasingly abstracted schema; for example, menu forms part of the overall schema of restaurant, which may itself become subsumed into a more abstract schema of the service economy. The point is that when teachers are chunking up the content into teaching units, this is far more than an administrative exercise to accommodate holidays or exams; this is about defining the units as coherent, meaningful chunks of learning. The word often used to describe this is 'cognate' where items are linked together by some underlying association. When we are chunking up the content then we are looking to identify connections which are sufficiently strong that they could form the basis of a schema or be subsumed into an existing schema.

It also follows from this that if these connections are sufficiently significant, we should also build in opportunities for students to revisit them so that eventually they can become automated. This is the rationale for Chambers' advice that it makes sense to chunk up algebra and revisit it at regular intervals. As Ollerton advises secondary maths teachers:

> When concepts are integrated into different topic areas and become part of what happens in mathematics classrooms, right from the very first lesson in Year 7, students expect to draw upon different skills and concepts at different times in a range of contexts. This is quite different to teaching concepts in separate, fragmented and isolated ways. (2006: 150)

At this stage, you might develop ideas for how to tackle a particular issue in class, but that detail relating to activities and sequencing can come later. The first stage is to ensure you can establish these cognate chunks as the building blocks of the plan. As with the rest of this process, some teachers will identify these chunks automatically with little conscious thought, but others (especially people new to teaching or new to a subject area) will have to spend some time sorting out what these chunks might be.

Strategy 1: Looking for conceptual affinities

The most obvious way to work from the huge brainstorm you have to a more tightly defined set of cognate chunks or modules is simply to start looking for connections and to try to group some of the content together. Figures 4.3 and 4.4 provide an example of how this might work for a history scheme of work on 'empire'. In one example the connections revolve around the concepts of slavery, whilst in the other example, the connections are related to the idea of trade. These connections might emerge through (i) simply reflecting on your knowledge of the area, (ii) looking for logical connections where you are searching for similarities, (iii) looking at textbooks or the wider literature to identify recurrent key concepts, or (iv) from talking to experienced colleagues and then applying their suggested themes to your content. At this point it doesn't really matter what you might actually teach; the point is to reduce this brainstorm to a smaller

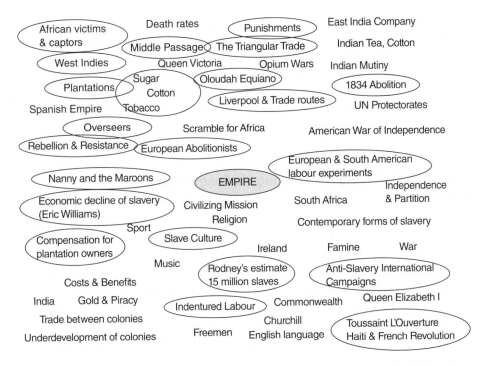

Figure 4.3   A brainstorm with connections to the concepts of 'slavery' highlighted

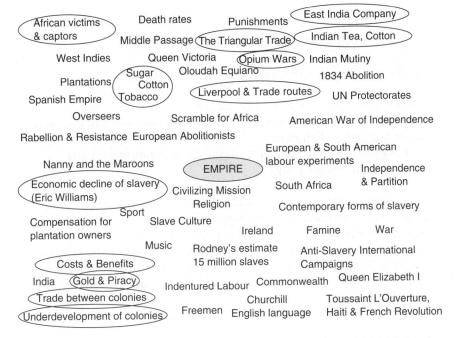

Figure 4.4   A brainstorm with connections to the concepts of 'trade' highlighted

number of concepts. These concepts or themes are likely to provide the building blocks of the scheme. In this history example, just identifying these two themes shows the kind of take the author has on imperial history, and as it stands, there are some areas that have not been included in the themes. This could prompt the teacher to think about whether they would therefore ignore some of the content, or devise another theme that would accommodate this additional knowledge.

Strategy 2: Identifying the learning challenge to find your focus

In relation to science Leach and Scott adopt a different strategy to get to the same point. They note that one way to think about how to organise the material is to start to assess the 'learning demand', which they define as the gap between the way a concept is discussed in social language and the way it is discussed in school science language (2002: 125). For example, we talk about 'suction' in everyday social language whilst scientists talk about 'differences in air pressure'. This is a clue to help the teacher think about the different conceptual tools available in each type of language.

 Case Study   Assessing the learning demand

Leach and Scott suggest the following approach:

1. Identify the school science to be taught.
2. Consider how this area of science is conceptualised in the everyday social language of students.
3. Identify the learning demand by appraising the nature of any differences between 1 and 2.

    As an example think about the nature of gravity versus common sense understandings of how things influence each other. This requires students to take on the concept of 'action at a distance' i.e. gravitation forces can operate between objects without them touching. This is likely to challenge the student's basic assumptions about the nature of the physical world. (Leach and Scott, 2002: 128)

And they provide an example of how this would work with a sequence of lessons on electric circuits:

School science language

- current as flow of charge;
- current as the means of energy transfer;
- current as being conserved;
- the supply of energy as originating in the electrical cell;
- energy being transferred in resistive elements of the circuit.

Everyday social language

- Batteries run out.
- Electricity makes things work.
- Current, electricity, volts, power are the same kind of thing.
- Electricity/electric current flows.

Learning demand

- Develop abstract scientific concepts of charge, current, resistance and energy in the context of explaining the behaviour of simple electric circuits, and differentiating between the meanings of these terms.
- Understand that the current carries energy in the electric circuit and that it is the energy which is 'used up' (transferred) and not the current.
- Be able to visualise what is happening in simple series circuits, with different combinations of cells and resistances and to predict and explain their behaviour.
- Understand that the electric circuit model based on concepts of charge, current, resistance and energy can be used to predict and explain the behaviour of a wide range of simple circuits.

These four areas might be the main themes you want to develop in your medium-term plan, and around which you start to plan sequences of lessons.

Source: Leach, J. and Scott, P. (2002) Designing and evaluating science teaching sequences: an approach drawing upon the concept of learning demand and a social constructivist perspective on learning, *Studies in Science Education*, 38, 115–142.

It is evident that thinking about the particular way in which language is used to represent concepts in subject disciplines provides some crucial clues about what to focus on, what the main chunks might be and what material might be marginal. So far, then, we have suggested two main strategies to adopt to make decisions about chunking and junking. First, you can look for similarities between the items in your brainstorm and group similar or related items together to form a chunk. If there is a strong connection it could form a theme or even the main focus of your plan. Second, you could think about the peculiarities of the subject lens on this topic – what is different about the way your subject considers this area compared with the way people would talk about it in everyday language? A third option might be just to reflect on the key concepts or problems that emerge in the literature relating to this area of subject knowledge. What are the areas of contention or debate that might provide useful points to focus on in order to explore deeper understandings of the topic and the subject? Out of this analytical process you should be able to turn your brainstorm into a more manageable set of core organising themes or ideas. You then need to be ruthless about cutting out elements that do not help you grapple with the main theme. Shiv provided a good example of this in her rejection of any significant new knowledge about the body because she wanted to focus on investigation skills with her primary science class. In our history example the teacher might decide to focus on trade and they may therefore decide that they only want to focus on a few key economic concepts. In order to really develop these concepts they might limit their material just to cover two key locations and one or two commodities, rather than try to do justice to all aspects of imperial trade. This approach would help you cut out case studies or examples which essentially repeat the same basic concept or idea. The clarity emerges from within your theme, because you identify strong connections to bind ideas and acts together, and from without because you cut out excess material to make the boundaries of your teaching clear and avoid getting bogged down in excessive detail.

 Activity

Connelly and Clandinin (1988) discuss the 'null curriculum' which is the curriculum we choose to exclude:

1. Review a scheme of work and list all the things that could have been included because they are relevant but were not.
2. What is the significance of these missing perspectives/elements?
3. Which, if any, would you want to include and why?
4. Are there any other elements in this scheme of work you would like to cut, because they do not seem sufficiently important? What difference would this cut make?

| ![] | **Activity** |

1. Review your brainstorm, highlighting possible themes and connections.
2. Identify the possible chunks, which could form the building blocks of the plan.
3. What content, if any, could you cut? This could be because it doesn't connect to any important chunks, or because it seems redundant or repetitive.

When we spoke to Andrew about how his planning had evolved over the years he was frustrated that the national literacy strategy had influenced his planning adversely (Chapter 2). Whatever the intention of the strategy, he was clear that it had the effect of fragmenting his planning, spreading his focus too thinly across too many objectives and preventing him from developing a coherent big picture. When he discussed the plan he was currently developing he was very much clearer about what he would *not* be doing in his scheme of work on debating:

> *You wouldn't do anything else that you were teaching specifically as an objective, you wouldn't say suddenly, right, we're going to look at semi-colons. It's just not relevant. It might come out of what they have written but you wouldn't have that as an objective for the whole class. You might teach it as and when it emerges from the students' work; for example, if I have 30 students of varying abilities, my own feeling now is that it is absolutely pointless doing a lesson to those 30 students on the semi-colon, because some will know it, some won't and actually it's such a small aspect of the subject, to have a big focus on it becomes a bit irrelevant. It needs to come in with certain targeted interventions with certain pupils. And by all means in your lessons have a mention of it. I just think the kind of lesson where your objective is to be able to use the semi-colon effectively in a sentence reduces the outcome of the lesson to something that is too small and actually too irrelevant to the wider context of what they are trying to do in terms of creating meaning in the English classroom.*

Step 5: Identifying a big question or a big picture

By this stage you should be edging towards some clarity about what the medium term is about and what it is for. We should have a good answer for the question, 'Why are we doing this?' It is perfectly possible to develop and teach a medium-term plan without having an overarching question, as long as there is a clear framework for the learning and you can explain this and the rationale for it to the students, that big picture will probably be good enough. But there is something intellectually satisfying about having a big question about which you care enough to want to find out the answer. Therefore we would recommend that, if possible, you try to devise a big question, or series of big questions, to help generate some momentum for the learning.

In Vicky's interview she talked about the kinds of questions that serve this function:

> *I was speaking to a colleague who has just retired, and she said the politics and sociology specifications have been de-politicised. So, whereas in the 1990s there might have been a question like 'Is civil disobedience ever necessary?' now that's not really touched upon ... not that I think we should promote civil disobedience, but I think when you are doing a politics course, you should be empowered to make good political decisions or have the confidence to take political action at some level. Most politics teachers I talk to agree this pressure groups unit is the one kids find most engaging, because in a sense it's the coolest unit, there's quite a lot of good stuff to talk about, and quite strong examples that the kids can engage in – they like it.*

It is apparent in the extracts we have already quoted above that Vicky is always teaching with the big questions in mind, and in this unit thinking about 'How do people make a difference?' and 'Do some people make more of a difference?' Questions also emerge out of the recognition that there is a gap in our knowledge or some form of inconsistency that needs to be resolved. Therefore some of the best questions are the ones that students recognise as arising out of their own confusion or misunderstanding (Tanner and Jones, 2000). In the *Truman on Trial* resource Anna spoke about earlier in this chapter, her big question is 'Were the Americans justified in dropping the atom bombs on Japan?' and pupils encountering this for the first time will be easily prompted to ask 'Why did they drop the bomb?' simply by examining some of the effects. In the history examples in Figures 4.3 and 4.4 each theme might also yield different and specific questions, such as 'Why didn't slavery end in 1834?' or 'Who benefited most from the empire?' These framing questions are often called 'enquiry questions' precisely because they provide the overarching question to guide a sustained period of investigation and thought.

While recognising the value of a good question as the starting point, Leach and Scott's focus on the language demands of science led them to focus more on the big picture, or big story in their case:

It seems to us that central to any teaching sequence is the way in which the teacher works with students to 'talk into existence' the scientific story ... The activities which are often used in science lessons (experiments, demonstrations and so on) are important, but only insofar as they can act as points of reference in the development of the scientific story. (Leach and Scott, 2002: 124)

Drawing on Vygotsky's distinction between spontaneous concepts, which are picked up unconsciously through day-to-day interactions, and scientific concepts, which originate in particular disciplines and which are learned though instruction, they argue that different subject communities develop their own uses of language. They conclude:

The different social languages and speech genres which are introduced and rehearsed on the social plane of the school classroom ... offer the means for students to develop a range of distinctive modes of talking, thinking and knowing about the world. (2002: 120)

They also reiterate that 'learners will not stumble upon the formalisms, theories and practices that form the content of science curricula without being introduced to them through teaching' (2002: 121). For them, the scheme of work is also about helping the pupils to tell the story in the right kind of language (the language of science), and this approach can be helpful in any subject. The motivation is to enable children to grasp the big picture so they can recount it accurately, in the appropriate subject conventions.

Conclusion

In this chapter we have tried to explain how you might move from a blank sheet to a clear statement defining what your medium-term plan is about, what it sets out to achieve and what you are not trying to do. Unless you can achieve this clarity the rest of the planning process is likely to become increasingly confused – reflecting the initial confusion. Or you are likely to end up simply rushing through endless lists of content, because you have to 'cover' it. In essence steps 1–3 prompt you to add in as many relevant dimensions as possible, and steps 4–5 require you to impose some kind of intellectual order on the result. Some of our readers will complete this articulation stage of the planning process in less time than they spend reading the chapter. Others will take longer because they need to read, consult with others and try out a variety of ways to achieve the desired clarity. The key point is that anyone who sets out to write a medium-term plan has to be able to articulate a clear statement about their purpose. Once this is achieved, the next challenge is to think about which route will provide the best learning journey for your class, and this is what we turn to in the next chapter.

Further reading

Bruner, J. (1960/1977) *The Process of Education*, Cambridge, MA: Harvard University Press.
Bruner's classic short book sets out some important principles that should inform curriculum design, including the notion of the spiral curriculum.

Leach, J. and Scott, P. (2002) 'Designing and evaluating science teaching sequences: an approach drawing upon the concept of learning demand and a social constructivist perspective on learning', *Studies in Science Education*, 38, 115–142.
This is one of the clearest and most compelling accounts of the planning process we have found in the literature. It combines practical suggestions with theoretical insights in a way that clearly demonstrates the intellectual work required to plan effectively.

CHAPTER 5

ALIGNING THE LEARNING STEPS

By the end of this chapter you will be able to:

- define the learning intentions for a medium-term plan;
- sequence learning steps or chunks so that they lead to the intended outcome;
- understand the contribution of each phase or chunk of learning to the whole;
- explain to others how you intend to move learners on from where they are to where you would like them to be.

Introduction

Earlier in this book we used the metaphor of planning a journey and argued that setting out on a sequence of lessons without thinking clearly about the desired outcome and a plan for getting there is as reckless as setting out on a hike with no map, destination or route in mind. You're sure to end up somewhere, but it will be somewhere unknown, possibly of little interest, and you may not feel that you benefited from the experience. This chapter is about becoming even clearer about the destination and working out a logical route, a series of steps that will get you from where and your learners are now, to where you reasonably expect they could be within the time available, without losing them along the way. We start by considering the learning journey as a whole, then focus specifically on the need to develop a very clear statement about your learning intentions – the destination of the journey. We then consider a number of examples of medium-term plans from teachers from different age phases and subjects and reflect on the kinds of routes they planned through the content and their reasons for choosing their approach. Finally, we end by focusing on two important dimensions of planning: the first relates to the initial phase of the plan and the importance of informing learners about the journey to come, and the second concerns the importance of re-visiting prior learning. By the end of the chapter you should be able to develop a sequence of steps that forms the structure of your medium-term plan.

The learning journey

Figure 5.1 demonstrates in a very clear and literal way how one teacher has envisaged the learning journey for a medium-term plan in Key Stage 3 history, focusing on the reign of King John. Banham (2000) maps out a route which appears to logically flow from one issue to the next. The plan starts with the traditional story of King John (widely held to be the worst king of England), then, once the story is secure, pupils are encouraged to look at the evidence supporting this interpretation. Next they consider the context in which John was ruling and come to appreciate the difficult situation he was in. With this understanding of the context, they then look again at key moments in the story of John's reign, and start to think about the options open to him and come to their own evaluation of his decisions. Having begun to form their own opinions about John's reign, the class then looks at how the reign has been interpreted by others at different times and, finally, they are encouraged to put this all together in an extended piece of writing, which considers the extent to which John was a good or bad king. Banham was worried that the lack of time available to history teachers to cover the whole of the medieval period might lead to a superficial coverage, as teachers attempted to cover everything that seemed important. His solution was to nestle mini-overviews within a depth study, for example a wider consideration of the nature of medieval monarchy or a consideration of the types of evidence available for historians to work with. This eight-week medium-term plan (about half a term) provides a satisfying depth study for secondary school pupils and enables them to achieve a significant piece of historical work. It also lays the foundation for a subsequent medium-term plan, which re-visits the theme of medieval monarchy and explores this in greater depth. The plan builds a sense of historical events, allows pupils to use their history skills to interrogate sources of evidence and historical interpretations, extends their appreciation of change and continuity in society and in historiography, and builds literacy skills. As Banham says, by the time they get on to the next unit of work, the learning can be accelerated because the pupils already have some contextual knowledge, they have begun to use the skills of non-chronological analysis, and they are motivated to know how other kings compared with John.

Any number of routes are possible, but some will be more interesting, more challenging and more satisfying than others. Plan a journey which is too simple and too slow, and you will bore pupils and lose their engagement. Plan

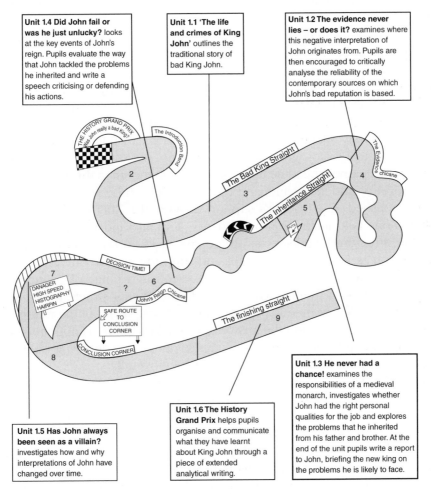

Unit 1.4 Did John fail or was he just unlucky? looks at the key events of John's reign. Pupils evaluate the way that John tackled the problems he inherited and write a speech criticising or defending his actions.

Unit 1.1 'The life and crimes of King John' outlines the traditional story of bad King John.

Unit 1.2 The evidence never lies – or does it? examines where this negative interpretation of John originates from. Pupils are then encouraged to critically analyse the reliability of the contemporary sources on which John's bad reputation is based.

Unit 1.3 He never had a chance! examines the responsibilities of a medieval monarch, investigates whether John had the right personal qualities for the job and explores the problems that he inherited from his father and brother. At the end of the unit pupils write a report to John, briefing the new king on the problems he is likely to face.

Unit 1.6 The History Grand Prix helps pupils organise and communicate what they have learnt about King John through a piece of extended analytical writing.

Unit 1.5 Has John always been seen as a villain? investigates how and why interpretations of John have changed over time.

Figure 5.1 A learning journey (Banham, 2000)

a journey which is inaccessibly difficult and progresses too fast, and they will be defeated and fall behind. Finding the right level of challenge is important and this must be related to the class you are teaching. Published resources like Banham's are undoubtedly valuable starting points, but they must be incorporated into your own medium-term planning, not function as a replacement for real planning. The purpose of constructing your own plan should be to think clearly about how you are going to secure progress. Progression could be characterised in any number of ways, such as building new knowledge step by step, or deepening pupils' understanding of a familiar area by problematising it and thinking more critically, or developing skills, either by using them in a new context, or at a higher level, or working increasingly independently. In order to achieve this, you need to have a clear sense of what your class could achieve with your guidance and the best way to help them achieve it.

This final point reflects the Vygotskian idea of the Zone of Proximal Development (ZPD), which, as we mentioned in Chapter 1, is a way to conceptualise the learning journey between a learner's starting point (what they can do now) and the end point, which is established by the teacher making a judgement about what the learner could achieve with support. The gap between these points is the ZPD; the next stage in a learner's development. Through carefully planning support the teacher can guide learners through their ZPD to achieve progression. By practising, rehearsing and consolidating this learning, learners become increasingly independent in this newly acquired skill or level of understanding, and thus the ZPD can be re-assessed and new goals established. The teacher's support through the ZPD can be direct, such as one-to-one talk, instruction or guidance, and also indirect, for example by providing structured worksheets, progressive tasks and questions, or differentiated resources. These planned steps and support strategies are often referred to as 'scaffolding' for learning, and can be seen in a range of contexts, most obviously in writing frames, which provide the overall structure required for higher-level work, but merely prompt learners to think about the required elements, rather than tell them the answers. Vygotsky's theory is not only relevant for its application to planning individual activities or resources, it is also helpful for thinking about the nature of the journey overall.

Figures 5.2 illustrates one practical way in which people have applied this notion of scaffolding to the practical job of medium-term planning. In Figure 5.2, Wilhelm et al. (2001) have used the ZPD idea to outline an overall model of progression in reading, in which the teacher maps out a clear path from the first stage, teacher reading to children, to the final stage, children choosing to read independently. Clearly this is not going to describe a single scheme of work, and some children will take years to make the learning journey, but the point is that it provides teachers with an important tool to use to plan a sequence of activities. An early years teacher would be focused on the left of the diagram and plan a sequence of activities across these stages, while a secondary school teacher with a class in which some pupils are not yet free readers might find themselves focusing on the right hand stages of the diagram to think about a suitable sequence of activities.

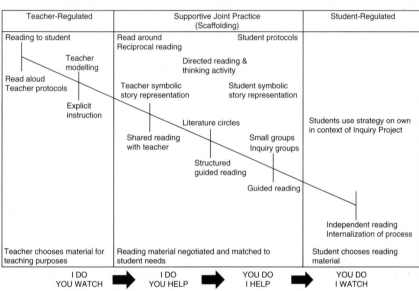

Figure 5.2   Scaffolding reading (Wilhelm et al., 2001)

Being clear about your destination

In order to plan the steps required to cross the ZPD, you need to clearly define the desired outcomes. If, for example, like the secondary design and technology teacher Trebell (2013), you want to focus on a very specific aspect of your subject, such as creativity in design, it makes sense to define what this means and what you want pupils to achieve. Trebell took the decision in one scheme of work not to ask pupils to actually make anything so they could really focus on the design process and not limit their creativity by restrictions about access to resources or their limitations in terms of practical skills. She concluded that the work was creative, responded to user needs and was feasible as a potentially manufacturable product, and that the class engaged with the task through an iterative process of design development. These features would be the characteristics of her stated destination.

You should aim to identify a reasonable statement about expectations from your knowledge of the class and the relevant curriculum frameworks within which you are designing a scheme of work. For example, courses leading to examinations have grade descriptors linked to them, which provide some indication of different levels of outcome. Lower down the school system teachers have traditionally had access to national curriculum attainment targets with levels, but from 2014 in England, teachers will lose these level descriptors for each subject, and schools are being encouraged to develop their own approaches to assessment. It remains to be seen what this will mean for national benchmarking, but there will probably be enough identifiable resources for you as a beginning teacher to help you get some indication of the kind of standards you might expect from children in a particular age phase and subject. This may take the form of exemplification files within schools, which collect examples of work at different levels of attainment; it is also highly likely that tests and assessment criteria will continue to be developed. There will be much more to say about levels of attainment in Chapter 7, when we focus on assessment, but the point to make here is simply that these frameworks can be useful for the new teacher to start to calibrate their expectations against experience.

Here is an example, drawn from the AQA English Literature GCSE specification for examination in 2014, to illustrate the kind of information you can find:

- Extract from grade A descriptor: 'They identify and comment on the impact of the social, cultural and historical contexts of texts on different readers at different times.'
- Extract from grade C descriptor: 'They show awareness of some of the social, cultural and historical contexts of texts and of how this influences their meanings for contemporary and modern readers.'
- Extract from grade F descriptor: 'They are aware that some aspects of texts relate to their specific social, cultural and historical contexts.' (AQA, 2012: 29)

While examples such as this might help a secondary English teacher to begin to think about their expectations, these are so broad that they are of limited practical use. Apart from knowing that you would have to consider the social, cultural and historical contexts in which texts were produced and read, it is not entirely clear how a pupil working at grade C level would 'show awareness' unless they 'identified and commented' on these criteria, in which case, why would they not be working at grade A expectations? The detail is likely to be gleaned from exam-paper mark schemes and examiner reports, highlighting where pupils did well and where they struggled. In this example, one might also look back at Key Stage 3 attainment targets and note that at level

4 students were expected to 'understand that texts reflect the time and culture in which they were written' (QCA, 2007). So, while not providing a blueprint, such statements do provide some clues about the kinds of progression that a teacher might expect to see.

What is probably most important at this stage is to narrow the range of learning outcomes you want to focus on. In the previous chapter we encouraged you to consider the broad range of learning that you might want to promote through a scheme of work and now you need to pin it down to specifics. This enables you to focus on what core content and skills you will aim to develop. There may well be many other things which are learned, but not everything needs to be recorded and shared with pupils. This is a chance to highlight the main issues and your priorities. Andrew, a secondary English specialist, highlights this in his interview about constructing a medium-term plan for 'debate' in English.

> *Personally I am really unsure about flagging up specific objectives for individual lessons at the beginning. If you are really interested in developing debating, then it has to happen holistically over a series of lessons over weeks, rather than, this is the one today, bang, this is the one for tomorrow, bang, we'll come back to this one, bang. You may well have a small selection on a screen, and say today we are going to definitely focus on these two but let's not forget the other ones because it all links together. You can't do a speech that only shows good use of the second-person pronoun; you are clearly doing lots of other things when you are doing any speech. Now clearly, you would need a lesson where you are looking at pronouns, they are very important linguistically in giving speeches – How are you talking to an audience? Are you using 'we'? Are you saying 'I'? – so you do need a focus on that but if the entire lesson is given over to that it becomes a really dry lesson and so it needs other stuff in there as well.*

This is rather different from the way that learning objectives are used (and abused) in many classrooms today. Andrew is suggesting that they can be used across sequences of lessons to help learners to focus on important underlying issues that inform the whole medium-term plan. This reflects the position advocated by Morrison et al. (2007), who argue that learning objectives have three purposes:

(1) To help the teacher to focus their teaching and select appropriate activities and resources.
(2) As a framework for assessment and evaluation.
(3) To guide the learner.

If a sequence of lessons all tackle the same theme there may be no need to separate out different learning objectives for every lesson in order to meet all these criteria.

Planning a route

Kranch (2012) argues that not only is it important for teachers to chunk the knowledge pupils will encounter (as these chunks form the building blocks of schemas), but that the order in which learners encounters these chunks is also important. The 'correct' order maximises the chances that these chunks will add up to functioning schemas that will enable people to develop expert interpretations. Learning in the wrong order can limit later developments because it may require the total re-organisation of learning to date in a specific area, which is difficult and time-consuming. It is much more likely that learners will attempt to learn new content through the lens established by prior learning, and if the wrong chunks are in place or have been incorrectly understood, they may hinder the acquisition of new learning and limit the development of effective schemas.

In his own research Kranch prepared three versions of the same teaching topic with the same content being delivered in three different sequences. This experiment showed no demonstrable differences in learning outcomes but it did demonstrate that learners reported finding some sequences more difficult than others. A significant limitation of the experimental model adopted in Kranch's project was that the learning resources consisted of 52 items to be learned through a sequence of web pages, which were presented in different orders. Learners had to work individually through the material in one sitting; therefore this variation did not take place over an extended period of time (participants varied between 30 minutes and three hours). This is different from thinking about sequencing activities over days or weeks and then using and re-using prior knowledge. In effect all he did was alter the sequence within a single-lesson plan, and so it is even more significant that he concluded the order of activities in such a short timescale led students to experience the learning as more or less difficult.

One conclusion to draw from this example is that teachers getting the sequence wrong does not mean that pupils will not learn; it just means the learners have to do more work themselves to achieve the learning and it also means they learn despite your planning rather than because of it. Getting the sequence right is important therefore to ensure that your input actually enhances and maximises learning, rather than creating unnecessary difficulties. Teaching is about much more than merely being on hand to present information in relatively haphazard ways. Most children would learn something from conversations with people who were more knowledgeable about a topic than they were, or by observing people who were better at some form of skill than them. Effective teaching implies a more coherent plan for the development of learners' knowledge, understanding and skills. It implies a clever plan and the cleverness rests in part on an understanding of the learners and their needs, and in part on the nature of the area to be learned.

There are any number of ways in which demand may be increased and therefore progress planned. Meiring and Norman (1999a, 1999b) provide secondary language teachers with some very specific advice about how to sequence A level specification topics to secure progression, starting with family and school, working through individual issues, and up towards more complex issues such as terrorism. There is clearly a logic at work here and it seems partly to do with building on familiarity at Key Stage 4 but is also partly a judgement about the inherent demands of each topic; some have a heavy factual demand (such as units on politics in France), whereas others demand a more nuanced and discursive treatment (such as a discussion of terrorism). While their list of topics is very firmly rooted in a specific syllabus, others have attempted to disaggregate the underlying factors that make some topics more or less demanding. The following list is also taken from suggestions by modern languages experts, but is relevant to many other subjects:

- from familiar to new vocabulary;
- from familiar to new language structures;
- from simple to complex language;
- familiar language in an unfamiliar context;
- increased range of topics;
- from specific to general themes;
- from concrete to abstract ideas;
- from factual to imaginative topics;
- from classroom learning to outside real-life experiences;
- from straightforward to controversial aspects;
- from short to longer spoken and written texts;
- from implicit to explicit knowledge of grammar;
- from scripted to authentic language;
- from familiar to unfamiliar topics;
- from teacher-led to independent learning.

(Adapted from Morgan and Neil, 2001 and Pachler et al., 2009).

As we saw in Chapter 4, Leach and Scott (2002) respond to this challenge when they discuss the inherent 'learning demand' of the science topic to be taught. They argue that teachers need to make decisions about:

- the subject knowledge content to be addressed (conceptual and epistemological, referring to the nature of subject language);
- levels of intellectual demand associated with each element and therefore the allocation of time and attention;
- the way in which the big story will be staged, the lines of argument to run through the sequence;
- the nature of classroom talk (the balance between exposition and exploration) at different points in the sequence.

These decisions are illustrated in the following case study.

 Case Study   Rationale for a teaching innovation about the interrelationship between science and technology

Hadjilouca and her colleagues (2011) wanted to encourage secondary school pupils to explore the changing nature of the relationship between science and technology. Their motivation for exploring both subjects together is an appreciation that science and technology experts have to increasingly work together to solve complex problems, such as climate change, and that therefore schools should equip pupils with an understanding of how they can collaborate. They note that pupils are hampered in their ability to connect the two because they lack a clear sense of the parameters of each and of the nature of their inter-relationship; for example they frequently mistake design for the output rather than the process, or assume that technology relates to manufactured objects while science relates to the natural world. They also note that until the Renaissance, these two areas were rather separate and that since then there has been debate about how the two areas inter-relate. They conclude that some of the most important aspects of the inter-relationship now include science's contribution to the development of technology through providing models and theories which underpin technological innovations and by posing challenges, such as the need for new measurement instruments. Similarly, technology contributes to science through providing increasingly accurate instruments for measurement and experimentation and generating new research questions.

In order to achieve their aims they outlined a scheme of work that starts with a group challenge to devise a means by which someone in the seventeenth century could observe animals from a distance without disturbing them. Having responded to the technical challenge to construct a device, pupils are then encouraged to conduct a series of scientific investigations, modelled on Galileo's experiments to improve the telescope. These involve investigating the influence of a range of factors on the magnification provided by a lens.

The authors argue that by requiring pupils first to respond to, and reflect upon, a technological design challenge and then move into a linked scientific enquiry, they should be well placed to launch into the third phase of the scheme of work, which is to discuss the inter-relationship between technology and science.

It seems obvious why these authors chose this route in their planning, but it is worth highlighting that they actually defer discussing the inter-relationship between science and technology (which is after all the focus of this plan) until the final phase of the sequence. They took the decision that this discussion would be too complicated and too abstract as a starting point. Thinking about the learning demand, it makes much more sense to start with a concrete example from history, and then draw out the significant themes as opposed to starting with rather abstract themes and definitions and then think about how they might be applied. This mirrors Banham's approach in his King John scheme of work (Figure 5.1), where the depth study (in this case Galileo and the telescope) includes elements of the broader theme, which are explored in greater detail later.

Source: Hadjilouca, R., Constaninou, C. and Papadouris, N. (2011) 'The rationale for a teaching innovation about the interrelationship between science and technology', *Science and Education*, 20 (10), 981–1005

In some subjects, such as maths, knowledge seems more obviously cumulative, and early mastery of basic skills, such as counting, sets the scene for continued rapid progress, whereas a failure to grasp these fundamentals holds learners back (Aunola et al., 2004). In such areas the sequence between learning steps may seem fairly obvious; for example, in primary maths one scheme of work specifies the following sequence for counting, partitioning and calculating:

- Read, write and order numbers on a number line.
- Count forwards and backwards on the number line in single digits and in multiples of ten.
- Partition three-digit numbers into multiples of 100, 10 and 1 in different ways.
- Round two- and three-digit numbers to the nearest 10 or 100.
- Add and subtract mentally one- and two-digit numbers.

- Partition, round and order four-digit numbers.
- Recognise and continue number sequences formed by counting on or back in steps of constant size. (Adapted from: www.teach-maths.co.uk)

We could debate the order of one or two of the steps but it is unlikely that anyone would decide it would be useful to start with the final stages and work backwards, because the latter stages require the earlier stages to have been accomplished. Similarly, Chambers (2008) provides an example at a higher level of demand in secondary maths:

- In the case of multiplying out brackets, one might consider first dealing only with linear factors containing positive coefficients and positive integers such as $(x + 3)(x + 6)$.
- When the pupils have shown success they can move on to consider cases such as $(x + 4)(x - 5)$; $(x - 2)(x - 1)$.
- Questions of the type $(2x + 1)(2x - 5)$; $(4 - 3x)(2 - x)$; $(x - 1)(3 + 7x)$, where the extra difficulty comes from coefficients of x other than one, and different orderings of the terms within each factor, can then be pursued. (Chambers, 2008: 64)

In this way such learning is seen as cumulative, with earlier steps providing an essential foundation for subsequent steps.

It is not this straightforward for all subjects, or even all aspects of maths, and there is always a planning decision to be made about something, even if it is only the duration of each of these steps, and the order to tackle content within each sub-topic. For example, in maths many teachers setting out to teach about Pythagoras' Theorem might simply explain it, demonstrate it and give students the opportunity to use it, but it is equally possible to set up an investigation to allow children to explore the connections between the sides of a right-angled triangle and try to identify the relevant rules for themselves. Reigeluth (1981) points out that the layers of knowledge, or chunks, can be connected in different types of sequences, including:

- forward chaining: presenting them in the order the teacher sequenced them;
- backward chaining: presenting them in reverse order;
- hierarchical sequencing: presenting all the major sub-steps separately before integrating them into a step in the sequence;
- general to detailed sequencing;
- simple to complex sequencing.

This implies that we might be able to articulate a direction or shape for the sequence, from top to bottom; from beginning to end; from big picture to detail and so forth.

Activity

Once you have agreed what your medium-term plan is about (by satisfactorily completing the articulation phase) sit down with a group of teachers or student teachers involved in the same age phase or subject area and agree what the reasonable outcomes or expectations are that you should be aiming for, and how much time is reasonable for this sequence of lessons. Then devise your own plan for the best way to sequence the content and compare your solutions.

- How much do they vary?
- To what extent is the sequence driven by the logic of the topic?
- To what extent does the sequence reflect people's own experience of learning this topic?
- To what extent does it reflect people's own understanding of the topic/subject?
- Is any solution obviously better or worse? Why?

(Based on a suggestion in Connelly and Clandinin, 1988)

As we have already suggested, and the activity may have demonstrated, there is rarely one obviously correct way to plan the learning journey. The important thing is to develop a clear rationale which provides a coherence to the learning. In the following examples we illustrate a number of ways in which experienced planners perceive the shape of the learning journey they have planned.

Anna (secondary humanities)

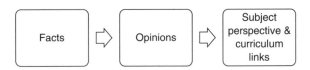

Figure 5.3 The shape of Anna's plan

Anna planned a series of lessons to explore the bombing of Hiroshima and Nagasaki, but she wanted it to be used by a range of teachers across several subjects. In her plan the children encounter the event itself and then think about how a particular subject lens could be applied to it. Her final phase therefore includes four distinct lesson plans, from which teachers select an appropriate lesson to enable the students to complete the sequence with a distinctive type of task associated with their curriculum area.

> *My idea was to have one totally fact-based lesson. Get them to do a fact-finding mission to find out what happened from scratch through a carousel activity and different artefacts. Quite often lessons in all sorts of subjects include activities for sorting out facts from opinion, but I wanted to start just with the facts, the bare facts, and then introduce the opinions that interpret those facts. The second lesson was for them to be exposed to different points of view and to understand that there are very different points of view around whether it was necessary or not to drop the bombs and the reasons for and against. I've done that through differentiated activities for lesson two. And lesson three was a way of tapping more firmly into the curriculum and making it easier for teachers to use.*

Andrew (secondary English)

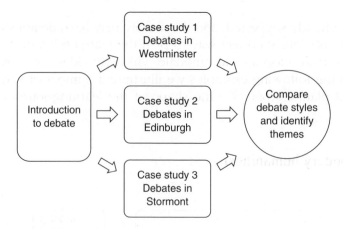

Figure 5.4   The shape of Andrew's plan

In Andrew's medium-term plan he is more squarely focusing on the language and form of debate in the secondary English classroom. He is keen to situate the learning in an analysis of how debate happens in the real world, and identifies a number of case studies in which students can encounter real parliamentary debate.

If you are looking at different forms of debate you clearly need to engage with different forms of debate before you can go on to how you use language in a debate. You need some of the content up front ... In English there is a distinction made between a whole-text approach or a sentence- or word-level approach. My preferred strategy would be beginning with a whole-text approach. It might not be a whole speech because they can be really long, but something you've got that is a coherent whole. This resonates with my reading of Vygotsky and the relationship between language and thought. Your thought process operates with wholes, so even if you are articulating a small bit, your head has the whole in there somewhere. If it doesn't it can't connect it properly. So if we can't give children the whole, then what they're articulating really comes from nowhere and is parroting what the teacher expects them to say. You can tick the box, but has any real learning taken place?

I think the approach allows students to engage with the material in their terms much more. If, as a teacher, I said this is how we do debate in the UK and we're going to focus on that right now, you make that into what debating is, whereas if you have an overview and you say, after that overview we'll try different ones, maybe we'll all try the same one or maybe students can choose which one they have their topic debated on. I think the more the students can be encouraged with your guidance to lead lessons the better.

These case studies then may be encountered in a sequential way, or the class could be divided into three groups and encounter one case study each. Andrew was also considering whether to choose speeches or episodes of debate which would illustrate other dimensions that he could pick up in the final part of the sequence. One example of an important theme that could be deliberately planned into these case studies is gender.

At a conference someone presented research on how women participate in the different parliaments and assemblies around the UK and you can't really look at gender in debate until you have an overview of the different ways of doing it. Otherwise you just see that women in Westminster do not intervene as much as the men, but so what? What this research found was that in Westminster women do a lot less of the barracking and are far less likely to intervene when someone has got the floor, but that is absolutely not the case in Northern Ireland, Wales or Scotland where women are as likely as the men to participate. So, that comparative element aids learning – if you have an overview it's easier to have an opinion on a single focus than if you start with a single focus.

In this way Andrew is adopting a shape and a logic to his sequence that allows him to start and end with an overview. By selecting a series of case studies which will provide students with a range of experiences (they will experience different forms of debate and critically analyse them) he is ensuring that when the students return to their overview at the end, they will be able to add depth and subtlety to their understanding of debate. Andrew had worked for several years as a PGCE tutor and to explain his approach to planning in a little more detail he shared an example of a student teacher he had been supervising.

As an example I observed a student teacher getting frustrated with children not being able to articulate what the student teacher wanted to articulate. I was watching a class with an image of the Harry Potter book cover on the board and the teacher wanted them to analyse it and the students were giving responses which didn't go beyond the train is red, he's wearing glasses ... and she got incredibly frustrated and thought, the children can't do anything, the response student teachers often have, but then I encouraged her to try with a different class providing two different covers and it's in that difference that articulation and learning occurred. So, when there's not a train in the next one they're suddenly able to be more articulate about why a train is there, when the colours have changed they are suddenly able to be much more articulate about why the dominance of blue might mean something that the yellow in this one it seems not to. When they've only got one model they really struggle to offer reasons.

By sharing this story from a very different context, Andrew illustrates how thinking at this general level of structure and shape for a sequence of learning activities can be useful for a teacher. While the skills and language objectives in his plan are almost entirely unrelated to those being pursued by his student teacher, he recognises that there is an underlying approach that can be transferred between schemes of work. That underlying approach concerns the need to relate examples to the whole and to relate examples to each other in order to encourage greater depth of analysis and to enable pupils to develop their thinking. The technical language and concepts will be easier to teach if they can be attached to existing ideas, rather than being taught in the abstract. In other words, I can understand what rhetoric is when I have just used it; I can understand symbolism, after I have decoded a symbol.

Shiv (primary science)

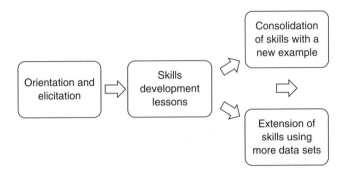

Figure 5.5 The shape of Shiv's plan

Shiv's planning overview looks deceptively simple. She started with an initial lesson which served several purposes:

They had just had the summer holiday and the first lesson was just about body parts and naming body parts and that was really just to remind them that this was science and we are doing something about the human body. I wouldn't call it a throwaway lesson but it was a lesson about making sure they had the vocabulary, and about putting the children into groups. They worked in pairs and threes and I was experimenting with groups of children to see who worked well together, and who had remembered things. If you think about the constructivist ideas, your first lessons are supposed to be orientation and elicitation: orientation, this is science; elicitation, we're doing the human body, what do we remember about the human body? I didn't keep any formal records, I was just seeing the range of knowledge, seeing where to pitch the coming lessons, getting a handle on where we all were, in terms of the dynamics of the group.

The middle block of lessons tackled the main substance of the medium-term plan, which related as much to maths and measurement as it did to science. Significantly, though, an aspect of the structure for the sequence was provided by a model for science investigations which was adopted throughout the whole school (this was discussed in Chapter 4). This gave Shiv a starting point: '... the first questions were always what do we have to find out, and how could we find it out ... so this was starting them all off with the process of doing an investigation'. In addition to these clear maths and science themes, Shiv also wanted to develop a Personal, Social and Health (PSHE) dimension, and so planned for opportunities to develop this as well, through encouraging the pupils to think about personal differences and similarities. The following sequence therefore addresses three curriculum frameworks but does this through developing a relatively simple series of tasks which develop all three areas simultaneously – the learning is multi-dimensional, but the tasks are relatively straightforward.

> *Basically the focus of these lessons was to do different things, to look at different aspects of investigation skills, and so all the following five lessons really they were just pegs to hang on different investigation skills. The first one was making measurements and comparisons, so I thought because it was about the human body it was quite important that we were able to make accurate measurements. It also happened that the class were doing measurement in maths ... and what we did in the second lesson was we ended up making a little booklet, 'All About Me', where we took measurements of our height, our hands, our feet, all of these things, and put them into a booklet. We talked about how to measure accurately, some children used standard measures, some non-standard measures, and for those children they put it in their booklet as 'so many cubes long' and then I got a more able child to work with them to convert it into centimetres and so they had two measurements, so we were able to work wherever they were at. But the other idea was that once they had established all this information, later on, as the weeks went by, doing different investigations, the groups wouldn't have to always get every child ... for instance if one group in the following week wanted to ask 'do all the brown haired children have blue eyes?', instead of looking at every child they would be able to collect these booklets in and look through the booklets ... so they would be able to use these booklets as a resource as well ... It fits as well with PSHE because it was that sense of characteristics, skin colour, eye colour, hair colour, so it was a chance to deal with those issues as well, you know are we all the same ... the PSHE topic was Good to be Me, what makes me special and why am I valuable, so it linked into that as well.*

> *Basically, letting children investigate, that was the format for every week but the challenge got slightly harder. So the next week we looked at a slightly different way of phrasing the question. So in week 3 it was 'What is the most popular eye colour, etc.?' but the next week we looked at 'Who has the biggest hand span/smallest feet, etc.?' so we were looking at different questions and saying things like, well do you just do a tally chart, will that work, and we said oh no, now we have to rank the numbers from smallest to biggest and for some of the children that was quite*

challenging, and so I think for this one I put them into big groups of four or five so the range of ability was bigger, to help them. I think I said if you choose hand span, just do it for the five children in your group and see if you can order that information, and if they were able to order those five I'd let them get a couple more. If they were struggling we'd look at that ... I remember some of them had hand-span information and they couldn't order it so we converted the measurements into cubes, and then we put the towers next to each other so we could see which was biggest, so we made a visual representation of hand spans because they weren't able to do it in abstract way, and then they were able to order it from biggest to smallest.

It is clear to see how each lesson builds on the kinds of approaches and skills that have been developed in the previous lesson, and how the demand is being increased over time. This is reflected in Shiv's focused interventions with groups where pupils struggled with ranking numbers, but also with a new grouping strategy, to enable pupils to support one another. At this point in the plan Shiv identified an opportunity to split the class and let those who were now struggling spend some more time getting to grips with the skills and consolidating their attainment, while others could develop greater independence and push themselves a little further. This illustrates how differentiation can be planned at the scheme of work level, rather than just in individual lessons, tasks or resources.

By that point, this is week 4, the class had kind of split really. You could see those children who were ready to go on and come up with more challenging questions and those children who had reached their level, those for whom this was as far as they were going to go this half-term ... in the following week when I did something more challenging, I had about a third of the class almost repeat this lesson again with a different idea but I split them up because I realised the next step was too hard for some of them. The next lesson was looking at a more complex question. Exactly the same idea of investigating ourselves, but 'Do children with the something have the something?' for example, 'Do children with the longest arms have the longest legs?', so this may be looking at two sets of data so it was much harder to see links. Basically I had about two-thirds of the class doing that ... you know exactly the same, put them in groups, let them pick the question they wanted to investigate and then let them do it. I had to spend much more time with the groups who were doing the harder investigation actually looking at ... because the human body being what it is, the data weren't always very neat ... And then we talked about science in the real world and you don't always get an answer to your question and the more difficult a question is the harder it is to find an answer. We were going into this idea that science isn't always about being right or coming up with an answer and that sometimes you can't even come up with an answer. That's something I'd want them to have for later in the year, you know, to recognise that 'what I did, didn't answer the question' ... it's good to say 'this investigation didn't work because ...'

Vicky (A level politics)

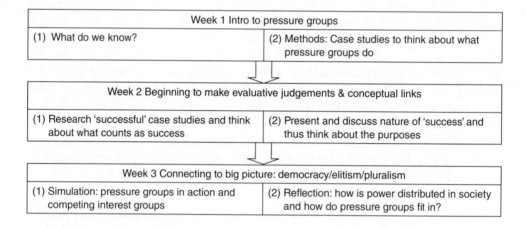

Figure 5.6   The shape of Vicky's plan

Vicky's A level politics was rather different in that it was clearly constrained by the A level specification and the need to get through the content specified by the exam board and relate that content specifically to the form of assessment used in the exam. Nevertheless, there was a need for her to impose a shape on the content which scaffolded her pupils' progress towards more complex and nuanced political discussions. In Figure 5.6 we have shown lessons 1 and 2 from each week, but there was a third lesson planned which functioned as a mop-up, revision and assessment focus. This meant she planned the first two lessons as opportunities for substantial input, information processing and thinking, and then used the third to re-visit anything that was causing particular problems and plan and practise exam answers, with the 5-mark questions appearing in week 1, the 10-mark questions in week 2 and the 25-mark essay in week 3.

Like Shiv's year 1 class, though, Vicky started with an elicitation and orientation lesson:

Hopefully together we'll create definitions of pressure groups, as a class. I think it's good practice to get kids developing their own definitions of the terms we are working with. In the second lesson we look at the different methods pressure groups use to make change … we start using the concepts from the first lesson to look at different pressure groups … we look at their aims and think about how they go about achieving them … another one of the thematic issues for this is how do you determine the success of a pressure group? So we start in the second lesson looking at different methods different groups used and then looking at the democratic functions that those groups establish, so for example they educate people, they represent minority voices … we are trying to scaffold now, getting into the third lesson of the week, how do we know if change has been achieved? There's Operation Black Vote, who are quite an interesting group because they are an insider group trying to represent a minority voice. I don't know how successful they have been but it's an interesting group for us to look at, partly because most of our pupils are black and so it feels very relevant to them and then that's quite a good way to start thinking about that democratic function, about how minorities get represented in a political system because political parties, we found out in the elections unit, with first past the post system, don't represent people properly, so here's a little way of people getting representation. I am totally committed to anti-racist teaching so I teach relevant case studies in every unit I teach. The specification doesn't tell you to do that kind of thing, so you could get through a politics A level without teaching about racism once, which I think is strange.

In the second week I just want to get the kids to apply what they have learnt in the first week to one of the thematic issues – Are pressure groups successful and what determines the success of a pressure group? – which is kind of a 10-mark question that has been put forward as a 25-mark question too. So, initially we would have an ICT room booked and they work in pairs to answer a set number of questions like, what's the aim of the pressure group, what type of status do they have, what's their historical context, what's their ideological belief, what's their membership like, how rich are they, what actions have they taken and have they had any success? One year I gave them the pressure groups I thought they would find interesting, in the second year I let them choose what they wanted. I'm not sure it made much difference really, you know a lot of the time the students don't want to choose or don't know what to choose, but in fact some of the boys were really interested in business and so I helped them to develop this by looking at the CBI and corporate lobby groups ... In the first part of the lesson we will build on the previous week's discussion of methods and look at lobbying and the different methods that pressure groups use, then I pair them up to start their research, then they finish that before the next lesson so they are ready to feedback in presentations in the second lesson. This enables us to apply the concepts to the various presentations.

In the third week the big question is 'Who accesses power in a democracy?' What is pluralism and what is elitism? I am lucky that I have a friend who is a campaigns officer for Greenpeace who is a very clever activist and he agreed to come in to visit. So we decided to have some fun and design a game. In the first year this ran, we organised an enrichment session for all the AS politics classes. So we started looking at elitism and pluralism, which is the main assessment objective for the pressure groups unit. It does ramp up a bit here because we learn about pluralism but we have been scaffolding what it means, because hopefully they have got the message from their presentations that there are loads of ideas and everyone is vying for attention for their ideas in a democracy. The pupils have some understanding of democracy already and so the idea of pluralism builds on that. I also want to ensure I start to put in some of the ideas from A2 into AS so it doesn't come as such a shock, so for example here I use a very abridged reading from Mill about the need for toleration of different ideas, to help to broaden out the appreciation that pluralism is about the free market place of ideas.

Once again the pattern in this scheme of work is very clear. Pupils build up their understanding of pressure groups starting from their own definitions and developing a more nuanced account through a series of case studies. Then through the simulation they have a chance to apply some of their learning to date and begin to experience what pressure group activity really feels like. Vicky is alert to this affective dimension to the learning, and to the fact that this presents a challenge to the young people that is about identity and belonging as much as it is about the politics A level syllabus. She is aware that the next step in the learning requires them to acknowledge an idea that may cause them to question some core values and assumptions about the way the world works, and therefore how they may work in the world.

The first lesson is quite full on, it's quite hard. I think elitism is probably the most difficult idea for the students to grasp. They don't really have any real concept of politics, democracy can be a platitude, you know, democracy is really good, because people can make change. But when you start saying, you know class is a major factor in whether you have access to money, status and power … that's hard to accept, it's hard to communicate and it's hard to demonstrate because it's hegemonic – because lots of the kids fully believe that business is the most important thing in society, it's a hegemonic idea, but that's my own political stance on that, but that's really hard to grasp because it really means them going, 'Oh what, this is all really complicated then', when it seems just normal, of course people with money get to do stuff. Many of the students think that we live in a meritocracy, if you get out and work hard you'll get here and here, but then being confronted by elitism, they think that's really unfair, but we live in a democracy, it's not supposed to be unfair, but they're young and they want it to be black and white and I think it's actually a really nuanced thing, elitism.

It is evident that Vicky's planning incorporates a detailed grasp of the curriculum requirements, a clear commitment about the purpose and nature of a politics education, and a keen awareness of the ways in which politics challenges young people's world-views. This short medium-term plan aims to accommodate all three in a way that is also accessible and enjoyable.

Michael (secondary history)

Michael discussed his history department's medium-term plan for the first year of secondary school. He illustrates how important it is to understand the subject at the deeper structural and procedural level, and not be tempted into planning just for 'coverage'. His interview illustrated how the medium-term planning ensured coherence at several levels.

(i) Thinking like a historian

First, the medium-term plan provides a coherent template for how to do history, much like the science investigation template used by Shiv in her Key Stage 1 example.

The scheme of work starts with 'what is history' because this is the first scheme of work we teach the students in secondary. When we introduce the pupils to these skills, such as using evidence, we tell them these are skills they will be using in subsequent topics. I frame it in terms of: 'You are now historical detectives, and what do detectives do? Well they examine evidence and listen to different sides of the story before they make a decision about what happened and that is what you have to do as historians ...' We keep referring back to those initial skills. We often start a lesson by looking back at the 'history skills pizza', where we describe the five or six key skills as slices of a pizza.

(ii) Working with evidence

One of those key skills in the history pizza relates to pupils' ability to work with sources, and within this the school has developed a more detailed model that can be used throughout various topics.

When we teach source work, we use the acronym ADAPTL, which prompts students to consider author, date, audience, purpose, time and limitations. If you look at the kind of source questions we ask our students in year 8, they are essentially the same kind of questions they will be asked at GCSE and AS level.

(iii) Conceptual themes

The plans also reflect teachers' awareness that history is more than just a story of unfolding events, but requires a more sophisticated conceptual understanding to make meaningful connections and interpretations.

Within each year group in Key Stage 3 chronology is important, each year covers distinct periods of time, starting with the medieval period, Reformation, Glorious Revolution, etc. ending with twentieth-century history. But within each period we don't necessarily stick with strict chronology. We might adopt different themes, such as how do things change after the Norman Conquest? What long-term consequences can we trace between the Reformation and contemporary society?

Each of the examples above provides the essential overview that would enable you, as the teacher, to realise what contribution to the whole is made by each of the elements. At the outset you can only make an informed guess about the period of time required to do justice to each component. This is an aspect of planning that simply becomes easier with experience, the best indicator of how long a chunk of learning will take is how long it has taken in the past, precisely the indicator you do not have access to at the beginning of a teaching career. This makes it even more important that you understand the contribution of each stage and can therefore respond to pupils' engagement with it, either speeding up a case study if the salient points have been grasped, or slowing down an essential stage where learners are experiencing problems. In Anna's example, a group with low reading ability might take longer on the first stage, in order to establish a secure comprehension of the relevant facts, and the teacher may have to plan several activities to provide them with access to the key information, while a group of competent readers might only require a single short lesson. The length of the stage changes because the teacher is clear about the required outcome from that stage. Similarly, if we take Andrew's debate plan, if the first case study was proving more difficult than he had thought, he would have the option of only using one other case study, which might have the impact of keeping the scheme of work within the overall time available but also simplify the analysis slightly by introducing fewer themes. Thus differentiating at the level of the scheme would take minutes once this overarching learning journey was worked out, but could have profound effects on the learning.

 Activity

Identify a scheme of work that you are developing, or take an existing example from the department where you are teaching. Devise a flow diagram, along similar lines to the ones we have provided above for the medium-term plan, to show how the chunks and themes fit together.

Is it possible to describe the learning with clarity or does this prompt you to return to the plan to clarify the structure and underlying themes?

Ask a colleague to do the same activity. Do you agree or have you discerned different chunks and themes within the plan?

Previewing your journey

In the early stages of a medium-term plan it is generally useful to share the big picture with those you will be teaching. At a general level this can be interpreted as simply explaining to the learners what the scheme of work is about, but it can also be interpreted in a much more specific way, as providing a framework for the learning – a structure within which new knowledge could be organised. This second meaning reflects Ausubel's work on 'advance organisers' which he argued should be seen as introductory material presented in advance of the learning material itself and at a 'higher level of abstraction' (1963: 81). Ausubel was partly interested in how 'expository' teaching (presenting and explaining) could lead to 'reception learning'. This is different from models of active experiential learning, but he stressed that if the learner was not intellectually engaged and working actively on the new content, then no learning would result. Similarly to Vygotsky's starting point for the Zone of Proximal Development, Ausubel emphasised that 'the most important single factor influencing learning is what the learner already knows' (Ausubel et al., 1978: 163), which means it is important that the teacher's plan relates the subject content to the learner's prior knowledge. This serves to 'anchor' the new learning to existing knowledge structures (Entwistle, 1988).

Ausubel insisted that advance organisers should be more abstract because they were intended to provide an overarching structure within which learners could interpret new information and make sense of it. It follows therefore that the teacher must do more than simply preview the learning in a brief summary of what is to come. The advance organiser should preview the kinds of structural, conceptual content that will form the schemas into which new material will be subsumed. Now, this definition is rather vague and is clearly open to interpretation, and this was recognised by Ausubel who argued that advance organisers could only be devised in specific contexts, reflecting both the specific content to be learned and the prior learning of the students. Story (1998) reviewed much of the evidence relating to the development and use of advance organisers and found that, despite this inherent flexibility and openness to interpretation, there was a small but consistent improvement in learning across a range of studies, where advance organisers were used. Advance organisers appear to secure this progress by helping the learners to understand and recognise the significant features of the learning (Story, 1998: 259). As Gurlitt et al. (2012) argue, this approach seems to work not only because it anchors new learning in prior learning, but also because it helps learners to generate provisional structures for new learning, which might be seen as proto-schemata.

Ausubel himself advocated simply telling learners about the learning, the key features and significant concepts that would help them make sense of and organise the material. In Andrew's secondary English scheme of work discussed above, this might involve flagging up three big ideas, gender, rhetoric and influencing others, as themes to pay attention to in the case studies, and key concepts to be returned to at the end. Others have developed concept maps or graphic organisers to achieve the same result (Novak, 1998). These can be as sophisticated as graphic representations of the topic being studied, identifying various levels of concepts organised hierarchically and with appropriate links and relationships identified. Or they can also be much simpler constructions, such as a Venn diagram; for example, in the case study of technology and science discussed earlier in this chapter, a Venn diagram demonstrating each area as a distinctive discipline, but with an overlapping space in between, would help the students to understand the purpose of building a telescope and also help them begin to think about the connections between science and technology before they arrived at the final stage of the medium-term plan.

There is a risk here that by starting a teaching sequence with such an abstract and potentially incomprehensible conceptual model, learners can be deterred and alienated. This would negate all the positive effects discussed by Andrew and Vicky of building up the activities to secure increasingly complex thinking and performance almost unconsciously. However, here is the significance of Ausubel's warning that we should not just set out the abstract map of the topic, but should do so in a way which reflects and connects with the students' current level of understanding. Ivie (1998) outlines the following as constituting a typical teaching sequence that would derive from Ausubel's approach.

- The teacher ascertains if the learner already possesses relevant concepts in his or her cognitive structure.
- The teacher provides appropriate advance organisers, which are used to anchor the new material within the established cognitive structure.
- The teacher presents the new material in an organised fashion, checking to make sure the learner is subsuming the new information under appropriate organisers.
- The teacher provides sufficient practice so that the material is thoroughly learned, becoming an integrated part of the learner's cognitive system.
- The teacher guides the learner through a problem-solving situation that utilises higher-order thinking skills.

This sequence is similar in some regards to Smith's (1996) popular accelerated learning cycle, which starts by connecting the topic to prior learning and then previews the new learning by providing the 'big picture'. For our purposes the important point to make is that it starts and ends with the big picture. The acceleration is supposed to be secured in part because the learner is made aware of the purpose of the learning and the contribution of the learning step to the overall journey.

Revisiting familiar territory

In reflecting on the pupils' learning in her primary science sequence of activities, Shiv was very clear that this had to be seen in the context of a whole year learning about the nature of science and the basics of numeracy. She felt that this was just a first foray into the school's model of science investigations, and did not assume that the children would know and understand the stages of investigation by the end of this unit. Similarly, when discussing some of the specific numeracy skills, she was aware of the need for caution in assessing the impact of her lessons.

> *Teaching children to rank numbers once doesn't mean they can rank numbers. In six weeks' time, when we come to rank numbers again, then we'll see who can rank numbers. Just because by the end of that day we all did it, doesn't mean to say we all learned it. It means we've all had an experience of it … If you've got any kind of constructivist model in mind you have to come back, because the experience thing is not the same as internalising and learning.*

This resonates with Bruner's (1960/1977) image of the spiral curriculum, which is the model he used to describe how these key concepts and skills would have to be planned into the curriculum repeatedly. The idea is not that teachers have to endlessly repeat content to 'drill' it into pupils' heads; rather that teachers have to repeatedly return to the core organising principles of knowledge and skills, to ensure that they are deeply understood, soundly internalised and developed progressively. Perhaps Shiv's year 1 (age five–six) primary class will get a sense that there is a logical sequence to a science investigation; by the end of primary school, they may be able to work increasingly independently in this framework; by the end of secondary school they may see how the sequence applies to a range of increasingly complex experiments and enquiries and will add some specific terminology to describe it; and in further study perhaps pupils can also become increasingly aware of the cultural context in which scientific investigations are conducted and in which scientific knowledge is constructed. The point is that each successive return to the idea of scientific investigations builds on the prior learning and builds up more complexity. Similarly, Michael's history pizza sets up the essential history skills, and these will continue to be important, but the acronym ADAPTL will be used differently; for example, a postgraduate response about the limitations of a source will be more sophisticated than a secondary school response and will consider it in the context of the historiography of the period. The prompts to ask certain questions of sources will always be relevant but the depth of understanding and the context will develop.

 Activity

Review your medium-term plan to clarify where you intend to consolidate or extend prior learning, or where you will introduce new learning. Colour code your plan to highlight where you will:

- Revise and re-use prior learning.

  Have you thought about how you will re-connect to this previous learning? How do you plan to re-use this learning?

- Extend a concept or skill previously learned.

  How do you plan to extend the learning? Will you introduce greater complexity or sophistication through adopting higher expectations? Will you provide a new context in which to apply this prior learning? Will it need to be combined with other knowledge to be effective?

- Introduce a new concept or skill.

  How will this be introduced? How will this connect to the big picture? What kind of 'advance organiser' might help the students to understand the significance of this new content?

Conclusion

Alignment means getting your lessons lined up in the right order, but, as we have seen, what constitutes the 'right' order is far from simple and is a matter of professional judgement. It requires you to have a sound grasp of the topic or subject being taught and a working knowledge of the learners for whom you are planning. We urge new teachers to undertake some of this work collaboratively because it is much easier to be aware of your own assumptions, strengths and weaknesses through comparison with others' perspectives. We also believe that the discussions that arise through collaborative planning are essential elements of professionalism because through these discussions we are forced to explain ourselves, take account of others and explore deep questions about learning and teaching. It is also a pragmatic strategy for avoiding obvious pitfalls in your planning. If you get the alignment wrong at the planning stage it is very likely this will have negative effects on the learners, and so taking the time to discuss ideas, consider alternatives and clarify the underlying rationale for a plan should help to bring clarity and coherence to the classroom. A well-aligned plan functions as an advance organiser for the teacher, as well as offering advance organisers to learners.

Further reading

Leithwood, K., McAdie, P., Bacia, N. and Rodrigue, A. (eds) (2006) *Teaching for Deep Understanding: What Every Educator Should Know*, Thousand Oaks, CA: Corwin Press.

This useful collection of essays and case studies explores the concept of 'deep learning', which is perhaps much mentioned elsewhere but less frequently explained.

Wilhelm, J. D., Baker, T. N. and Dube, J. (2001) *Strategic Reading: Guiding Students to Lifelong Literacy, 6–12*, Portsmouth, NH: Boynton/Cook Publishers.

We recommend this book for all teachers as a great introduction to developing pupils' literacy across the age range and across subjects. It also exemplifies the notion of planning for progression.

CHAPTER 6

CHAPTER 6

ACTIVATING THE LEARNING

By the end of this chapter you will:

- understand the relationship between individual activities and the plan as a whole;
- be able to select appropriate activities to promote the specific learning you want to focus on;
- identify strategies for beginning to teach a unit of work;
- understand how pragmatic factors, such as time and pupil behaviour, can influence your choice of activities.

Introduction

This chapter does not aim to provide a comprehensive list of teaching strategies. There has been a proliferation of such books in recent years, with some based on experience, such as *The Teacher's Toolkit* (Ginnis, 2002), and others exploring strategies through research evidence, such as *Visible Learning* (Hattie, 2009). Rather, we want to think about some of the factors that might help you make decisions about what types of activities to include in your medium-term plans. In order to do this we deal with three broad areas, beginning with clarifying the purposes behind your choice, moving on to consider some of the general approaches to designing learning activities and finally thinking about some pragmatic issues relating to how to make work achievable for you and your pupils.

The purpose of activities

Researchers visiting one class studying Latin observed pupils constructing salt sculptures of Pompeii. While the teacher clearly expected pupils to be learning about Roman culture, when asked about what he had learned, one boy said, 'the salt cracks if you don't use enough water'. As Smith and Ragan (1999: 17) observe, 'too often teachers think first of designing activities during instructional planning ... it is also not uncommon for the goal to become lost from the activity'. In many ways this is not surprising as there is an overwhelming imperative to keep the pupils occupied and to keep up some kind of momentum, but this can also lead to 'busy-work' where the classroom is buzzing with activity, which ultimately leads to little learning. Children often collude with this kind of time-filling activity, because it can be pleasant enough to complete some low-level task whilst maintaining conversation with one's friends. However, as Dave (one of our teacher interviewees) points out in his discussion about the use of practicals in science lessons, 'we don't do practicals for the sake of doing practicals, but because it helps with the learning and moves the learning on in some way. It's not to keep them busy, it's about making a point.' Our first point is therefore the most basic one: the activities you select within your medium-term plan are first and foremost *learning* activities, and the learning intentions should have been clearly established by your completion of the articulation and alignment phases of planning. In short, you already know what you want children to learn at each stage, and what kinds of knowledge, attitudes and skills you want to promote; now you need to identify the optimum kinds of activity that will enable those intentions to be achieved.

Some of these activities will already be emerging, perhaps in rather vague terms, from the previous planning phases (Ollerton, 2006), but now you need to start pinning down specifics. You must select or create activities that enable pupils to engage with the precise intentions, and unless you are constantly checking for that connection it is all too easy to end up with vaguely related activities, which are all loosely about the same topic, but which do not clearly lead to your desired outcomes. Tyler (1950) summed this up a long time ago with the key observations that:

1. The activity must provide the student with the opportunity to engage with and learn about the objective.
2. The activity should provide the student with the opportunity to experience satisfaction at achieving the objective.
3. The activities should be achievable.
4. There are many ways to achieve the same objective.
5. Any activity will (potentially) lead to more than one objective.

Once you have identified what needs to be learned, Chambers (2008) suggests listing all the ways it *could* be taught as the first step in determining the optimum teaching approach and avoiding making lazy assumptions or repeating the same style of lessons. He argues that teachers need to become aware of the variety of possible approaches and weigh up the pros and cons of each. This is easier for experienced teachers, who may have taught the topic differently over the years and gained some sense of the strengths and weaknesses of the methods they have used in the past and the conditions in which some approaches work well. For newer teachers, and student teachers especially, this phase might require further reading and observations of colleagues. Some schools and departments have open cultures, where colleagues discuss the variety of pedagogical approaches that could be adopted to teach a topic, while others tend to default to 'safe' strategies, or dismiss the variation as reflecting nothing more than teachers' preferences (Scott Douglas, 2014). In these latter examples, you will have a harder job to compile the alternatives, but you should always at least consider a few different approaches, to reassure yourself that you understand why an activity appeals to you.

Tanner and Jones (2000) address an audience of maths teachers, but their advice on the matter of choosing teaching strategies is more broadly applicable. They recommend that teachers should plan to:

-   use a variety of strategies to reinforce the concepts or skills being developed;
-   bring misconceptions into open discussion;
-   require pupils to explain their thinking to each other and to the teacher;
-   require pupils to listen to each other's methods and try to understand them;
-   encourage pupils to reflect on their own strategies and to adopt more effective ones;
-   encourage pupils to try to predict where errors may occur;
-   use errors as teaching points.

They recognise that what pupils have done in one activity can be recycled in subsequent activities; for example, solve a problem, then explain how you solved the problem using mathematical terminology, then compare methods and decide which is best, then apply that method in a new context and then teach someone else your method. This is five activities, but they are related, and the previous activity becomes the raw material for the next one. If the pursuit of pace, progress and variety leads you to devise lots of separate activities, you are likely to be planning and making resources during every spare waking moment. In fact the learning is often served best by several closely related activities, and in this example, all the teacher is required to produce in the way of teaching resources is the original problem, and the subsequent activities are reliant on the teacher devising a process and providing instructions.

Lawrence Stenhouse led an influential curriculum development project in England in the 1960s and 1970s and subsequently focused his account of the curriculum as a process rather than simply a product. Stenhouse urged teachers not to become entirely obsessed with measurable, or observable, objectives which are defined in behavioural terms. He argued that teachers also need to plan for rich activities which allow for individualised and unpredictable outcomes. While he argued that the process model should replace the behaviourist outcomes model, we would urge that teachers should simply recognise that while the behaviourist outcomes model is dominant in the current climate, it is not without problems and it is not the only possible route to meaningful planning and learning. In helping to illustrate how teachers might consider richer, open-ended learning tasks Stenhouse borrows a list of criteria (1975: 86–87) for identifying activities that seem to have inherent worth from Raths (1971), who wrote an article entitled 'Teaching without specific objectives' in which he argued that, all other things being equal, one activity is more worthwhile than another if it fulfils one or more of the following criteria:

- The activity permits children to make informed choices in carrying out the activity and to reflect on the consequences of their choices.
- The activity assigns to pupils active roles in the learning situations rather than passive ones.
- The activity asks pupils to engage in enquiry into ideas, applications of intellectual processes, or current problems, either personal or social.
- The activity involves children with real objects, materials and facts.
- Completion of the activity may be accomplished successfully by children at several different levels of ability.
- The activity asks pupils to examine *in a new setting* an idea, an application of an intellectual process, or a current problem which has been *previously studied*.
- The activity requires pupils to examine topics or issues that citizens in our society do not normally examine, and that are typically ignored by the major communication media in the nation.

- The activity involves pupils and teachers in risk taking – not a risk of life or limb, but a risk of success or failure.
- The activity requires pupils to rewrite, rehearse and polish their initial efforts.
- The activity involves pupils in the application and mastery of meaningful rules, standards or disciplines.
- The activity gives pupils the chance to share the planning, the carrying out of a plan, or the results of an activity with others.

While one may argue with any of these criteria, the point is well made that teachers' selection of activities is potentially incredibly powerful. What pupils are asked to do obviously has implications for motivation, engagement and levels of interest. It also has implications for the kinds of skills that students will be using, and the ways in which they will be required to think and use (and develop) their knowledge. It also has significant implications for how students will experience learning in your lesson and how these experiences will add up over time.

Underpinning all of this is a key question that exercised Stenhouse when he was director of the Humanities Project (1968–1973) and the school-leaving age was being increased. He was preoccupied with the kind of young adult schools should be helping to turn out into society. He was interested by the idea that teachers in secondary schools had to wean students off dependent relationships and prepare them to think and learn independently and co-operatively but not to require the direction and authority to do so. Indeed, Stenhouse thought it was important to somehow use schooling to help young people to become less susceptible to authoritarian modes of teaching. Clearly, then, this kind of long-term objective for education can only really be achieved through the selection of appropriate modes of working, and by the teacher providing (and then removing) sufficiently supportive structures to facilitate this level of independence. There is no reason to believe that this will happen by accident and every reason to tackle the selection of activities seriously and systematically.

In the following extracts from our interviews we highlight some of the ways in which these experienced planners have sought to be very clear about why they have selected specific activities. In the first example, Anna reflects on her scheme of work on the use of the atom bomb in Nagasaki and Hiroshima. In the same way that Stenhouse was driven by a clear overall educational purpose, to promote young adults' autonomy, Anna is driven by her commitment to peace education:

I feel strongly about student-led activities. I don't see students as a cup into which the teacher pours knowledge. The teacher should be a facilitator so, by adopting a carousel approach, the kids actively gather knowledge. This can be a very good way of getting kids engaged, and to see this as an issue that they may find interesting. If they are on their feet, and are engaged, hopefully they are less likely to be bored.

This leads to Activity 1: Carousel with groups working through different resources to understand what happened.
Rationale: To secure basic comprehension and pupil engagement, through active participation.

As a peace educator I want to promote moral reasoning and empathy. I feel very strongly that you shouldn't ever tell children what to think, you should be giving them information and enabling them to make up their own minds. Through the characters created in the resource, I wanted to have a person representing each viewpoint so that the students could look at the issues through a critical thinking approach, but also understand the human perspective. The characters enabled me to personify the view, which is better than presenting a series of viewpoints in the abstract.

This leads to Activity 2: Read and respond to role cards.
Rationale: To promote moral reasoning and empathy through understanding multiple perspectives on a single event.

There is an alternative Activity 2, which is designed for students who may find the debate format too challenging. In this alternative students are given a card with one fact about their character, then as a group they have to piece together the story of the character. Then they are given a bingo-style card and they have to go round the class and circle whether each of the six characters is for or against the bombing and why, so that fosters the skills of questioning and critical thinking.

This leads to Activity 3: Debate or bingo activity to complete profile and compare characters.
Rationale: To promote questioning and critical thinking through a comparison of perspectives and development of pupils' own ethical response.

In the next example Andrew, our secondary English teacher, makes a similar point about the need to be crystal clear about the learning intentions, whilst devising a sufficiently flexible task so that pupils can encounter the topic and make sense of it on their own terms. It would be possible simply to teach the conventions of debate from the front, or pre-determine the list of characteristics of various debates and ask pupils to memorise them, but he adopts a more active approach:

The key in planning the unit was really to allow the students to see what the different forms of debate are. So the plan is to produce lots of video material to offer as models. I think one of the key things for English teachers will be stressing the differences between debates and speeches. English teachers can do speeches until the cows come home, whereas debating contains speeches but, depending on what form of debate it is, it also has various codes and different ways of using language and the need for listening and responding is much clearer as well. So, the activities, wherever possible, will offer material to the students that they are going to engage with and extrapolate ideas from ... Through that combination of visual material and discussion, that's really led by the students, you've got your starting point.

This leads to Activity: Group analysis of different forms of debate.
Rationale: To understand the relationship between a speech and debate and the conventions which shape debates.

Learning demand

In Tyler's list, discussed earlier in this chapter, we noted that tasks should be achievable, and Wilhelm et al. (2001) argue slightly more specifically that this requires the teacher to make a judgement about the learners' current level of attainment and the stage they could achieve with the support of the teacher. This reflects their commitment to Vygotsky's social constructivist approach, and especially his description of the zone of proximal development (ZPD). Wilhelm and his colleagues argue that teaching and learning within the ZPD should be 'hard fun', which is to say it should be challenging for the pupils because it is genuinely at the edge of their current ability, but it should also be engaging and motivating. Reflecting on his own teaching, Wilhelm recalls being flushed with pride when the whole class handed in excellent projects with no apparent difficulty, but on later reflection he suspected such perfection was only possible because the pupils had already mastered all the skills and knowledge required, and so in fact those perfect assignments were proof that he had taught them nothing new. There was no evidence of struggle, error, correction, provisional understanding; in short, no evidence of the process of learning.

This has important implications for thinking about the level of demand of the activities you select or design. Being realistic about the level of demand enables you to put in place appropriately scaffolded activities, which enable pupils to achieve overall objectives which might feel out of reach if they were just presented on their own, but which can be achieved with the appropriate stepping stones in place. Thinking about reading is a useful illustration of this point. It is fairly common for secondary school teachers of subjects other than English to see texts as problematic resources in classes where pupils are not confident readers. A common response, which we have frequently seen with student teachers, is to continually re-present and simplify the text to reduce the level of reading demand to a point where there is no challenge. This is problematic for two reasons. The first is that it doesn't make the learning 'hard fun' because it pegs the pupil to their existing level of attainment and provides no reading challenge. The second problem is that reducing the level of linguistic complexity often also reduces the level of conceptual complexity in the subject being taught, and therefore teachers may find themselves over-simplifying content because they are avoiding demanding subject specific language. As Wilhelm et al. (2001: 19) point out, 'one of the problems with reading is that the processes are internal, hidden and abstract', and therefore the correct teaching response is to analyse the text, identify the problematic features, clarify the key elements and then design a series of specific activities designed to scaffold the pupils' access to the text and the key ideas therein. All teachers need to think about what kind of steps they could plan in a sequence of activities to overcome obstacles to learning, rather than assume the optimum strategy is to work around the obstacles; if everyone takes this approach, pupils will never improve.

Grenfell and Harris (1999) illustrate how this kind of approach might influence the kinds of activities designed for each stage of the plan:

1. Consciousness/awareness raising (including brainstorming strategies).
2. Modelling.
3. General practice.
4. Action planning, goal setting and monitoring.
5. Focused practice and fading out the reminders.
6. Evaluation.

Towards the end 'the teacher seeks to withdraw gradually the scaffolding provided by the reminders and to establish whether the strategies have been assimilated and can be deployed effectively' (Grenfell and Harris, 1999: 80). By providing a clear, progressive structure and teaching students about this explicitly, they are introduced to the range of learning procedures that will eventually enable them to become increasingly independent learners. While there may be a case for 'learning to learn' in separate study skills classes, there is value in subject specialists using these strategies because, by teaching these skills and strategies within subjects, students can become accustomed to using the strategies in specific circumstances. This reflects Grenfell and Harris's observation that simply introducing strategies does not render them useful or usable; this requires carefully constructed opportunities for practice and explicit instruction and feedback.

In these examples the level of demand is varied by the amount of scaffolding, but Sweller at al. (1998) also point out that some material to be learned is intrinsically more cognitively demanding. In a modern language lesson, simply learning vocabulary presents learners with a relatively low cognitive load because the words can be learned individually in a sequence, whereas when they are working on grammar, for example, making sure they understand the order in which those words fit into a sentence, this places a higher cognitive load on the learner's working memory because they have to process the words together and consider the relationships between them, rather than one by one. Maths tasks tend to require a high level of element interactivity, which may explain why it often feels like it is more challenging (Sweller et al., 1998: 260). For example, when balancing both sides of an equation, a student who has not automated the appropriate mathematical schema is placing a great burden on their working memory, and as a consequence may take short cuts, for example simply mimicking the teacher by moving a number over, rather than understanding the need to balance both sides of an equation. It may be that a student cannot really fully understand the relationship between various elements until they have built a higher-order schema. This means that teachers have to recognise that the level of difficulty or demand of an activity is not merely a reflection of how well the teacher has planned the activity, it is also determined by the level of schema development a learner brings to the task, and the level of automaticity they have developed.

One implication of this which has been trialled in experiments is to develop goal-free tasks that distinguish between problem-solving tasks and more open-ended activities. For example, a pupil could be presented with the following problem:

A car is uniformly accelerated from rest for 1 minute. Its final velocity is 2km/min. How far has it travelled? (Sweller et al., 1998: 271)

As the authors point out, it may be possible for a pupil to calculate the answer, recalling certain elements of prior learning, but this is quite demanding on working memory. An alternative, goal-free approach would be to simply present the following to pupils:

A car is uniformly accelerated from rest for 1 minute. Its final velocity is 2 km/min. Calculate the value of as many variables as you can.

While this approach feels counterintuitive to most teachers, the authors point out that the second version only requires the pupil to explore one step at a time. They do not need to simultaneously hold the problem, the desired end goal, and recall the required sub-steps. Being free to explore the problem is likely to lead the pupil to calculate the same answer, but in a way that reduces cognitive load and encourages schema formation. They therefore recommend that maths and science teachers use this method sometimes as well as specifying the goal.

For similar reasons they argue that sometimes learning can be facilitated more easily by providing examples of annotated worked examples rather than only encouraging pupils to solve their own problems. By enabling them to repeatedly see the correct processes being used, pupils can derive and internalise the correct schemas more efficiently than if they have to devote their working memory solely to the task of problem solving. While too many worked problems may result in a loss of engagement and motivation, the authors demonstrate that some of the benefits can be replicated if teachers design partially completed problems, with a gradual reduction in the degree of completion over time to encourage pupils' engagement and task completion.

Moving from maths to English, Andrew's interview also illustrates how he is engaging with the idea of an appropriate level of demand for pupils:

> *When you are looking at linguistic features, you can often overlook language itself, which is more important I think. So actually, why is this is an effective use of language? Beyond the fact that it uses triplicates or there are oppositional phrases … No one looks at a great Obama speech and says it was great because he listed three things … In the resource I would like to use examples of people using features which do not work to great effect … You know, why, when Thatcher said 'You turn, the lady's not for turning', why is that a great piece of rhetoric? It's quite hard to say. It's not that she's used word play, you turn is like a U-turn, big deal. How do you get students to articulate why rhetorically that's really fantastic beyond actually explaining the play on words? It's very difficult. In selecting examples you have to think carefully about what will work in the classroom, so in order to understand the Thatcher speech you probably need to understand that it's about the shift from consensual politics to conviction politics, but you can't really put that into a scheme of work, so that may not be a good resource for this plan. Because so much depends on context, you might decide in the classroom to use an extract from a blockbuster movie like* Independence Day *where the President's speech only lasts about 30 seconds but contains all those rhetorical devices, is far better than any politician could deliver but is pure cheese as well.*

Here Andrew is really grappling with the precise nature of the learning he wants to encourage and the best type of resource that might help him. He is aware that traditional forms of teaching linguistic features might actually miss some of the really important learning, but that language is really much more subtle and complicated than might first appear. The first step is to know what kind of formulaic activities he will not use (such as spot and reproduce the rule of three), and then to move on to think about what kinds of activities he might use. This leads him to speculate that it might be useful to look at failed examples, where the rules are being applied but unsuccessfully. It also leads him to select some unlikely possible sources, such as the speech from *Independence Day*, because it will enable him to make a point without getting bogged down initially in context. As Sweller and his colleagues were devising ways to reduce the need for pupils to simultaneously hold multiple maths functions in their working memory, Andrew is also aware that the level of new contextual information required to understand the use of language in the Thatcher speech is probably excessive for pupils starting with almost no cultural references. He decides to simply sidestep the issue and use a completely different type of resource to get at the same point. Another response might be to use a speech delivered in a context more familiar to the children. Because Andrew is designing a plan for other teachers to use, his flexibility is limited, but a classroom teacher devising their own activity would be able to pick a speech from the week's news and build on the fact that the children already understand the context.

 Activity

Describe a task you have used in the classroom. Explain exactly what purposes it served and what contribution it made to the pupils' learning.
   Now think of a way in which you could have increased or decreased the level of cognitive demand, by adapting the same task rather than replacing it.

Activities that activate prior learning and preview future learning

In the previous chapter we discussed Ausubel's suggestions about advance organisers, which clearly indicate that a medium-term plan should start with some deliberately constructed activities to put these structures in place. As we saw, Ausubel argued this could be done fairly simply through explaining the main concepts, or themes, to be covered, while others have developed alternative activities, such as graphical organisers to preview the learning, or the use of key concepts (Gurlitt et al., 2012). Writing about modern languages teaching, Meiring and Norman (1999a, 1999b) suggest creating a topic organiser template, so that pupils can collect key grammar points, vocabulary and topic-related ideas, which may inform their writing and speaking. This kind of template requires the teacher to apply their own knowledge of the kinds of information that could be collected and their ideas about the best way to collate it for future use. In our interview with Dave about his science unit with year 8 (12–13 years) boys, he reported a similar idea:

> *I made little booklets that structured their writing and helped me provide them with support, e.g. key words, but it also allowed them to work at their own pace. I didn't have to keep stopping and starting the lesson to give instructions, they could see where they were going.*

This was devised primarily as a tool to support pupils with limited writing skills, but one of the key advantages is that the booklets previewed the whole activity and provided a very tangible scaffold for the pupils so that they could work through the tasks without having to work at the same pace as everyone else, and without constant recourse to their teacher for instructions.

In a similar vein Wilhelm et al. (2001: Ch. 4) write about *frontloading* their teaching so that pupils are introduced to some of the key themes ahead of the main period of teaching. In their book, most of the examples are related to teaching literature, as they are largely concerned with promoting advanced level reading, but they draw on a range of familiar strategies, for example the K–W–L grid. This is a simple device, which draws pupils' attention to what they already know about the topic (the first column is labelled K for 'know'), what they want to learn (the second column is labelled W for 'want') and what they have learned (the third column is labelled L for 'learned'). The first two columns can be completed as part of the frontloading period, while the third is a useful final activity to ensure pupils think about how to connect up their new learning with their prior knowledge, and of course, to make sure they answered the questions they had at the outset. The first column helps the pupils to activate their prior learning, and also helps you to identify any gaps or misconceptions. The second column helps to engage the pupils and arouse their curiosity, it also enables you to adapt your planning to incorporate issues that are of interest to the pupils. Completion of the third column can help pupils to think about the topic as a whole, and can be used as the basis for a new concept map of the topic, to ensure that new and old information are synthesised.

Rita mentioned this in her account of planning in the early years. For her this initial phase of the unit serves an organisational and a learning purpose:

> *Towards half-term, we told the parents in a newsletter that next half-term our theme would be transport. We told them where we were at with the planning, for example we had already discussed with the children how we*

were going to set up the role-play areas, so we would have a fire station and rockets, and then the children are really excited, so when they come back for the new term, they are really excited about this new topic, and it's almost like pre-teaching, which can be helpful to some children with English as an additional language. It also gives us an opportunity to collect resources, and to involve parents in bringing in whatever we need.

Several of Wilhelm's other frontloading activities are designed to generate predictions about what pupils are about to learn. In relation to preparing to read a novel, this can take the form of providing pupils with quotations from characters, or giving them events to sequence. In other subjects, you might suggest certain possible scenarios and ask pupils to discuss which they feel are most likely, returning to their predictions during and after the teaching to compare with the new material being learned. Predictive activities can be useful ways to start a scheme of work because they draw the pupils into the learning and start to secure interest and engagement; they also establish at least one form of motivation, because the pupil is keen to know if they 'guessed' right; but they also serve a valuable role in requiring the pupil to draw on previous learning in order to extrapolate from what they know and to provide a reasonable justification for their prediction.

Other frontloading activities might include asking pupils to consider their opinion about a topic before the new content is considered, with a review at the end to reflect on the personal significance of the learning. This also helps pupils to think about the preconceptions they might bring to the new material. Drama techniques can also help in terms of preparing pupils for some of the issues that might arise in the subsequent teaching: for example, to explore emotional themes that will be significant in a novel; or key ethical dilemmas that will emerge in the study of history; or even key ideas about the physical world ahead of a science unit – while there may be inaccuracies in asking children to role-play atoms, it can be useful to preface their thinking about theoretical and abstract concepts with some concrete starting points.

 Case Study   The power of failure

This short article by Collins reviews the papers in a special issue of the journal *Instructional Science*, which focused on the question of how to teach maths problem solving when there is a canonical solution for the pupils to learn. Obviously the teacher could just teach the solution directly

(Continued)

(Continued)

to the pupils but these articles explore a teaching method which requires pupils to struggle to solve a novel problem before being given the solution. This is based on the idea that an initial phase of 'invention' and 'productive failure' followed by a second phase of instruction in the actual solution may be more effective than just direct teaching. One problem with this method is that pupils need to be confident and sufficiently well briefed to really explore alternative solutions in the initial phase and the journal includes research which suggests the following strategies may be helpful in developing this basic first phase:

(1) Role-play scripts.

Teachers promoted scaffolded paired talk about potential problem-solving strategies by providing role-playing scripts. These helped pupils to understand the exploratory phase and they gradually internalised these forms of exploratory talk.

(2) Prepare cases for analysis.

Teachers also provided meta-cognitive scaffolding and alternative cases for the pupils to compare. This involved pupils being given four different ways to solve the problem and using sets of scaffolded questions that would (i) encourage the pupil to compare the cases methodically to identify a preferred solution; (ii) guide the pupil to develop an individual justification for their preferred solution; (iii) provide suggestions for peer interaction to help pupils compare answers.

(3) Vary the type of ability grouping.

In this example mixed-ability groups were found to be better at promoting a more varied exploratory initial phase, whereas pupils grouped with others of a similar ability tended to produce a narrower range of solutions.

(4) Use varied representational scaffolding.

Collins also suggests asking pupils to produce a variety of representations (line graphs, scatter plots, calculations, etc.) as a general method to help them consider different possibilities.

There are questions the teacher needs to consider such as the balance between individual, paired and group work; and the balance between free experimentation and being given some prepared resources to respond to.

Collins also speculates about whether such an approach could be useful in problems where there is no canonical solution.

Teachers need to choose the right kind of problems for this teaching method and this is related to the pupils' prior knowledge. If the students have too much knowledge, then the problem is too easy, and pupils will simply solve it without any struggle. If they do not have enough knowledge to make sense of the problem, then it will be too difficult, and they may become discouraged. This resonates with our ongoing discussion about positioning the learning within the ZPD, so that it is 'hard fun'.

Source: Collins, A. (2012) What is the most effective way to teach problem solving? A commentary on productive failure as a method of teaching, *Instructional Science*, 40(4), 731–735.

Big and small activities

The National Strategies in England gave rise to a rather formulaic approach to lesson planning, which has left a residue in many schools embodied in the three-part lesson. This typically includes three separate activities in the main phase of the lesson plus a starter activity and some form of plenary. In an hour-long lesson this typically means each substantial activity lasts 10–15 minutes, which really is not very long for a sustained, in-depth engagement with anything. On the other hand, the recipe was adopted largely because it can be helpful to change activities regularly to maintain pace and avoid boredom. One way to remedy the potential fragmentation that derives from such a lesson structure is to ensure that all the activities are closely related, and that there are obvious connections between them. Another approach is to deliberately adopt overarching tasks that are themselves bigger than single lessons, so that pupils can begin to experience a more sustained form of learning. Some people are too quick to assume children have short attention spans, but observe a young child playing with Lego or an older child playing a computer game and it is clear that they can sustain close attention to a task if it is sufficiently stimulating and relevant to them. There is no blueprint here, having several short focused activities in a single lesson is not necessarily better or worse than devising a single extended activity to run over several lessons. Each brings different advantages and disadvantages, each requires a different approach to teaching, and a different approach to learning. We raise it here as a separate point simply because we think the default assumption in many schools is to adopt the former model of activity planning, and we want to encourage you to consider when you might adopt the latter.

One of the most obvious methods for adopting longer activities that run over time is the 'project'. A project provides pupils with time to focus on a topic of interest to them and to explore it with greater freedom than if their teacher sets all the tasks one by one. One review of projects developed across different age groups and subjects in the USA and UK concluded simply that there were three basic rules for high-quality project work:

1. Exhibition – there should be a public audience for the work, so children know the work will be seen (and judged by) a real audience, other than their teacher.
2. Multiple drafts – making the time for pupils to revise and improve their work means they have the opportunity to produce a piece of work they can feel really proud of. It also enables the teacher to make an additional kind of assessment judgement about how well they can respond to feedback and improve their performance over time.
3. Critique – the process should enable pupils to feedback to one another and get accustomed to making evaluative judgements. In High Tech High, the basic rules for critique sessions are: be kind, be specific, and be helpful. (Patton, 2012)

Projects are also powerful because they encourage pupils to focus on the process of learning and presenting what has been learned as well as on the actual content.

Clearly if you are planning a project as a learning activity you cannot simply tell the pupils to get on with it; there would need to be careful planning around supporting the process, setting goals, helping pupils manage their time, enabling access to appropriate resources, helping them to develop assessment criteria, and so on. Projects can be scaled up or down, and it may be reasonable to build in a project element to a larger scheme of work, or even make a whole scheme of work project-based. However, there are other ways in which you can start to think about learning activities stretching beyond a short period of a single lesson. Shiv, in her account of her primary science medium-term plan, makes an important point about the nature of learning activities. She used a basic investigation method to measure parts of the body and look for relationships between various measurements. Although the unit went on for six lessons, she is clear that the basic activity structure was similar across most of the lessons:

In year 2 (six to seven-year-olds) I wanted them to think of their own questions and so the reason I gave them more freedom and put them in smaller groups was that I was trying to let them take the next step ... the reason why the process was similar from week to week is that I was trying to enable them to make intellectual jumps really. Even from year 1 (five to six-year-olds) they had been doing investigations, they had those skills – what I was trying to do was get them to take more ownership and do more of the process. The repetition every week was just to give them something familiar, so while we developed that aspect of it, the actual 'right, once I know my question, here I come, tape measure, clipboard here I go', once they had got through those steps they knew what they were doing … I don't think they thought they were doing the same thing every week. I couched it in those terms but each lesson was sufficiently different that they didn't think like that … They are always delighted in science to get their hands on things and work in mixed ability groups.

So for Shiv, there was value in re-using the same underlying activity structure lesson after lesson, but the variety was provided by the nature of the question to be investigated and the degree of freedom the pupils had to determine what to investigate and how. In the following extract, Dave makes a slightly different point about learning activities in a science unit with year 8 (12 to 13-year-olds) in secondary school.

Some of these objectives carry over from lesson to lesson that links to what is called 'deep learning'. The two big activities up front are investigations. You can't do an investigation in 25 minutes. It has to span a period of time to allow pupils to truly investigate. And one of the things we do is, rather than packing up at the end of the lesson, we give them a tray and say it doesn't matter where you got to, just put your stuff in the tray, put your name on it and then you just collect it at the start of the next lesson – the pupils are not waiting for me to give an instruction. Now that really does work and it doesn't mean they all have to get to same point at the same time.

Here, then, some activities are simply too big to fit within the artificial confines of a timetabled lesson, but a reasonable organisational step enables pupils to simply pick up where they left off. Dave also accompanied this strategy with lesson by lesson reflections from the children, so they recorded what they had done and what they had learned at the end of each lesson. A quick review of these entries before the next lesson enabled him to plan an early intervention for any groups who were struggling or developing misconceptions.

Types of approach

As we saw in the previous section, there are decisions you may make about which type of learning activity to use that could have significant implications for your planning. Using a project-based approach, or even planning science investigations that run across several lessons, requires a different type of planning and therefore different types of instructions for the pupils. In her early years setting Rita embraced a play-based approach, but even here there were three distinctive types of activity which informed her medium-term planning and the children's experiences:

1. Child-initiated: for example, they might spot a broken chair in the role-play area and decide to fix it. This is often spontaneous and teachers have to observe and adapt. It can't really be planned for.
2. Adult-initiated: for example, setting up resources to promote a particular type of play or activity. These can be planned, but children will exercise some choice about whether and when they engage with these planned opportunities.
3. Adult-led: for example a carpet-time session, where children have much less choice.

The literature is full of different approaches to learning; for example, Reigeluth (1999) lists the following teaching activities: apprenticeship, debate, demonstration, field trip, game, group discussion (guided or open), interview, laboratory work, lecture, panel discussion, project (individual or team), seminar, simulation, case study, role-play, brainstorm, tutorial, Socratic dialogue, drill and practice. But here we want to name just a few general approaches to illustrate the scale of decisions you might consider when thinking about the kinds of learning activities that will promote the learning you are aiming for. There are other approaches in the literature, but we have chosen these as examples of the kind of overarching 'big' activity approaches that indicate the importance of thinking beyond single short activities within a lesson. For each there are different implications for your planning, for how you support the pupils and for the kind of instructions you must provide (Butcher et al., 2006).

(i) Learning through experience

In Chapter 1 we said something briefly about the tradition of experiential learning, which can be most briefly described in a simple cycle (see Figure 6.1, adapted from Dennison and Kirk, 1990). It is clearly the case that much of what we learn in life is learned through experience; that much is obvious whether we are talking about learning to teach, drive a car, write academic essays, or be successful at job interviews. While there are books written about all of these topics, and specialists who can teach you about them, there is really no learning as powerful as the experience of being: in the classroom as a teacher, behind the wheel of a car as a driver, at the keyboard framing a paragraph, or in the hot-seat being interviewed by a panel, and the opportunity to reflect on that experience to think about how you will improve. If we have learned from our reflections on those experiences, we should be confident that the next similar experience will be better; our lessons improve, our driving becomes more fluid and confident, our marks improve and we get the job (eventually).

Figure 6.1   Simplified experiential learning cycle (adapted from Dennison and Kirk, 1990)

There are some obvious issues here in relation to teaching and learning in schools. The first and most obvious observation to make is that schools are not really set up to foster this kind of learning. The artificial division of the day into subjects and lessons sits uneasily with the reality of experiential learning, and of course putting children in a building away from the rest of the community also reduces the accessibility of meaningful real-life situations in which skills and knowledge might be built. This does not mean though that experiential learning has no place in schools, just that we have to think creatively about how to build on this cycle. It may be that in practical subjects, such as design and technology or physical education, it is relatively easy to build in these cycles of activity, so that pupils have the opportunity to complete the cycle several times; for example, a sequence of lessons in which pupils repeat similar cooking techniques to build up mastery, or a sequence of lessons on a sport, where pupils build their skills and understanding by reflecting an aspects of their performance. It is also sometimes possible to plan a unit of work around some form of core experience, for example through negotiating a collapsed timetable day, so pupils have an extended period of time to do something, or through planning some real action-oriented outcome to a unit, as frequently undertaken by citizenship teachers helping pupils to engage in some form of political action. For example, in one school pupils actually started their own local youth club through lobbying the council, finding appropriate premises and advertising the service. It may also be that you try to use some form of simulation to build on some of the features of experiential learning.

In her Politics A level medium-term plan, Vicky used a simulation to provide pupils with a relevant learning experience:

> *The simulation in week 3 was designed to provide everyone with some kind of experience of direct action. The scenario is that oil has been discovered near the college and then the cohort was split into different groups to decide what should happen. We gave points to everyone who managed to get the media group to cover their activity or gain the support of a politician or voters. One group were so frustrated that they took direct action, to make a ring of people around the BP area, to stop their lobbyists getting to the media group. It demonstrated a range of methods, it enabled the students to use their prior learning but also introduced an experiential and emotional element – they saw some things very clearly, such as how money buys you press releases.*

The point here is clear – that the experience, even in a simulation, involves thinking, doing and feeling. The debrief from such activities needs to focus on each of these three dimensions: What did you do? How did you feel? Why did you do it like that? What did you learn? In Vicky's example, we can see that some pupils used their emotional response as a stimulus to physically intervene in the work of another group, and of course in doing so, these pupils learned a very powerful lesson about direct action. It is important, though, to remember that the learning is not the same as the activity. To facilitate experiential learning the teacher has to make time and devise teaching processes that promote pupils' reflection on that experience so that they can articulate what they have learned and integrate it with their prior learning.

If you decide to use experiential learning as a key learning activity in your medium-term plan you will need time for the activity, the preparatory phase and the reflection phase. These phases require different forms of teaching, with the preparatory phase involving more direct input from the teacher, and the subsequent phases requiring a more facilitative role. You need to be clear about time, resources and style of teaching, and plan carefully for each.

(ii) Direct teaching for knowledge acquisition

This model of teaching is more akin to the expository teaching espoused by Ausubel, which we discussed in the previous chapter. While much of learning theory is concerned with participation and experience, Ausubel was interested in how teachers could develop the ways in which they presented and structured information to enable pupils to learn effectively. While it might not be the most commonly promoted form of teaching in the literature, it is probably still the most common form of teaching in schools, and is what schools are best suited to. This is the default model we have had in mind in this book, although we think the principles of medium-term planning hold equally true for any approach to teaching. This model also clearly works when done well, because this is ultimately how most of us learned things in school and university. The key when adopting this approach is to think clearly about how you sequence the new content, how you introduce it, how you relate it to the learner's existing knowledge, in short, how you explain progression.

Here is one example from Rubia, about secondary maths, which exemplifies this kind of approach. She is discussing how she sequenced activities within her plan to build on year 10 (14 to 15-year-old) pupils' prior learning of shape to introduce them to GCSE level knowledge.

> *When I teach a topic such as corresponding and alternate angles I use my visualiser a great deal, like a YouTube tutorial. So ... the girls had spent a lesson doing flip learning, we'd gone to the computer room and they worked through a MyMaths programme on quadrilaterals, and the following lesson they were asked to fill in a worksheet with the shapes on them. They had time to think back and fill in as much information for each shape as they could remember from the previous lesson, so it might be ... a rectangle with dashes for equal sides and double dashes for the opposite equal sides, arrows to show parallel sides or simply write in sentences or bullet points, key facts that they could recall. The process would have involved initially working on their own, then they discussed it with a partner, comparing and discussing differences and finally going through the task as a whole class with feedback from individuals. This final process would have involved me asking questions like, what do those labels mean, or how are those lines different? Again, getting them to think about how they are remembering key facts. New information would be included, such as how to recognise parallel lines and corresponding and alternate angles. Again we did this by working through an example on the visualiser. They have their sheets and mini-whiteboards and I might ask them to find this line, and find other parallel lines. I would then nominate students to come up and indicate their answers at the front. This creates an environment where everyone is engaged. If there was one piece of equipment that has transformed how I teach shape activities, transformations, bearings and so on, it's the visualiser because they can literally follow me as I go along.*

Here we can see why this kind of teaching really can be effective. In the first activity students are working through online material independently, being introduced to some key ideas. Then Rubia tests their recall and understanding. Then she models how this information can be used, building in time for inter-action between her and the pupils as well as for interaction between the pupils to encourage them to talk about what they are doing and allow any problems to come to the fore through such comparative conversations. The use of struc-tured worksheets and mini-whiteboards allows her to see if pupils can follow the instructions and begin to apply the knowledge correctly. Clearly here the implications for planning are quite different; Rubia has to sequence the activi-ties carefully so that information is provided in several ways before pupils are asked to use it, and so that she carefully moves between independent work, whole-class work, paired talk, and so on. Teacher explanation, modelling and instruction are crucial at each stage of the lesson and require resources and instructions to be planned clearly in advance.

(iii) Discovery learning

Discovery learning is, in many ways, the opposite of expository teaching. Whereas the latter introduces pupils to the main idea to be learned and fol-lows up with examples to reinforce the basic message and ensure pupils can apply it correctly, discovery learning is a more inductive process in which pupils arrive at the main idea more or less independently. This makes the process more open to error, although of course correcting errors can be as helpful in securing understanding as confirming success (Glaser, 1966). Bruner (1961) argued that essentially discovery learning is useful because learning discovered by the learner has a more powerful impact on the learner; because it is intrinsically motivating; and because it requires pupils to draw on prior knowledge and therefore ensures new learning is better connected with existing knowledge and more likely to be remembered. We include it here because it is useful to prompt yourself at the planning stage to think about whether you want to provide all the content up front, or whether you want the pupils to have to work for it, and to generate some of the substantive content themselves. From what we have already said, it should be evident that we take a fairly pragmatic approach on this; simply put, there are times when this approach works well and times when other approaches might be more appropriate. The following examples show how two teachers make this decision:

> Sometimes, when we begin learning about circles, I might ask each mem-ber of the class to bring in round objects, we will then spend a lesson tak-ing measurements and try to work out the relationship between diameter and circumference. They may know about the number pi but they may not always have worked out the link to circles before those lessons.

In this first example, Rubia gives an example where she would use a discovery method to enable children to 'discover' pi and its relationship to diameter and circumference. But in the following example, she starts to think about possible limitations to this approach.

Students might be expected to find out whether a particular shape might tessellate, so in order to investigate that, they would need to know key facts … They need to know what an angle is, and how to use the protractor to measure angles. They don't need to be told the angles around a point add up to 360° – they could do an investigation and then work it out, by comparing what is common between the shapes that fit together … [But] we often have debates about VAK learners but we don't talk about learners who don't like investigating – some learners just like to have key information in place, which they can test out. There can be a joy in just applying principles you've been taught and working that through. That's another part of differentiation, you know, really understanding your group, and how they enjoy learning and then guiding them to new ways of approaching a problem. Once again the learning process simplifies down to the confidence of the individual. A student could sit there in an investigation thinking I don't know where to start, some don't have the skills necessary to get involved and investigate, and they need to be taught those skills. Some students are overwhelmed by investigative tasks and although risk taking is a good skill to develop, throwing students in at the deep end still requires a well thought out support system from the teacher's side.

Here Rubia makes two valuable points. One is that not all children enjoy this type of learning, or find it preferable to other approaches, therefore one cannot assume it is always intrinsically motivating. And the second is that the teacher cannot assume pupils are able to embark on a discovery activity or investigation without receiving clear instructions and guidance. Therefore, the teacher's planning must address this by teaching explicitly about the processes to be applied, or the parameters within which to experiment. In the following example, Dave also reflects on some of the limitations of using this method when teaching year 8 (12 to 13-years-old) pupils about electric circuits:

The notion of a series circuit, which is one that just goes round in a line, is OK – you can probably get that easily. In my experience teachers then talk about parallel circuits without students really knowing what these are – in my view you have to teach that, you can't discover it, you can do that in a number of ways. You can set up a number of circuits around the room without telling the pupils what kind of circuit it is, and say things like, right remove that bulb and see what happens to the other bulbs, so you can guide them to the learning but I think it's one of those things that in the end you probably just have to say, right OK, what kind of parallel circuit is this? They can then tell you what the features of that circuit are, but I think the number of students that could point that out by themselves would be quite low.

While Dave was happy to let the children 'play around' with the equipment to establish how series circuits worked, he was less convinced that the same approach would be as helpful in establishing an understanding of parallel circuits. Therefore he adopted a different approach to the kind of activities he adopted for each aspect of content. This kind of mixed economy is common in classrooms, but it is useful to think consciously at the planning stage about the overall balance, and the variety of approaches you want to incorporate within a single scheme. Will one model dominate, or will you draw on one or more types of activity throughout the sequence of lessons? The decisions you make at this stage will make a significant difference to how effectively you help the pupils to learn, but also to how much they enjoy the learning, and how well equipped they are to embark on future learning.

Pragmatic choices: behaviour, relationships, time

The discussion so far has been largely concerned with how to make decisions about learning activities in relation to the content to be learned and the process of learning itself. But it is also important to note that the decisions you make about learning activities will also make a difference to how you ask pupils to behave, the kind of relationship you will set up between yourself and the pupils and your expectations about relationships between pupils. If a class is loud and confident, then planning a debate lesson will be easy; if they are quiet and reserved, you might need to adjust your planning to provide more preparation to build up their confidence, or even opt for an alternative kind of activity to engage with the same kinds of objectives. You also need to think carefully about when you will set an activity as an individual task, a paired activity or for group work. You should have a good reason why one task is aimed at individuals as opposed to groups – how does that foster the kind of learning and thinking you want to promote? But you may also need to adapt this in the light of the class you are teaching; for example, an excitable group who are difficult to settle after break-time may benefit from an individualised settling activity at the start of the lesson, rather than a whole-class brainstorm in order to establish a calm atmosphere. Starting with a whole-class discussion might be justified in terms of activating prior learning, but might also set you up for behaviour difficulties and therefore be counter-productive. It is important therefore to plan for lessons that are realistic and which will be manageable. Incorporating these kind of strategies at the medium-term planning stage means you can build up some familiar routines to establish effective relationships.

Time and resource constraints will also play a part in determining what counts as realistic and manageable learning activities. This latter point is well made by Rubia, a secondary maths teacher, when she reflects on the nature of her current teaching timetable:

> *As we operate on a two-week timetable, it becomes natural to work in two-week sections, but it also depends on each individual teacher's timetable. My timetable, for example, does not incorporate a non-contact each day, I get three on Thursday in week B. So generally I do my planning for the two-week cycle at the same point in week B for the whole fortnight ahead. I also collect the majority of the resources that I may need at this point. When non-contacts are more evenly spread out, planning can also be more evenly spread out on a weekly basis.*

Michael, a secondary history teacher, makes a related point about time, when he talks about the timing for specific types of pupil activity throughout the year:

> *Another popular activity is the building of a castle. We do this after the January exams when teachers are quite busy marking and writing reports. This means it's useful to have a student-centred task for a week. Teachers set this process up very clearly so each member of the group is assigned specific roles, to ensure the project runs smoothly.*

So, some choices will be influenced by the pragmatic time constraints of managing your workload. Others may relate to resources, with the most obvious issue being whether you will be working in the classroom alongside other staff, or whether you will be the only adult. Shiv taught her primary science lessons whilst covering for a colleague's preparation time and so she was teaching the whole class of 6-year-olds on her own. This meant that she had to come up with a form of activity which would free her up to support pupils who needed extra help:

> *You get it so they are quite independent and … you have got the chance to go and do some input where it will help the most. You've got this class of children all busy in twos and threes all collecting information and*

your job is to go to each little group and facilitate what's going on ... I had to do things that worked with one adult. Strangely enough the more independent, the more you let them go, the better it got. It seems counterintuitive, because I think if you were by yourself you would want them all sat at tables but I found that was hellish. The more you let them be practical and get them with their own sense of purpose, and then you facilitate it all, you had 30 children in a science lesson and that was working ... The way that I ended up working with lots of small groups has come through experience. There's an element of pragmatic thinking – how am I going to manage these 30 children? You need to run a classroom where you know all 30 children are going to be engaged.

In a very different kind of pragmatic reasoning, Vicky talked about the kind of overall attitude she wanted to promote in her A level politics class:

I am quite interested in our classroom having a sense of community. I have become more interested in this, so in my A2 class this year, all of the definitions we have, we have made together, because we haven't used textbooks ... In week 2, when we use ICT-based research, it's the same kind of thing – we're creating knowledge that we can use. The kids don't interpret it like this but the hope is that we are researching this and when we report back it will be knowledge that we have accumulated together about the wider world ... It's quite dictatorial isn't it if I'm always choosing, like you must know about Apartheid, and you must know about Climate Camp, and you must know about the Suffragettes, and it gives them the chance to say, well, actually, Vicky, you need to know about Tescopoly ... and that's the whole point that we learn something together. I think it's important that there's a sense of communal learning, as a group we bring things in together.

For Vicky, it was important to teach in a more open way, sharing responsibility with the learners, because this was the kind of relationship she wanted, and because she felt it important to encourage them to take more initiative for their own learning. This is clearly a useful experience for those considering university as the next step in their education. By contrast, Dave's low-attaining group of 12-year-old boys presented him with another kind of challenge when he was considering introducing long practical activities stretching over several lessons:

In my school, where the behaviour can be challenging, you can't just do this and expect it to work automatically. These pupils were not used to independent working and they do have to be trained in that kind of work; for example, the two initial investigations were very similar, which meant what they applied in the first one, they could apply in the second one. I'd like to think if I taught them again, and I used a similar approach, they would buy into it because it's quite powerful.

As with Shiv's earlier account of working with science investigations in primary school, Dave reiterates how important it was to devise activities that were sufficiently similar so pupils could recognise the activity and begin to apply the same approaches they had learned in previous activities. This kind of consistency and consolidation can only be maximised if it is planned in at the early stages of planning.

Conclusion

Many student teachers struggle to think of varied ways to teach a topic. In the early stages of teaching, when there is often a focus on individual lessons, there is simply a limited repertoire available to them, and therefore the idea of collecting examples of teaching activities takes on some urgency to avoid lessons becoming boring and repetitive. However, in this chapter we have argued that there should be more strategic reasons behind the selection of learning activities within a medium-term plan. Teachers should be clear why they have selected specific approaches to learning activities, how these optimise the learning and what contribution they make to the pupils' development of skills and their overall approach to study. Teachers should also be able to use their planning to ensure deadlines do not bunch up together, that work is spread out manageably and that they devise teaching approaches that will work for the pupils in their classes. In this way medium-term planning removes a lot of chance and uncertainty. It also means teachers can devote the bulk of their time to teaching, assessment and feedback during the working week. If the plan is not already in place, the teacher has to spend time planning lesson by lesson, and we do not believe there really is time for such detailed planning alongside the regular teaching week.

Further reading

Laurillard, D. (2012) *Teaching as a Design Science: Building Pedagogical Patterns for Learning and Technology*, Abingdon: Routledge.

This book is doubly useful, both as an exemplification of how teachers have to make decisions at a fairly high level about the kind of learning they want to promote, and how they can use technology to enhance their teaching.

Sweller, J., van Merrionboer, J. J. G. and Paas, F, G. W. C. (1998) 'Cognitive architecture and instructional design', *Educational Psychology Review*, 10(3), 251–296.
This is a challenging but important article which sets out some of the principles that should inform planning.

CHAPTER 7

ASSESSING THE LEARNING AND ADAPTING THE PLAN

By the end of this chapter you will be able to:

- understand the importance of learning intentions and success criteria, both at the medium-term planning level and in individual lessons, in framing learning opportunities that help pupils make progress;
- develop success criteria at the product and process level;
- recognise the role of feedback at task, process and self-evaluation levels;
- consider how best to use different types of feedback to move learning forward and to make suitable adaptations in planning to facilitate further progress.

Introduction

In previous chapters we have focused on the process of planning your teaching, with the intention that you can maximise the chances of pupil learning. The crucial question in the learning cycle will always then be, 'How do we know any learning has happened?' As you will discover in your teaching career, beautifully conceptualised learning objectives, thoughtfully differentiated activities and professional looking resources do not necessarily make for effective learning. They might make for ordered classroom experiences in which children seem to make progress and, dare we say it, have fun. However, unless you have clear strategies which enable you to delve effectively and efficiently into what the learners are actually getting out of the lesson, you (a) won't have an accurate picture of learner progress and (b) won't be able to capitalise on this accurate picture in order to make effective adjustments to future planning. In our experience, student teachers often inaccurately estimate the type, depth and breadth of learning of their pupils and this is often the result of having ineffective ways to measure learning.

In this chapter we will explore how to get an accurate picture of pupils' learning and how to use that feedback to adapt your teaching and planning. Assessment provides you and learners with an accurate picture of learning that can then be used in different contexts: at the point of learning, between learning episodes and over the medium and longer term.

Assessment considerations underpin our other As

While assessment is at the end of our *planning* process, we want you to consider assessment as a fluid, dynamic process that is central to the *learning* process and underpins our other As, not as something that only ever comes at the end of a learning episode. In order to do it effectively, assessment has to be woven through the different stages in the learning cycle.

Assessment is clearly part of the three planning stages we have already considered. The 'articulation' element requires you to consider the content and type of learning to be developed, from what might be an infinite number of learning possibilities. The 'alignment' element requires a consideration of progression routes; in other words, how pupils will use each stage of the sequence to consolidate and move on in their knowledge, understanding and skills. When you are aligning the learning steps you are deciding what your learning intentions will be and how these develop across the sequence to build to answers to your key questions. The development of learning intentions should lead to the development of success criteria that can be used by pupils and teachers to measure where they are at and where they need to get to. The 'activation' stage requires you to decide how to ensure that learning can occur and be consolidated, using tasks and techniques that will allow you to identify whether learning is successfully being achieved.

The next logical stage on from this, and the assessment information generated by children undertaking tasks and the discussions and feedback surrounding it, is the 'adaptation' element which we will also consider in this chapter.

Assessment as a professional skill

Sadler (1998) has identified a number of attributes and skills that teachers bring to the process of assessment. It is worth exploring this in a little more detail because these are the key aspects which you will need to develop as a new teacher:

Teachers bring to assessment:

- superior knowledge of what is to be learned;
- attitudes and dispositions towards teaching and learners;
- skill in task and test construction;
- deep knowledge of appropriate criteria and standards;
- expertise and evaluative skill based on prior reflective practice;
- framing feedback for learners.

(Sadler, 1998)

Superior knowledge of what is to be learned

Teachers bring a high degree of knowledge of what is to be learned, including factual knowledge, conceptual knowledge and procedural knowledge (for instance, assessing the different ways things might be done and the appropriateness of these). This allows them to confirm the levels of correctness of learners' responses in context, or 'whether the idea of correctness makes any sense in the context'. A key part of our 'alignment' phase is, of course, the ability to 'chunk and junk' relevant subject knowledge in the context of your medium-term plan, but inevitably as a teacher you will need to be able to tap into your broader subject knowledge when teaching a sequence of lessons in order to deal with questions emerging from pupils or to increase the cognitive challenge for those learners who are making rapid progress. This links to our earlier discussion of Hussey and Smith (2003) in relation to the need for teachers to recognise, deal and capitalise on emergent learning outcomes as they arise.

Attitudes and dispositions towards teaching and learners

This is a broader skill set, relating to the teachers' attitudes around learner achievement, setting appropriate challenges, empathising with learners' academic and social needs, and considering how to help learners to improve. It also impacts on the nature and style of feedback and personal reflections on the impact of their own practice.

Skill in task and test construction

This skill set touches significantly on our 'Activation' phase. Teachers bring skill in being able to develop tasks and techniques 'to elicit revealing and pertinent responses from students' (Sadler, 1998: 80). Sadler suggests that this requires a broader view of learning over a period of time. The selection of tasks requires 'refined subjective judgement' as teachers need to ensure that tasks are dissimilar from those attempted in the past, but similar enough to allow for the 'transfer or extended application of learning'. While teachers will also use their knowledge of learners to make adaptations to the design of tasks, Sadler suggests that the one-way direction of this (the teacher setting a task which the learners do) is problematic if it is the entirety of assessment practice. Instead, he argues that 'a strong case can be made that students should be taught to change their pattern of thinking so that they know not only how to respond to and solve (externally sourced) problems but also how to frame the problems themselves'.

Deep knowledge of appropriate criteria and standards

Sadler suggests that criteria and standards might exist either in the form of clear statements of standards (for example examination mark schemes, attainment levels) or in a form that is unarticulated and thus more difficult to share. The changes to the national curriculum in England in 2014 brought about a shift from a heavily prescribed set of national standards embodied in attainment level descriptions for every subject and relevant phase, to an unarticulated form in which the attainment target for all phases and subjects became simply 'pupils are expected to know, apply and understand the matters, skills and processes specified in the relevant programme of study' (DfE, 2014). This 'flat' attainment target clearly gives a greater level of autonomy to teachers to use their subject or age-phase knowledge to deconstruct its meaning and identify the implications for curriculum planning, learner progression and their formative and summative assessment systems. But it could also lead to greater variation in the expectations of standards between schools. Whatever view you hold of this, there is no disputing the fact that teachers will need to use their own subject knowledge and professional skills to interpret and codify these expectations in a manner that will support planning and assessing.

Sadler also states that teachers bring a set of expectations to this process. These expectations include 'generalised expectations' based upon knowledge of the cohort of learners they are teaching, and expectations based upon how the learners will respond to the task they have planned, based upon recent teaching and their experiences with differing and possibly less demanding tasks. Therefore, Sadler is suggesting that the teacher, over the course of a sequence of lessons, is incorporating progressively more challenging learning activities and techniques. This is an important point, because in your own planning you will need to ensure that the cognitive challenge increases over the course of the sequence of lessons. A way of checking this is to think about whether your pupils could successfully undertake a task at any point in the sequence. If the answer is yes, then it's probably the case that you need to rethink it. Always consider what knowledge and skills the pupil is bringing to the task before they set off to complete it, what new skills and knowledge they'll acquire once they've worked on it and what that will allow them to do next.

Expertise and evaluative skill based on prior reflective practice

This skill set is based upon teachers using their own prior learning drawn from their teaching experiences to consider how learners might approach tasks including the skills, processes, conceptions and (mis)understandings they bring. Sadler indicates that teachers make hundreds of qualitative judgements each year, giving them regular, constant experience as assessors. The need to make such judgements 'demands that teachers attend conscientiously to the features of student performance'. New teachers will be less likely to have a deep sense of this, so you will need to engage in discussions with more experienced teachers about the likely way learners will approach tasks and the outcomes you should expect. Looking at a range of pre-existing assessed tasks, for instance in exercise books, as part of that conversation is also likely to support this process of calibrating your expectations.

A connection between this skill set might be made with Hattie's assertion that assessment provides feedback for teachers about their impact on learners. Formative assessment evidence provides teachers with a deeper understanding about the impact on learning, facilitating more meaningful discussion between teachers on collective next steps (Hattie, 2012).

Framing feedback for learners

The final skill set that teachers bring is their ability to provide feedback to learners in a meaningful way. While at a basic level this might be through confirming the 'correctness' of a response, it might also be automatic through using a computer program or a self-scoring system. For effective formative assessment, there would need to be greater sophistication in the type of feedback provided including evaluative feedback and non-evaluative descriptions of the work, linked to criteria with suggestions for future improvement. The type of feedback will 'also draw on a knowledge of those persons' previous performances as well as their personalities'. You will need to have a clear understanding of not only the most suitable form of feedback in relation to learning intentions, but also of how to formulate that feedback so that it motivates learners, and that relies on good knowledge of them as people as well as learners. We will return to this point later in the chapter.

Essential strategies of formative assessment

In Chapter 3 we looked at the Assessment Reform Group's five principles of effective formative assessment. In this chapter we move from these principles to consider practical strategies that should inform how you plan for assessment at the medium-term level and how you review your plans in the light of assessment feedback. Wiliam (2011) presents what he sees as the five essential strategies of formative assessment:

1. Clarifying, sharing and understanding learning intentions and criteria for success.
2. Engineering effective classroom discussions, activities and learning tasks that elicit evidence of understanding.
3. Providing feedback that moves learning forward.
4. Activating learners as instructional resources for one another.
5. Activating learners as owners of their own learning.

We are going to use these five principles as a framework for good practice as well as using our case studies to highlight how teachers have used such strategies. The first two strategies clearly embody the principles of alignment and activation, while the latter three strategies will involve teachers and pupils making suitable adaptations to learning. We will therefore combine principles 3, 4 and 5 to provide an overarching explanation of our adaptation element.

1 Clarifying, sharing and understanding learning intentions and criteria for success

In Chapters 3 and 5 we explored the critical importance of getting your learning intentions right and in sharing these with learners in a meaningful way. From an assessment perspective, learning intentions help to clarify learning goals, while success criteria provide a way of guiding the process of achieving these goals and checking the extent of achievement. Meaningfully sharing these with pupils, through ongoing dialogue and active engagement, will help pupils to have greater ownership over the process of achieving the goals including self-managing and regulating their own work in pursuit of these (Sadler, 1989). In our experience, all too often student teachers share their intentions by putting objectives on the board, reading these out and getting pupils to copy them, but then do little to get pupils to use these to guide their contributions and work.

Hattie (2012) outlines three questions which should guide teachers and pupils alike:

1. Where am I going?
2. How am I going to get there?
3. Where to next?

'Where am I going?' clearly refers to the need for clear and unambiguous learning intentions. These should be communicated consistently to pupils: at the start of a new sequence of learning (setting out the overall learning goals for the sequence of lessons); at the start of each lesson (setting out the individual goals for the lesson; in the context of the overall sequence learning goals); and at regular points in each lesson.

As we discussed in previous chapters, it can be difficult to get learning intentions right and the advice varies, whether you are consulting the academic literature, learning toolkits or observing school practice. Sometimes such advice is contradictory. Even the terminology tends to differ, with terms such as aims, objectives and outcomes used in a variety of ways. We have certainly seen schools where all three are used in lessons, with little contribution to achieving clarity. Having said this, the bottom line is that you and your pupils need to be clear about the essential knowledge and skills to be developed across your sequence of lessons. This emerges from our articulation and alignment phase and must also be realised in everything that is done in and between the sequence of lessons.

Intentions that facilitate formative assessment

Whichever format you choose to articulate your learning intentions, there are three principles rooted in research into effective assessment practices that should guide your decisions about what goes into these.

a) Your intentions should allow pupils to demonstrate what they have learned in a qualitative rather than a quantitative way

Many learning intentions are often too heavily based on developing a certain amount of knowledge rather than a quality of knowledge. Take, for instance, the following learning intention:

'To know the causes of the English Civil War.'

It would be difficult for teachers to be able to establish meaningful formative feedback opportunities that might follow on from tasks that deliver this intention. It's unlikely that a history teacher would spend a whole lesson running through some key causes; it's far more likely that the teacher would get pupils to consider different types of causes, assessing each for the greater contribution to the war finally breaking out. However, this intention fails to capture those essential historical skills and therefore leads to a disconnect between the intention, what pupils do and the feedback that could help them develop their understanding and skills in relation to the historical concept of causation. Therefore, the future use of this knowledge may well be very limited. A better objective such as 'To be able to assess and justify the importance of different causes of the English Civil War' would at least allow feedback on the ability to consider relative importance in causation.

By thinking forward to the type of qualitative, formative feedback that learners might be able to take from individual lessons as a result of the intention being realised, you will certainly find that the purpose of the lesson is clearer and the learning transfer is more obvious throughout the sequence. If feedback can only be given on how much has been learned, arguably something is not quite right with the intentions and the activities that exist to deliver these.

b) Learning intentions should be de-contextualised

Clarke (2005, 2008) and Wiliam (2011) have both discussed the problems with contextually rooted learning intentions. Take, for example, the following learning intention:

'To learn about what an MP does.'

This learning intention is clearly rooted in a specific context, in this case the UK Parliament. While the context certainly provides a hook for learning, linking to something that the pupils may know something about and will have some opinions on, this hook may well become the focus rather than broader conceptual or skills learning. The measure of such a learning intention can only really be in terms of the quantity of new knowledge (knowing the things they do) rather than deeper learning measured through a conceptual understanding of democracy, or the skills they used to identify the knowledge.

Here are two more ways of framing this same learning intention:

Better:

'To be able to outline the responsibilities of elected representatives in a democracy.'

(Context: MPs in Parliament)

Best:

'To be able to use an enquiry technique in order to identify the responsibilities of elected representatives in democracies.'

(Context: MPs in Parliament)

The second intention is better. It is now decontextualised and it can broaden pupils' understanding of the role and responsibilities of all elected representatives in democracies, allowing further knowledge transfer. It also allows the possibility for transfer across contexts, so pupils can draw from wider national or international examples. However, when thinking about the type of feedback the pupil could receive in order to improve in the subject, it is still limited because it tends towards the ability to recall a number rather than the way they went about identifying this new knowledge. This is the key difference with the third intention. The addition of the process of enquiry into the intention suggests qualitative feedback can now be given that can develop a pupil's citizenship skills as well as developing their effective conceptual understanding of democracy. It is easy to break this intention down into process success criteria and for any feedback to be used by the pupil in future enquiry work (and not only in citizenship lessons). It also makes it easier for the teacher to identify the kinds of learning opportunities they need to provide and the kind of feedback the pupil can receive whilst they learn. Importantly it also makes it easier for pupils to monitor their own progress throughout the lesson. In the context of medium-term planning, it would be easy to break down different enquiry processes throughout the sequence of lessons, with an overarching learning intention for the sequence including the development of enquiry skills. Each lesson could develop a different enquiry skill, so that by the end of the sequence they could become very proficient at using enquiry in future units of work.

In history teaching, many teachers use an enquiry-led approach to medium-term planning, using an enquiry question that underpins the sequence of lessons and is shared with pupils at the start of the sequence of lessons. In an example in *Teaching History* (Wrenn, 2004) teachers developed a medium-term plan with the enquiry question of 'Joan of Arc: saint, witch or warrior?' A key focus of the enquiry was developing pupils' ability to understand the historical concept of interpretation over time, building to a final assessed extended piece of writing in which the pupils engaged with this question. Each lesson deliberately built in tasks that developed their ability to analyse interpretations in order to recognise the reasons why there might be differing interpretations of Joan of Arc, including the impact of historical context. This also included ongoing peer assessment and self-reflection over the learning journey, encouraging pupils to be aware of their learning about historical interpretations as a general concept as well as the specific history relating to Joan of Arc.

c) Your intentions should clearly align with success criteria

Success criteria provide teachers and pupils with a tangible way of recognising whether intentions are being achieved. Often success criteria are discussed in relation to individual lessons or tasks, but we believe it is possible for teachers to identify broad indicators of success underpinning an entire sequence of lessons that can also be shared with pupils. Sometimes these are expressed as 'learning outcomes'. However you choose to do this, it is worth spending time trying to identify how you as a teacher and your pupils can gauge successful progress in line with learning intentions across the sequence of lessons and in relation to individual episodes of learning.

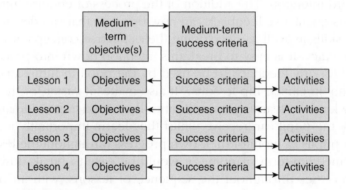

Figure 7.1 Linking medium-term intentions and success criteria to individual lesson intentions and success criteria

In Figure 7.1, overarching medium-term learning intentions and success criteria are used to frame the learning intentions and success criteria for individual lessons. In turn, these frame the learning that the pupils engage with.

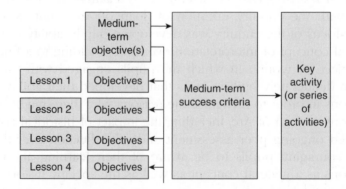

Figure 7.2 Linking medium-term intentions to an overarching medium-term success criteria and key activity

In this example, medium-term success criteria underpin the entire sequence of lessons. These success criteria, in turn, align with a key activity (or maybe a series of nested activities that make up an overall activity). This might be an extended project over a number of weeks, with pupils using the criteria to support their learning and to check their progress across lessons. It's possible to have a hybrid of the first and second examples, where the teacher breaks down overall success criteria that relate to a key activity into lesson-sized chunks, for instance to aid differentiation.

The decision for you as a teacher is whether you use overarching success criteria for an entire sequence of lessons that connect with individual lesson success criteria or whether you use this overarching success criteria as a way of gauging the successful development of knowledge and skills throughout (possibly even in relation to the production of one task that is worked on in every lesson). No one way is better than the other; the approach you take will relate to the phase or subject you work in, what you are trying to achieve with learners (which might relate to broader learning intentions outside of your immediate subject such as developing effective group work) and so on. While many schemes of work may break down the sequence into lesson by lesson steps (Figure 7.1), we have also seen in Chapter 6 how projects or science investigations can develop over several lessons and therefore might benefit from a single success criterion.

Product and process success criteria

It is also worth distinguishing between types of success criteria. There is the type of success criteria that focuses on what knowledge, skills or combination needs to be demonstrated at a set point, for example in a completed project report, as well as criteria that help pupils to know if they are on the right track. The former is often referred to as 'product success criteria' and the latter 'process success criteria'. Some teachers may choose to combine the two, while others might separate these out. However you choose to do this, it is usually the case that you can involve pupils in the generation of the success criteria.

Suzanne, a secondary school English teacher, developed a successful medium-term plan that used hip-hop music in order to develop her year 8 (12 to 13-year-old) pupils' ability to recognise and use poetic devices. Having learned and identified different poetic devices in a couple of lessons, Suzanne set a task in which her pupils were to write the lyrics to their own hip-hop tune. First, the class listened to Nas's 'Blood Diamonds are Forever', following the words on a lyric sheet, and identified the key poetic features as well as the political and moral themes (notably around blood diamonds and hip-hop culture). From this, the class developed a product success criterion for their own tune. Suzanne then worked with the class to break this down into meaningful elements that could guide the process of writing the song. The class was a single-sex mixed-ability boys group, with a range of special needs and behavioural challenges. She felt it made sense to break the criteria down further to act as a clearer checklist of what they would need to do and to keep them on track.

Product success criteria

Your song will have:

- an issue that's important to you;
- clear distinctions between verses and chorus;
- a range of poetic devices used;
- consistent rhythm.

Process success criteria

When writing your song, you should:

- identify an interest that's important to you (for example, violence, war, homelessness);
- choose the poetic devices you wish to use (look back at examples in your book);
- decide how many verses you are going to have and how many times you go back to the chorus;
- decide how many lines you are going to have in each verse;
- decide how you are going to make the verse different from the chorus;
- tap your verse out to check the rhythm.

The process success criteria worked effectively because they allowed the pupils not only to check that they were on track, but they also meant that over the course of a couple of lessons Suzanne could get the boys to give informal feedback to each other about the progress they were making. The pupils did a practice run with a partner who gave them informal feedback which they then used to finalise their lyrics.

Clarke (2008) argues that her research has shown that the use of success criteria is always more effective when generated by pupils. This is because in constructing criteria they are being cognitively challenged to identify the important knowledge, understanding and skills that need to be demonstrated. There are some prerequisites to this, some of which are shown in Suzanne's example above. First, modelling becomes important to develop a 'nose for quality' (Claxton, 1995). This might be done through looking at an existing piece of work, be it a piece of art, footage of a tennis player demonstrating a certain technique or a way of presenting findings from an experiment. Alternatively, it might be through comparing or contrasting two pieces of work of differing quality.

Alasdair, one of our interviewees who has worked as a primary and secondary school history teacher, discussed how looking for features of quality allows pupils to transfer learning across subjects:

> It's a way of getting the kids to think about the content of what makes something good and if you think about what makes something good you start identifying criteria and how you can make it better. And you start evaluating. It's an amazing way to get kids thinking … so we are doing 'Dulce et decorum est'. What makes a good poem? I started off with what makes a good poem, and they suddenly reeled off all this stuff from their English lessons and I'm going, 'Ah, yes, I love all of this'. Then I had to say … OK that's English, they're looking at metaphors, etc., what I'm interested in is about how poems help us to understand history so we'll have a list of their success criteria that comes from English and added stuff like is it realistic historically, how does it connect with things how they were, etc., adding in historical stuff. So it just gives you what I think is called transfer skills that you do in your history lesson, builds upon skills used in other lessons, so it's not some kind of foreign country where you don't really know what history is about, where you do all these things you do in English, you do in geography, etc. I did a lesson on graphs about causes of the war and we considered what makes a good graph. They said, 'Ah, this is maths'. And because we discussed what makes a good graph suddenly the history makes sense to them because they saw what they were doing. If I suddenly said, 'We're going to do some graphs', they'd have struggled with the graphs.

What is interesting about Alasdair's approach is that it does much to promote the transferability of learning across the curriculum and, in doing so, helps pupils to understand essential knowledge and skill connections across different areas of learning. This potentially allows them to engage in a more effective, deeper way with learning tasks. It also highlights the possible power in different curriculum areas working together to support knowledge transfer.

Second, Clarke suggests that the teachers in her research found using common success criteria was more effective than using differentiated criteria for types of learners. This is because 'it constrained pupils, lowered their expec-tations and overloaded short-term planning' (Clarke, 2008: 93). Instead, the teachers found that using differentiated activities and support to help all pupils meet the criteria was more effective. In Suzanne's class, weaker pupils found it more challenging to decide how to break down their issues into aspects they could develop through their lyrics. Her solution to this was to use mind-mapping techniques with those pupils. Likewise, she deliberately increased the challenge level for her more able pupils to ensure they used more com-plex poetic devices.

A third prerequisite in constructing effective success criteria is that they should avoid over-specificity. Specifying every single aspect we are looking for in a learning endeavour may well stifle creativity or prevent pupils dem-onstrating their knowledge and skills in a completely different way. It is also possible that pupils might do very well on the task at hand, but that there is little opportunity for pupils to transfer this learning to new topics and con-texts; the gains are therefore short-lived. A way around this can be to develop broader success criteria that specify the desired knowledge and skills that need to be demonstrated and can be demonstrated in a variety of ways. Pupils can even develop their own criteria based upon how they are going to show their knowledge, for example by choosing to show it via a speech, a poster, or song. As Wiliam states, 'we need to realize that process success criteria are, at the same time, both constraints *and* affordances for our students, and so we need to be thoughtful about how we frame them and how we use them' (Wiliam, 2011: 64).

Engineering effective classroom discussions, activities and learning tasks that elicit evidence of understanding

We now turn to Wiliam's second strategy to consider how teachers use a range of techniques to probe the extent to which learning intentions are being achieved. As we discussed earlier, assessment is a process, despite the fact that some reduce that process down to the summative assessment of a single task or test. While a sequence of learning is being delivered, a lot of implicit and explicit learning is hopefully being achieved in line with learning inten-tions. While the tasks pupils undertake give us some snapshots of whether learning is happening, they only tell part of the story. As Black and Wiliam (1998) state:

> Tasks have to be justified in terms of the learning aims that they serve, and they can only work well if opportunities for pupils to communicate their evolving understanding are built into the planning. Discussion,

observation of activities, marking of written work, can all be used to provide the opportunities, but it is then important to look at, or listen carefully to, the talk, the writing, the actions through which pupils develop and display the state of their understanding.

We use the analogy of using a fishing rod to catch fish in an ocean, compared with using a net. The point is that using single, end-of-unit assessment tasks to capture the entirety of learning will inevitably lead to limited information for teachers and pupils on what has been learned and next steps. If learning intentions are well established and linked to effective success criteria under-pinning a sequence of lessons, a range of formal and informal evidence can be used, drawn from extended tasks, class discussions involving probing questions, snapshots and personal reflections on progress. Sometimes these will be planned (for example tasks including self and peer assessment oppor-tunities), while at other times they may emerge from the learning process (for example using questions to probe understandings). All, if carefully thought about, can provide rich assessment information.

Capturing evidence of learning outside of 'assessment tasks'

A range of formative assessment techniques has been developed for teachers to be able to gauge the progress that pupils are making towards intended learning outcomes. For instance, a recent technique promoted by Dylan Wiliam is the use of lolly sticks, which can be used either to randomise who answers questions in lessons or indeed to include questions on the sticks which pupils randomly pick out. Some teachers use a traffic light system, where pupils give themselves red, amber or green against learning intentions. Teachers can use follow-up questioning to probe this further.

While these might seem rather informal, to be successful they need to have emerged from a carefully planned approach that seeks to identify evidence of learning. Sometimes these techniques are used in a well-intentioned way, but it can be difficult to see how the techniques lead to effective feedback for teachers or pupils because there isn't a clear link to what the pupils or teacher will do next. At other times, teachers might not probe or capitalise on the knowledge that pupils already have, or indeed the misunderstanding they might be bringing to the classroom.

Rebecca, a secondary modern languages teacher interviewee, discussed a medium-term plan in which a key focus was to develop her year 9's (13 to 14-year-olds) reading strategies in French. The context of the sequence was comparing life in three Francophone countries: Haiti, Ivory Coast and France. In her medium-term plan, she designed it so that every lesson and activity linked to the broader intention of developing these reading strategies. Her first lesson started with a discussion of vocabulary and structures that were going to be used throughout the sequence of lessons, allowing her to gauge what her pupils might be bringing to this new unit:

> *In a scheme of work like this in Year 9, you'd want to get the pupils to use their prior learning to predict the language and verbs they are likely to use in the scheme of work. Prediction is a useful thing and they quite like it. So, for example, we're going to be using words about what it's like to live in a hot country, so what words will we use, like 'sun'. This is a way of assessing what they know and don't know. If you identify they don't know some vocabulary, you know you are going to have to revise weather. Using texts can help to stimulate this revision, particularly if they can't produce the language themselves.*

In a similar way, our maths teacher interviewee Rubia discussed with us the use of mini-tests at the start of a sequence of learning:

> *When you come back to Shape 2 you might start with a mini-test to check and recall the main concepts. Those mini-tests are just as much for them as for you, so they can see what they have remembered. If they didn't know something, I wouldn't necessarily spend the next two weeks teaching it again, I might just say, well this is something that needs to be learnt and you do need to make sure to go away and do that – this would depend on whether or not it is a conceptual misunderstanding.*

In both cases, it is interesting that the teachers use these initial tasks to identify fundamental knowledge that pupils need to have if they are to be successful in the sequence of lesson. They differentiate between essential knowledge, which is so important that they will need to take remedial action, and other knowledge, which can be developed during the sequence. Without building in an opportunity to capture this from the start, it is likely that the rate of progress for the pupils would be affected. It also highlights the need for flexibility and adaptability; if pupils have a weak understanding of a key concept, teachers will need to build in additional time and space which they may not have initially planned for.

Capturing ideas and conceptions at different points in a sequence of lessons can also help pupils to reflect on their learning journeys and the progress they have made over time. In the 'Joan of Arc' history medium-term plan we discussed earlier, pupils were asked to summarise a personal interpretation of Joan of Arc which they popped in envelopes. At the end of the sequence they re-opened these and in their extended pieces of writing had to reflect upon their own shifting interpretations.

Dave, our science teacher interviewee from Chapter 6, looked for a range of ways to capture the learning journey that his pupils were making. As we discussed there, one approach he used was to use a reflection booklet at the end of each lesson. There were two specific reflective questions that pupils had to answer: What have I learned in this lesson? and, How do I know I have been successful in this lesson? Dave saw these as:

> ... *really good reminders for me to think about what they actually learned. This gave me an opportunity to write short comments for them to look at next time, and to intervene if there were misunderstandings. This really did prompt a dialogue ... I had a quick look through in between lessons and that enabled me to involve students in the starting phase of each lesson and ask the right people to contribute.*

A simple five-minute activity such as this involved pupils not only in judging their own progress against learning intentions, but also in thinking about the process that helped them make progress. Additionally, it provided Dave with an opportunity to address any key issues as well as involving the pupils in setting up the next step towards achieving the learning intentions for this sequence of activities.

Effective classroom questioning can play a significant role in identifying the type and quality of learning that is happening within and across lessons. However, research has shown in the past that the type of questioning asked in lessons is often focused on managerial considerations or those requiring closed answers. In their own study Brown and Wragg (1993) showed that less than 10 per cent of teacher questions promoted new learning, while Cazden (2001) has shown how pupils are often given one second or less to process questions and to respond. Wiliam (2011) argues that 'there are only two good reasons to ask questions in class: to cause thinking and to provide information for the teacher about what to do next' (Wiliam, 2011: 79)

While this isn't the place to discuss questioning techniques in detail, there are some principles which certainly do help with assessment. First, and crucially, the thing that many student teachers take a while to realise is that not every question needs to be answered at whole-class level. Using techniques like 'think/pair/share' (where pupils are given time on their own to consider their response to a question, before pairing up with a partner to consider this collectively before offering their response to the whole class) builds in sufficient time for individual pupils to think and respond, before engaging in comparative discussion. Likewise, questioning in small groups can also lead to greater participation and synthesis of ideas than that achieved at class level. Rubia, our maths teacher, indicates that such approaches also improve collaboration between learners:

Recently, through working with our primary transition teacher I have also incorporated a good deal more paired discussion work; paired talk between students for one minute to share ideas is a powerful tool – it breaks up the lesson but it also gives them an opportunity to check in with each other. I used to say, check your answers with someone, but the change in language to have a discussion has helped them to work better as a team.

Second, when questioning is done at the class level, using randomisation techniques (where random pupils are selected, often using interactive whiteboard software or lolly sticks), no-hands up questioning, hot-seating and mini-whiteboards, can help to get a better sense of what a range of pupils has actually learned. Leahy et al. (2005) suggest that by using these techniques at appropriately planned 'hinge-points', so called because the lesson might change direction depending on the feedback offered, 'teachers can make their teaching more responsive to their students' needs in real time'. Therefore, 'hinge-point questions provide a window into pupils' thinking and, at the same time, give the teacher some ideas about how to take the pupils' learning forward' (2005: 4).

Third, thinking more carefully about the type of response that (a) will help us to identify the kind of learning going on and (b) that will make pupils really think is likely to provide teachers with a greater grasp of what is actually happening with their pupils. Paul and Elder (2006) have developed a range of nine types of 'Socratic questions' that may help teachers in engaging pupils in deeper conversations about learning. They include the following types:

Questions of clarification

What do you mean by that? Can you give me an example?

Questions that probe purpose

What is the purpose of ...?
What was your purpose when you said ...?

Questions that probe assumptions

What is being assumed? Why would somebody say that?

Questions that probe reason and evidence

What are your reasons for saying that? What criteria do you base that argument on?

Questions that probe implications and consequences

What might be the consequences of behaving like that?
Do you think you might be jumping to conclusions?

Questions about viewpoints or perspectives

What would be another way of saying that? How do Hannah's ideas differ from John's?

Questions about the question

How is that question going to help us? Can you think of any other questions that might be useful?

Questions that probe concepts

What is the main idea we are dealing with?

Questions that probe inferences and interpretations

Which conclusions are we coming to about ...?
On what information are we basing this conclusion?

Using 'assessment tasks' to capture evidence of learning intentions

We are troubled by the idea of end-of-unit assessment tasks because, as we discussed earlier, they don't capture the entirety of learning against intentions. Worse still, there has been a tendency in recent times for schools to have teachers summatively assess these every half-term in order to generate a level or grade. These then get added to data management information systems, the number or grade becoming the sole measure of the success (or failure) of the individual pupil. This is hardly surprising, given the role of these numbers and grades in school inspections, school league tables and so on. However, we strongly feel that these do very little to help children develop as learners because the formative aspect tends to be overshadowed by the summative judgement. Nevertheless, there are ways to make sure that end-of-unit assessment tasks do have a formative feedback loop built into them from the start and that any judgements that teachers have to make at the end of the sequence of lessons are based upon both the task and the other sources of evidence taken across the sequence. Obviously, any task that is set has to be rooted in the learning intentions and success criteria set out for the medium-term plan.

Alasdair, our history teacher interviewee who has taught in primary and secondary schools, has developed an approach that puts the end-of-unit summative assessment task at the heart of everything he does throughout the sequence of lessons. The task is made clear to pupils from the start of his sequence of lessons and early on will develop the success criteria that underpin the task. He discussed with us two medium-term plans that he has developed for a primary and a secondary school that embody this approach.

For his primary history medium-term plan, Alasdair developed a local history topic based on Arsenal Football Club's Emirates Stadium, as the school was very close to the stadium. Alasdair worked with the headteacher of the school to develop a unit of work that aimed to explore a central question around 'What stadiums tell us about our society', with the Emirates Stadium being compared by pupils to the Coliseum in Rome:

> *The project would have two stages to it, first that we'd look at the Coliseum and get them excited about the history of Rome and the Coliseum and what went on at the Coliseum and then we would use that to compare the Coliseum to the Emirates. We'd do a site visit of the Emirates and then go and look at the key features of the Emirates and then talk about the fact it's football whereas the Coliseum had gladiator games, getting them to think about what that tells us about society in terms of leisure and entertainment.*

The headteacher was keen that the unit developed the pupils' literacy skills, so the eventual plan (and assessment task) was to get the pupils to produce a leaflet about the Emirates Stadium. However, there would be a formative task part way through that was to produce a leaflet about the Coliseum. This would provide pupils with a 'dry run' at the final task, on which they would receive both peer and teacher feedback. At the start of the unit, pupils looked through leaflets from historical sites, identifying key features and turning these into success criteria in groups. The various criteria were brought together to form one that underpinned the first leaflet, then this was slightly altered for the final assessment task as the context had changed.

Alasdair says that his approach to planning has changed in recent times, partly in response to the need for teachers to show tangible progression, but also since he has developed a deep interest in assessment for learning. So all of his planning now starts with the end of unit assessment task that is expected in his school and he works backwards, ensuring that pupils know what they are aiming to produce at the end, co-developing success criteria with them, building in a practice run using a task that requires them to use similar historical concepts and skills using the criteria, building in feedback on this and then using this to produce a final assessment task. Alasdair also uses his iPad, projected up onto the whiteboard, to show differing responses to the interim task and the final task, which can then be compared against the criteria by the whole class. This approach also allows for possible modifications of the success criteria, where pupils might have shown some original insight or technique that would be beneficial for other pupils to adopt.

Dave's approach to assessment appears more traditional, in the sense that the pupils completed a test in the medium-term plan he shared with us. Nevertheless, he demonstrates a wariness about relying too much on the end of unit test:

> *I think constructing a good test is incredibly difficult, but I would tend to start with closed questions, with some key words provided and gradually open up the questions and reduce the prompts. I also try to ensure tests include opportunities to use skills that have been taught, such as analysing data. I think a quick 20-minute test at the end is fine, if it really focuses on the core of what you want them know, and the results for this class were good. So the scheme of work was successful on that measure. But whether it was also successful in setting them up for future learning will remain to be seen. I'd like to think with the right prompt – remember the experiments with the lemons for example or the story with the frog – they can connect back to those narratives.*

Dave is using this test as a snapshot of the core knowledge learned in the sequence of lessons, which he connects to the other evidence of learning he has been collecting throughout (such as his reflective diaries and, as we will see, his rapid formative assessment approach). In talking about connecting with narratives, he is also using meaningful tasks that can root the type of conceptual knowledge that he will engage learners with in the future.

Adapting for learning: providing, facilitating and developing feedback opportunities and cycles that move learning forward

For pupils to make progress, teachers need to ensure that feedback is delivered to them in a timely way, highlighting aspects of quality and areas for development. This will impact on future planning, since teachers must provide pupils with opportunities to use this feedback to drive future learning. Harlen uses a thermostat analogy to emphasise the importance of this feedback for teachers:

> Just as feedback from the thermostat of a heating or cooling system allows the temperature of a room to be maintained within a particular range, so feedback of information about learning helps ensure that new experiences are not too difficult nor too easy for students. (2006: 104)

Much of what we have already discussed will provide teachers and pupils alike with feedback on the impact of learning, which then can be used to make effective adaptations to teaching and learning. As part of your medium-term planning, it's useful to identify the kind of feedback you are hoping to provide and utilise, as well as making decisions about who is best placed to make these adaptions: you, other pupils or the pupil themselves. Hopefully your medium-term plans will allow for a mixture of all three, with feedback not just emerging from what you say and do. Sadler (1989) has suggested that at the start of any new learning opportunity, a 'feedback gap' exists which teachers will need to plan to fill. The gap exists because the teacher has a sense of the attributes of quality they are looking for in pupils' work which pupils may not share. Thus, to promote effective learning:

> The indispensable conditions for improvement are that the student comes to hold a concept of quality roughly similar to that held by the teacher, is able to monitor continuously the quality of what is being produced during the act of production itself, and has a repertoire of alternative moves or strategies from which to draw at any given point. In other words, students have to be able to judge the quality of what they are producing and be able to regulate what they are doing during the doing of it. (1989: 121)

Table 7.1 Levels of feedback (adapted from Hattie, 2012: 116)

Levels	Teaching considerations/aspects	Feedback to learners
Task	How well the task has been performed; does it meet the product success criteria?	Where am I going? What are my goals? What does success look like?
Process	What are the key aspects and strategies that are needed to ensure learning can be demonstrated/a task can be completed? Might consider a range of approaches that can lead to the same substantive ends.	How am I going? What progress is being made towards the goal?
Self-regulation	The self-monitoring and assessment of the process and/or task. Learner knowledge of the necessary knowledge required to do this well.	Where to next? What activities need to be undertaken next to make better progress? What adaptations will be required next time?
Self	Personal evaluation and affect about the learning.	

Sadler's suggestion also highlights the different stages at which feedback might drive learning onwards. Hattie (2012) has identified four levels of feedback, which are summarised in Table 7.1.

The following sections identify the different levels of feedback that teachers can use to make adaptations. These adaptations can be 'in the moment' changes and interventions that you will introduce immediately during the lesson in response to pupil performance. Additionally, these adaptations might be made in the medium term as you return to your plan and revise aspects of it in the light of evidence of pupil progress.

Task-level feedback

This correlates with the type of feedback offered in relation to products of work, and as such relates to the production of product success criteria outlined earlier. As Hattie states, this tends to be the most common form of feedback in classrooms and can take the form of 'corrective feedback' or 'knowledge of results'. It also tends towards specificity, in relation to the qualities of the task, but is not always generalisable and applicable in future learning endeavours unless teachers can provide specific feedback that identifies such aspects. However, such task feedback is critical and serves as 'a pedestal on which processing and self-regulation can be effectively built' (Hattie and Timperley, 2007: 91). With the right criteria and teaching approaches, pupils (through self and peer assessment) and teachers can be involved at this level. In medium-term planning, the feedback provided in tasks is useful but only if (a) it happens in a timely manner and (b) you build in time for pupils to make use of the feedback that they are provided with. For instance, Alasdair's 'dry run' approach allows transferability of feedback to the process that pupils use in their final assessment task. Leaving substantive feedback to the end of a sequence of learning means that it is less likely that pupils can make productive and timely use of this feedback, unless teachers plan a way of revisiting this later on.

Process-level feedback

This type of feedback relates to the processes involved in the completion of the task, again linking to the process success criteria discussed earlier. Hattie suggests that this level of feedback is crucial because it can help to 'develop learning strategies and error detection, cueing to seek a more effective information search, recognising relationships between ideas and employing task strategies'. Furthermore, 'feedback at this process level appears to be more effective for enhancing deeper learning than it is at the task level, and there can be a powerful interactive effect between feedback aimed at improving the strategies and processes, and feedback aimed at the more surface task information' (Hattie, 2012: 119). Crucially, feedback on processes can be longer lasting and transferable across different contexts and curricular areas. Again, such feedback can be provided by teachers and pupils alike. Teachers can use evidence from this feedback to make suitable adaptations in planning, for instance where pupils are finding particular processes difficult to engage with.

Leahy and Wiliam (2009) have discussed the power of what they term 'rapid formative assessment'. This approach lends itself to feedback at the process level, while pupils are working towards a learning intention, and involves anything that allows for rapid intervention to correct misunderstanding, clarify ideas and concepts, facilitate a consideration of alternative approaches, apply ideas and processes to new contexts and so on. Their research suggests 'when formative assessment practices are integrated into the minute-to-minute and day-by-day classroom activities of teachers, substantial increases in student achievement – of the order of a 70 to 80 percent increase in the speed of learning – are possible' (Leahy and Wiliam, 2009: 15).

Dave indicates how he uses a rapid formative assessment approach in his own lessons through focused conversations with pupils:

In class I maximise the time available to talk to children about their ideas, and they are more likely to listen to me when I'm having a conversation with a small group. It's immediate diagnostic assessment with immediate corrections. The most important thing in a lesson is to get a student to explain why a bulb lit up, not assume that because they have done it, they must be a certain level.

Both Suzanne and Alasdair discussed their use of process success criteria stickers. These stickers used pre-set qualitative feedback statements that linked to the process success criteria set by the class. Such an approach is not only time-effective (saving time writing similar types of feedback in pupils' books) but also because it makes crystal clear where improvements need to be made (short and longer term). Alasdair explains that:

[On the stickers] you highlight all the relevant steps for them to move on, so … it's much clearer to them about what steps they need to take to show progress. In my experience with the kids they'll come up with a phrase like 'Oh yeah, I now realise what I have to do' because the quality of your feedback is good. The comments on my feedback stickers are much more prescriptive than ever before.

Alasdair also explains how he tries to separate feedback that is about learning in the subject from broader learning targets:

I have some stickers which are about basic literacy, you must use paragraphs, punctuation … I will sometimes put two stickers in their books. One is about the history stuff and one is the generic stuff. The trouble is you can end up overwhelming people … if they've written a good essay with punctuation errors, which do you focus on? For our purposes the quality of the history is crucial but at some point you might like to say this is what will make it smoother. So you've got to weigh it up.

This raises a good point about the kinds of feedback we offer to pupils and decisions about the point at which we give subject versus broader feedback that supports their learning. Some teachers may choose an approach in which they incorporate a broader learning intention (for example accuracy of punctuation) within the overall success criteria.

Rebecca discussed how she made use of peer assessment in order to support the process of annotating texts to identify grammatical structures. In her medium-term plan, she included a task where pupils were given different texts to analyse as a group. These texts were blown up in size and stuck on large pieces of sugar paper. Pupils were given highlighter pens and markers and used these to analyse the different structures being shown and to comment on these. Once they completed this, they visited other groups. This fulfils two functions. First, they give peer feedback to each group on the process they used, further annotating the texts on the sugar paper where necessary (thus providing instant feedback). Second, they also make a note of new structures and vocabulary they've picked up from the process of comparing and contrasting their own analysis with that of others.

You need to clarify the points in your sequence where pupils have to engage in specific processes. This will happen during the establishment of success criteria, but it can't stop there. Pupils need to make active use of the criteria and this happens when the criteria guide the types of things that they do as well as the supportive conversations that they have with each other and with you. Pupils may also find difficulty with aspects of the process; for instance, they may struggle with an aspect of research. In which case, you may need to make adaptations to your overall plan to tackle this. Helping pupils to recognise the steps needed to achieve something and the fact that we may have certain strengths and weaknesses in relation to these can develop a growth mindset, because we can focus our feedback on the weakest aspects and provide opportunities to improve on these in a timely manner. While the learning challenge remains, pupils are likely to be much happier when they can improve specific elements and see the transferability of the area in which they've developed.

Self-regulation-level feedback

This level relates to the pupils monitoring their own progress and evaluating their own learning. This self-monitoring can 'enhance pupils' skills in self-evaluation, provide greater confidence to engage further with the task, assist in the pupil seeking and accepting feedback, and enhance their willingness to invest effort into seeking and dealing with feedback information' (Earl, 2003: 25). Earl suggests that pupils' engagement in assessment in this way also develops vital life skills, encouraging them to take responsibilities for issues that they have control over. This level suggests that the sequencing of self-assessment needs to be carefully thought out. For instance, there may be times (as at the end of a sequence of learning) when it is better for pupils to self-assess once they have received feedback from their teachers and peers which they can compare against their own reflections of progress. At other points, possibly when completing a task, it might be useful for pupils to do a quick self-assessment and then to compare this with another pupil's assessment of their work. This would likely promote a useful discussion (which might draw out misconceptions about the process or the product), allowing for immediate corrective action to be taken.

Rebecca takes this self-regulation approach further in her modern languages medium-term plan. At the start of the sequence of lessons she facilitates the pupils setting personal learning targets for developing reading strategies, one of her key learning intentions:

> *I would start off their first lesson saying the next five or six lessons we are going to be developing reading strategies and you would make links to other areas like English in doing this as well. You would spend time in the lesson talking about reading strategies and what we mean by this, and part of that would be differentiated in that you would talk about the kinds of targets they might want to set for themselves so by the end of the six lessons this is what I want you to be better at ... That would need to be a thread you'd need to keep repeating or dropping back into conversations with pupils throughout the unit of work.*

Such an approach is powerful, in that it recognises that pupils will have differing starting points in relation to this topic and it also provides pupils with ownership over both the journey and the destination. Rebecca saw this as particularly important, as languages were taught in mixed-ability classes and the school required all pupils to study languages to the age of 16. Pupils can consistently assess their progress against their own targets during the sequence and at the end, and can consider the types of adaptations they might make in their future learning.

Self-evaluation at the medium-term planning level needs to play an active role in helping pupils to recognise the essential skills and knowledge they should develop in the future. This identification of next-step targets can also provide you with feedback on the extent to which pupils have actually understood and achieved your overall intentions. If self-evaluation happens at regular points during the sequence of lessons, this feedback is all the more useful to you.

Self-level feedback

This type of feedback is essentially praise, rather than focused on the learning. Hattie suggests that this type of feedback, while important in helping pupils to feel valued as people, should be kept separate from feedback on learning. Research has shown that this type of feedback has little impact on learning and in some cases can have negative impact, especially when pupils are less successful in meeting learning intentions. Teachers sometimes use praise to mitigate against features that have been less successful. While this is somewhat understandable, it is probably better to provide a positive learning environment in which pupils feel there is trust and recognition for the efforts they put in, whilst leaving this aside from the kind of feedback that teachers offer. Dweck (2006) also makes the point that praising pupils for the intelligence they have shown can have a negative impact on their motivation. This tends to manifest itself when they are faced with a difficult learning obstacle, leading to a possible drop in confidence since they believe that they don't have the intelligence to deal with the issue. Instead feedback should identify the process strategies used and the impact these have had on what they have accomplished (Clarke, 2008: 22). Overall, as Hattie states, 'the message is that for *feedback* to be effective in the act of learning, praise dissipates the message ... if you wish to make a major difference to learning, leave praise out of feedback about learning' (2012: 121).

Using feedback to make adaptations for learning

It should come as no surprise that your planning needs to allow space to respond to evidence from feedback, whether this is from your own assessment, or from pupils' peer or self assessment. Alasdair discussed with us how he leaves around three lessons spare in a scheme of work of 18 lessons. He sees leaving this space as important, because it provides space to deviate from the plan when needed to fill gaps in understanding, to pick up on areas that are worth exploring because pupils have a genuine interest in a particular aspect, and to spend time analysing pupils' work as a class in order to identify quality features (for instance during the mid-sequence assessment tasks or at the end of the sequence). Similarly in her politics A level classes, where new terminology and abstract concepts are common, Vicky planned time every week to deal with queries, misunderstandings or problems and ensured there was at least a part of every third lesson where no new content was planned.

There is little point building in thoughtful ways for pupils to receive feedback, if they then can't respond to that feedback. This takes us back to our issues with end-of-sequence assessment tasks. Teachers can spend a lot of time giving high-quality diagnostic feedback, but if pupils have little opportunity to respond to it, the gains from the feedback are likely to be limited. This will be compounded if the focus is on the product of learning rather than the process used to get there. Planning to use a blended array of feedback techniques at task, process and self-evaluation levels ensures that you deliberately prompt yourself and your pupils to respond to the feedback at the point of learning.

 Activity

For this task, we want you to use a pre-existing medium-term plan to identify assessment opportunities, the feedback that would follow and the adaptations that might be made.

1. Start with the medium-term learning intentions and compare these with individual lesson intentions. Are these aligned? Is there room to ensure these could be better aligned? Is it possible to identify success criteria that underpin the whole lesson sequence?
2. Now consider the learning opportunities and activities. Will these help to deliver medium- and short-term intentions? Are there opportunities for pupils to recognise quality learning and to turn this into process and product success criteria? What might be included in such criteria?
3. Now consider the feedback opportunities. What are the activities and focused questions that are asked of learners to help them move their learning forward in relation to the overall medium-term intentions? How will the teacher give their own feedback, for instance on finished products?
4. Finally, consider the adaptations that might follow. What might the evidence of learning show? How might this affect the overall medium-term intentions and the next lessons in the sequence? What might they need to consider changing for the next time the medium-term plan is revised and taught?

Conclusion

Thinking about assessment in terms of feedback in relation to learning intentions and success criteria helps to emphasise the point we made earlier in this chapter, that assessment is a process and not a thing we do to learners. It is perfectly possible to use a range of interesting learning activities with pupils across a medium-term plan, providing these activities (a) help pupils to achieve learning intentions; (b) have success criteria underpinning them to help pupils recognise how to achieve quality; (c) provide pupils with feedback from teachers and peers on how successful they have been; and (d) allow pupils to use this to evaluate their own learning progress. As we have shown, spending time helping pupils to understand both what is expected of them and the process that can get them to that point is time much better spent compared with filling lessons with lots of factual knowledge to acquire, because the longer-term learning gains will be greater and more transferable. Likewise, building sufficient time and flexibility into your planning allows you and your pupils to respond to feedback through a variety of adaptations and ensures that learning can be consolidated. These adaptations not only show that you are actually focusing on the impact of your teaching, they also help pupils to understand that you too are a learner who is engaged in self-assessment that drives your own practice forward.

Further reading

Black, P., Harrison, C., Lee, C. Marshall, B. and Wiliam, D. (2003) *Assessment for Learning: Putting it into Practice*, Maidenhead: Open University Press.
This book traces the Assessment Reform Group's work in implementing Assessment for Learning in schools. It provides a useful summary of their ideas as well as lots of examples from teachers about how they adapted their practice.

Clarke, S. (2008) *Active Learning through Formative Assessment*, London: Hodder.
Shirley Clarke's work is very accessible and practical, and really clarifies how to effectively integrate assessment into teaching and learning activities.

CHAPTER 8

MOVING ON

At the end of the final chapter you will:

- understand the overall process of medium-term planning;
- be able to critique examples of medium-term plans in progress and identify strengths and areas for improvement;
- be able to check your own work in progress to identify areas for improvement.

Introduction

In many ways this has been a book that has set out to state the obvious. We do not apologise for that; rather we see it as part of what experienced teachers must do in order to bring to the surface the accrued knowledge they have developed over years of practice. This is one of the most difficult aspects of initial teacher training for experienced practitioners, because eventually that knowledge becomes an almost invisible part of the background to how teachers work. When new teachers observe an experienced teacher ask a question of a particular pupil, it is impossible to observe the complex thought processes and judgements that enable that particular question to emerge, for that particular pupil, at that particular time. The chances are that the teacher will not be fully aware of what they have done or why. In reality, they draw on an in-depth knowledge of the curriculum (what knowledge must be learned?), attainment standards (what level is expected?), assessment mechanisms (how should pupils be able to demonstrate their knowledge?), the nature of the knowledge being learned (what is this knowledge and how does it fit into the topic/subject as a whole?), the pupil's own strengths and weaknesses (what have they found easy or difficult? What would help them to move on?), and the class as a whole (what do other people in this room need to hear to consolidate their learning?). All of this is balanced in the blink of an eye and the question emerges and has its impact on the learning. In reality, the new teacher seeking to replicate this process would take so long to work through these stages that the moment would be lost and the time for the question would be long gone. Therefore the student teacher's learning process in the classroom in reality is marked by approximating, guessing and having a go. Over time, the 'guesstimates' get better, fewer questions miss the mark, lessons start to feel more fluid and pupil learning becomes more evident.

Medium-term planning is helpful precisely because it provides a space for the new teacher to engage with the parameters for the learning: the curriculum, exam syllabus, pedagogic traditions, assessment requirements, prior attainment and so. In doing so it reduces the requirement to 'wing it' in class. Simply put, if you do not have the knowledge at your fingertips, you will have to make the time to work through it in advance so that you can still teach in an appropriately informed manner. By thoroughly planning in advance you can reassure yourself that you will be consistently focusing on the right kind of learning, in a sequence you have judged to be most likely to promote progression, and in a way you hope will be engaging for your pupils. The process of constructing a medium-term plan also enables you to have conversations with colleagues, in order to collect ideas for teaching before you enter the classroom. A good plan is helpful both because most of the potential teaching errors have been eradicated at the planning stage, and because it frees you to focus more on the day to day interactions with pupils, gauging how the learning is progressing and how you can finesse the plan to make it even better.

As we said at the outset, some of this learning comes quickly to many student teachers, but sometimes people experience blocks about part of the process, and sometimes it is just difficult to get started. Chapters 4–7 have outlined one way in which you could start from scratch and end up with a medium-term plan. In reality there is no simple linear process to follow; you might start at the end (perhaps with the exam paper) and work back-wards, or you might start with a fantastic activity (perhaps with the offer of a wonderful school trip) and work outwards from there. The point is that by the time you start teaching you should have brought all these dimensions of the planning process into alignment, so that you understand how the plan hangs together as a coherent account of learning. Figure 8.1 presents a summary of the elements that moves away from the idea of a linear process and demonstrates much more clearly how these elements are all required to support the pupils' learning. In the following section we pull together the key messages from each chapter into a checklist. This is designed to help you review your progress and ensure that you have considered all the essential elements before you start teaching.

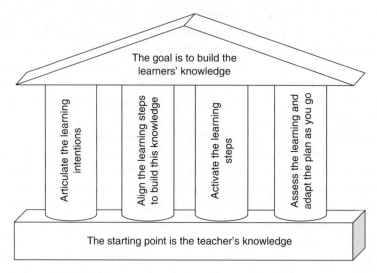

Figure 8.1 Summary of the five As

Summary and checklist

Articulation

It is essential that before you start teaching you have developed a clear definition about your learning intentions. In Chapter 4 we presented a process which started with expanding a list of all the relevant aspects of learning that could be included in a topic, and then suggested how you might reduce this to a manageable plan. We want to emphasise that every good plan is deliberately shaped out of an infinite range of possibilities. There is nothing 'obvious' about what is to be learned, how it is to be learned, or what contribution this chunk of learning makes to the broader project of education. Teachers have to engage with the process of prioritising, forging connections between important elements and discarding some possible aspects of the topic. This is a creative and profoundly intellectual exercise and requires knowledge of the subject to be taught, of the broader curriculum, of the values and purposes of education and of the learners.

1. Do you have a secure knowledge of the subject area you are going to teach?
2. Do you know how and why this subject content is important in the subject itself?
3. Do you know how and why this subject content is important in the school curriculum?
4. How does this subject content connect to other content that has already been taught?
5. How does this subject content connect to other content that will be taught in the future?
6. What key concepts or ideas are essential in order to understand the subject area?
7. What common errors or misconceptions are likely to arise in relation to this subject area?
8. How will the pupils' understanding of this subject area be assessed?
9. What skills will be developed alongside the subject area?
10. How will you divide up the subject area?
11. What are you not going to cover in this medium-term plan?
12. What is the big picture or the big question?

Alignment

Once you have established the parameters of your medium-term plan, clarified what's in, what's out and what the destination is, you have to define a route to move from here to there. In Chapter 5 we demonstrated this with a range of examples from experienced colleagues, each of whom had developed a clear learning journey for their class. The point we wanted to make was that the medium-term plan has its own shape and sequence, beyond the obvious linear logic of having to teach one lesson after the other. We argued it was important to have this map of the learning journey clear in your mind because it provides the route that enables learners to move on from one stage to the next. The correct sequence should enable you to move pupils on, from current levels of attainment to higher levels, by building their knowledge and understanding, so that by the end of the sequence they know more and can do more than they could at the outset. As with the first stage, this requires you to have an in-depth understanding of the subject to be taught and some understanding of the ways in which children make sense of the topic and build their own knowledge and skills. We argued that you should pay particular attention to the beginning and end of the medium-term plan to try to ensure the learning doesn't sit in a bubble on its own, but is connected with prior learning and provides a sound foundation for future learning. Ultimately, the learners are building their own knowledge of the topic in their minds, constructing and revising schemas, and moving closer to your mature understanding of the subject.

1. Do you have a clear statement about what you want pupils to achieve by the end of the sequence?
2. Do you have a rationale for your selected starting point?
3. Will your starting point enable pupils to see how this new learning connects to prior knowledge?
4. Will your starting point help to secure pupil motivation and engagement?
5. Do you have a clear sequence of steps leading from the starting point to the final destination?
6. Can you explain clearly how these steps connect together?
7. Is it possible to explain the logic of this sequence clearly to pupils?
8. Do you know where prior learning is being re-used?
9. Do you know where completely new content is being introduced?
10. Can you explain how new learning is being subsequently re-used, consolidated and extended?
11. Are you clear on where existing skills are being re-used?
12. Are you clear on where you are planning to extend and develop pupils' skills?

Activation

In Chapter 6 we turned to consider the learning activities that would help pupils to develop their skills and understanding. We argued that the clarity of purpose that you should have achieved as a result of the first two stages of planning will enable you to be very purposeful in your selection of appropriate learning activities. The learning activities are not just vehicles for the content, they also help to develop pupils' knowledge, skills and values, and so we also wanted to emphasise that this stage of the planning is more sophisticated than simply looking at a list of teaching activities and selecting a nicely varied range. Here we considered activities that stretched beyond the confines of single lessons and which must be planned across the medium-term, such as projects, investigations or experiential learning. We also focused on learning activities which 'front-load' the learning, helping learners to connect prior learning and future learning within meaningful schemas.

1. What range of activities do you plan to use?
2. Why have you selected these activities?
3. What activities have you decided not to use?
4. Why have you excluded some kinds of activities?
5. Is there an overarching logic to your selection of activities (for example, enquiry, co-operation, discovery)?
6. How do the activities enable pupils to improve (rather than simply re-use) their skills in this area?
7. Does each activity clearly relate to one of more of your learning intentions?
8. Are more challenging activities preceded by easier ones?
9. How do these activities help pupils to build their independence as learners?
10. How do these activities help to promote a positive classroom atmosphere?
11. What types of activities do you think will be easy for the pupils in this class?
12. What types of activities do you anticipate will be more challenging for these pupils?
13. Which activities will you find more difficult as a teacher?
14. What resources will be required for each activity?
15. Are you clear about how you will manage the processes involved in each activity?
16. Are you clear about how you will teach the pupils to complete each activity, and therefore teach the process?

Assessment and adaptation

In Chapter 7 we considered some of the principles that underpin effective assessment practice and applied these to the process of medium-term planning. Having discussed the importance of de-contextualised learning intentions, we argued that framing learning intentions by way of process and product success criteria helps pupils to recognise the key features of successful learning and provides opportunities for essential feedback to pupils. We made the point that aligning all the learning activities in a medium-term plan with learning intentions helps to provide you with a rich source of evidence on which to make formative assessment judgements. We also considered the different levels of feedback and their purposes both in helping pupils to progress and in providing you with evidence of the impact of learning that you can use to make further adaptions in the moment of learning and as you review how well your medium-term plan is working.

1. Are your learning intentions for the sequence and individual lessons de-contextualised and focused more on qualitative rather than quantitative learning?
2. Have you translated your medium-term learning intentions into medium-term success criteria?
3. Can your medium-term intentions and success criteria underpin the entire sequence of lessons or do you need to break these up further?
4. Have you identified the essential learning activities and tasks that will provide you with evidence of the extent to which learning intentions are being achieved?
5. What approaches will you take to co-generate process, or product, success criteria with your pupils?
6. What kinds of questions will you need to ask pupils to help promote learning in relation to the intentions?
7. How will you use pupil responses to questions and tasks to make adaptations?
8. How will feedback be given to pupils at task and process level and who will give this feedback?
9. How are you facilitating and building on self assessment throughout the sequence of lessons?
10. What adaptations could you make at the point of learning and in reviewing your overall medium-term plan?

Case studies

As we wrote this book we tried out our ideas on the experienced teachers we interviewed. They responded positively to the five As model and were able to discuss their own practice easily under those headings. We also tried out the ideas on student teachers and had the opportunity to summarise the model in lectures to primary and secondary student teachers across a range of subjects as well as in smaller workshops working with subject specialist secondary student teachers. In this section we present the work of two groups of student teachers at Queen's University Belfast. For each group there is a summary of the scheme of work they were developing for secondary school history and a brief explanation about how their thinking developed through their discussions. They were a mixed group of RE, politics and sociology teachers who were all studying history as a subsidiary subject as part of their PGCE. The medium-term planning workshops took place over four half-day sessions after their first school placement. Alongside sessions run by local teachers and a visit to the local museum, the students had about four to five hours in total to start with a blank sheet of paper and come up with a workable medium-term plan.

Activity

Read though the examples and think about areas of strength and possible areas to develop further.

Because of the limitations of time and space the students were not able to write down all aspects of their plans and so some of your suggestions may simply relate to areas that are not explained here, for example overall intentions and success criteria.

Try to come up three strengths of the plan and three areas for further detail/clarification.

Compare your priorities with someone else and with the checklist.

Group 1: Holocaust

The first group chose the Holocaust as a particularly difficult area of history that they may have to teach. As a group who were not history specialists they were aware this would take some careful thought and preparation. Figure 8.2 shows their initial brainstorm in the first session. You can see they were just noting down all the possible ideas they could think of that might be relevant. In the event, many of these ideas were later ignored or left relatively undeveloped. During their discussion, however, they became increasingly interested in the challenge of making the Holocaust relevant to young people now that the generation who experienced it was almost entirely dead. They did not just want to teach it as a harrowing historical event, but wanted to be more deliberate about what they could expect young people to learn from the study. This led them into thinking about why the Holocaust happened, how it could be explained in human terms. This in turn led them to think about their own background as sociology graduates and the kind of perspectives they brought to such difficult questions. And this finally led them to the focus on the theme of obedience to authority. Table 8.1 shows how these ideas finally emerged in the scheme of work they proposed at the end of the workshops.

Group 2: Home Rule for Ireland

The second group was formed of politics graduates and their initial brainstorm was very focused on the details of the political history they had learned at school and university (Figure 8.3). They were stuck at this level for quite some time and discussed whether to structure the scheme of work around a straightforward chronology or to divide the lessons to consider a series of key people. Eventually, as facilitator of the workshop, I (LJ)

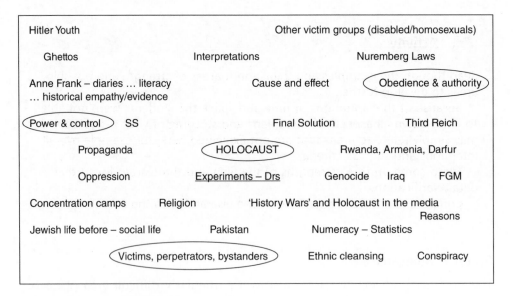

Figure 8.2   Initial brainstorm

intervened and asked them if there were any significant themes that they understood as the basis of the explanation as to why Home Rule was so significant yet failed to be implemented. This enabled the group to think about the content at a slightly more abstract analytical level and this informed the structure of the actual scheme of work they proposed in Table 8.2. This was an interesting process precisely because all the members of the group seemed to have stopped at the same point – simply adding more facts into the brainstorm and then looking for a way to sequence the content. They devised the themes that structured the final plan; it just needed a naïve outside question from someone who didn't know as much about the history of Ireland to encourage them to think about how this information could be 'chunked up' thematically.

A call to action ...

Medium-term planning may not seem like the most exciting aspect of teaching at first glance, but hopefully by now you will have developed an appreciation of the possibilities of doing it well. We are convinced that the more time that teachers spend on getting their medium-term plans right, the greater the learning gains for pupils and they'll find they spend far less time having to develop individual lessons. As we conclude our book, we'd like to leave you five key messages that collectively may serve as a call to action.

Table 8.1 Medium-term plan: did 'obedience to authority' allow the Holocaust to happen?

Target group: 13 to 14-year-olds
Duration: 6–8 weeks, 2 hours per week

Unit description: Using Milgram's iconic obedience to authority experiment as the initial stimulus material, this scheme of work approaches the Holocaust from a different angle. Focusing on media, power and control, the topic seeks to motivate students to investigate often overlooked aspects of the history

Cross-curricular links: English, Citizenship, Geography, ICT/Media Studies, Sociology, Politics

Week/Topic	Learning Objectives	Suitable Pupil Activities	Appropriate Resources	Assessment Opportunities
One: Conceptual Context	How does Milgram's study link to the Holocaust? Establish what is meant by the term power. Who ultimately holds the power?	Template for both individual and group feedback on Milgram's study. Case studies on power using modern examples of CEOs, businessmen, etc. to explore what makes a powerful person.	Milgram's obedience to authority experiment video clip. BBC Modern version of the experiment. Graham Norton's "Red Chair".	Formative assessment through oral feedback. Find examples of power from a newspaper/magazine: entertainment, political and sporting examples.
Two: Skills	Historical empathy. Cause and effect. Historical interpretations.	Fishbone on causes of First World War. Source work: written sources, media sources and visual sources. Silent discussion: use a picture on a large page of the Ukraine Riots/the Troubles/Night of the Long Knives. Each group will then give feedback on their views on what is happening in of these pictures.	Previous schemes of work from their last two years of history: be aware of what students have already studied and what historical skills they have already acquired.	Formative assessment through oral feedback. Formative assessment from the silent discussion.

(Continued)

Table 8.1 (Continued)

Week/Topic	Learning Objectives	Suitable Pupil Activities	Appropriate Resources	Assessment Opportunities
Three: Theme 1 Jewish life	The context in which Hitler came to power. Why did no one stand up for those being oppressed?	Question worksheet to go with the video. Investigating Jewish society fact file and research project on the jobs of Jews/position they held in society.	Video clips of Hitler at the time/Jewish life/German life.	Anne Frank Twitter diary: What would Anne Frank tweet if she was in hiding in the twenty-first century?
Four: Theme 2 Experiments	Why do we obey certain people in power? Who was Dr Mengele?	Case studies on Dr Mengele's experiments. Diary of how you would feel if you were Dr Mengele's assistant.	*Brown Eyes, Blue Eyes* (video clip). *The Debt* (film). *Dr Mengele's Assistant* (book).	Formative assessment through discussion and feedback.
Five: Theme 3 Propaganda	How the media attempted to control people. Propaganda v. stereotypes: an old phenomenon?	Using newspapers (*Guardian, Sun, Daily Mail*), students are to pick out stories and decide whether they are gossip or actual news stories. Analysing videos/posters of the time.	Propaganda videos. Posters. *Education for Death* (Disney propaganda cartoon). *The Sound of Music* (film).	Designing their own propaganda poster for recruitment during the Second World War.
Six: Genocide	How does obedience to authority affect us in modern society? Case studies on modern genocide.	Case studies on: Rwanda, Darfur, Armenia. Research project on modern genocide. The success criteria for this are the three skills which were outlined in Week 2.	*Hotel Rwanda* (film). Success criteria worksheet detailing the skills they need to cover in their research topic. *One Million Bones* (website).	Peer and self assessment of the research projects.

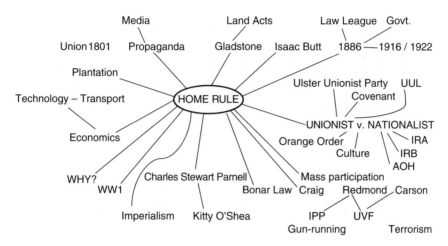

Figure 8.3 Initial brainstorm

See yourself as an active interpreter of the curriculum

As we discussed at the beginning, teachers have huge power over the way that any curriculum is realised. A curriculum is not meant to be a list of things to tick off, but instead it is a constructed description of knowledge and skills deemed to serve a particular purpose at a specific point in a child's life. While a curriculum may include a little or a lot of detail, it does not define the entirety of learning in any subject. As a teacher you should use the power that you have to critically interpret any curriculum and to frame the learning that follows on from that interpretation in meaningful ways for the pupils you are teaching. This happens in the way you map out learning across a phase of schooling (for example across a Key Stage) and at the medium-term level.

See yourself as a creator of meaningful learning opportunities

In critically interpreting any curriculum and translating it into long- and medium-term plans, you also have the opportunity to bring the learning alive through the way you deliver new knowledge and develop pupils' skills. Challenge yourself to find new ways for pupils to meet your carefully planned learning intentions through meaningful learning moments that leave pupils thinking and able to act upon what they've learned. In our experience, schools are often awash with technology these days that could, with a bit of planning, be put to effective use, but all too often the lessons feel to us little different from those we experienced as children. We have to consider the world that our children are entering as young adults and the way that their learning can be effectively harnessed in it.

Table 8.2 Medium-term plan: why was Home Rule not successful by 1914?

Target group: 14 to 15-year-olds (GCSE)
Duration: 6 weeks, 2 hours per week

Week	Learning Intentions	Activities	Assessment
1 Introduction to Nationalism.	Define Nationalism. Outline the three strands of Nationalism. Predict effect of competing Nationalisms.	Circular mind-map (groups). Post-it note activity.	Formative assessment – oral feedback.
2 Introduction to the reasons why Home Rule was unsuccessful. Nationalism in Ireland and the Catholic Church.	Outline why Nationalists in Ireland wanted Home Rule. Establish how Nationalists tried to achieve Home Rule. Evaluate role of Catholic Church in Nationalist politics (significance).	Card sort activity. Poster. Past paper essay question.	Essay question for homework. Oral feedback.
3 Strengths of Unionism.	Distinguish between Unionism and Nationalism in Ireland. Outline how Unionists try to abolish Home Rule. Evaluate strengths of Unionism 1886–1914.	Source work: Unionist and Nationalist propaganda. Case study of UVF.	Feedback from source work. UVF work booklet.
4 The role of the British government.	Establish the different countries within the British empire. Outline the role played by the British government. Predict what would happen to the rest of the empire if Ireland gained Home Rule.	Map work. British Foreign Secretary activity.	Class discussion. Feedback on activity.
5 World War 1.	Outline Unionist and Nationalist reactions to the First World War. Discuss whether the First World War was the most important factor in Home Rule not being successful?	Role play: Unionist/Nationalists. Design anti- or pro-First World War propaganda.	Questioning. Feedback from propaganda activity.
6 Evaluation.	Construct a PowerPoint of one of the four themes. Evaluate the significance of each theme.	PowerPoint. Walking debate.	Peer feedback from PowerPoint and debate.

Recognise planning should be dynamic and responsive

As we have taken pains to say throughout, the five As approach is one in which medium-term planning is an ongoing process. Medium-term planning is not about developing a template, filling it in and sticking in on a shared network drive. It is about a process in which your initial mapping of learning intentions and activities responds to the realities of delivery and the impact they are having on pupil progress. It requires an ongoing review throughout its delivery and then time to evaluate it in relation to the range of evidence that learners provide.

Appreciate that medium-term planning is best as a collaborative endeavour

As we have suggested, the international research shows that a feature of high-performing education systems is the commitment they have to collaborative planning and reflection. Teaching is always better when teachers can come together to decide on what needs to be learned in the medium term, the approaches that can deliver that learning and the way that they can assess the impact. It ensures that everyone knows the principles, has a stake in these and knows the kinds of things they should be asking themselves to judge success. Just as medium-term planning is dynamic and responsive to the impact it's having on pupils, so it should also reflect the experiences of the teachers that deliver it.

Remember that outstanding learning is more important than 'outstanding' lessons

Finally, we return to our message from the very beginning of this book. Our aim should be outstanding learning over the medium and long term that challenges learners, builds meaningful knowledge and develops transferable skills. The true measure of 'outstanding' is the progress that pupils make over a longer period of time rather than a lesson. Schools need to liberate themselves from a culture that measures teacher quality through comparatively tiny pockets of time and rewards a 'performance' rather than the vast range of evidence of pupils' longer-term progress. This includes analysing medium-term plans and engaging teachers in reflective conversations about their planning, reviewing pupil work (where possible) and identifying how knowledge and skills are developing, as well as talking to pupils, getting them to identify their own learning journeys and the impact of the teaching on this. School-management teams also need to consider how to support teachers to improve the way they conceptualise and deliver learning over longer periods of time.

We envisage intelligent teachers grappling with the nature of the knowledge and skills to be learned, conceptualising it in various ways and engaging in professional conversations about how best to proceed. Medium-term plans respond to your pupils' abilities and needs, your own developing knowledge and capacity, and the context in which you teach. It stands to reason that these plans can only ever be provisional and that they should always be dynamic documents. There is a quote that is questionably attributed to Abraham Lincoln along the lines of, 'If given five minutes to chop down a tree, I'd spend the first two minutes sharpening the axe.' While you might be itching to get into the classroom to teach lessons, we are suggesting that the equivalent preparation for teachers is to thoroughly plan so that your classroom efforts are incisive, efficient and effective. Otherwise, your teaching practice may become, like the woodcutter with a blunt axe, tedious, full of unnecessary exertion and ultimately unproductive.

Further reading

Hattie, J. (2012) *Visible Learning for Teachers*, Abingdon: Routledge.
This is fast becoming a classic text for teachers and offers ideas that might help you extend your repertoire of teaching strategies in the light of broader research evidence.

Kohl, H. (1971) *36 Children*, Harmondsworth: Penguin Books Ltd.
This book is a moving account of someone discovering how to teach children who have been let down by the education system. As part of his journey, Herbert Kohl discusses the ways in which he developed bespoke plans to meet his learners' needs and interests.

REFERENCES

Abrams, F. (2005) Cognitive conundrum, *Times Educational Supplement*, 20 May.

Allen, D. (2001) *Getting Things Done*, London: Penguin.

AQA (2012) *English Literature GCSE Specification 9710*, Manchester: AQA.

ARG (1999) *Assessment for Learning: Beyond the Black Box*, Cambridge: Cambridge School of Education.

Arriassecq, I. and Greca, I. M. (2012) A teaching–learning sequence for the special relativity theory at high school level historically and epistemologically contextualized, *Science and Education*, 21(6), 827–851.

Aunola, K., Leskinen, E., Lerkkanen, M. and Nurmi, J. (2004) Developmental dynamics of math performance from preschool to Grade 2, *Journal of Educational Psychology*, 96(4), 699–713.

Ausubel, D. P. (1963) *The Psychology of Meaningful Verbal Learning*, New York: Grune & Stratton.

Ausubel, D. P., Novak, J. S. and Hanesian, H. (1978) *Educational Psychology: A Cognitive View* (2nd edition), New York: Holt, Rinehart & Winston.

Bangs, J., Macbeath, J. and Galton, M. (2011) *Reinventing Schools, Reforming Teaching*, Abingdon: Routledge.

Banham, D. (2000) *King John: Teachers' Resource Book*, London: John Murray.

Barber, M. and Mourshed, M. (2007) *How the World's Best-performing School Systems Come Out on Top*, London: McKinsey & Company.

Barlex, D. (2005) The centrality of designing: an emerging realization from three curriculum projects. Paper presented at the PATT15 Conference – Technology Education and Research: Twenty Years in Retrospect, Eindhoven, the Netherlands.

Biggs, J. (1996) Enhancing teaching through constructive alignment, *Higher Education*, 32, 347–364.

Biggs, J. (2003) Aligning Teaching and Assessment to Curriculum Objectives, available online at: www.ucl.ac.uk/teaching-learning/global_uni/internationalisation/downloads/Aligning_teaching (accessed 17 November 2014).

Black, P. and Wiliam, D. (1998) *Inside the Black Box: Raising Standards through Classroom Assessment*, London: King's College London.

Black, P., Harrison, C, Lee, C., Marshall, B. and Wiliam, D. (2003) *Assessment for Learning: Putting It Into Practice*, Maidenhead: Open University Press.

Bloom, B. S., Engelhart, M. D., Furst, E. J., Hill, W. H. and Krathwohl, D. R. (1956) *Taxonomy of Educational Objectives: the Classification of Educational Goals. Handbook I: Cognitive Domain,* New York: David McKay Company.

Brown, D. and Clement, J. (1991) Classroom teaching experiments in mechanics, in R. Duit, F. Goldberg and H. Niedderer (eds) *Research in Physics Learning: Theoretical and Empirical Studies,* Kiel, Germany: IPN, 380–397.

Brown, G. and Wragg, T. (1993) *Questioning,* London: Routledge.

Bruner, J. (1960/1977) *The Process of Education,* Cambridge, MA: Harvard University Press.

Bruner, J. (1961) The act of discovery, *Harvard Educational Review,* 31, 21–32.

Bruner, J. (1978) The role of dialogue in language acquisition, in A. Sinclair, R. J. Jarvelle and W. J. M. Levelt (eds) *The Child's Concept of Language,* New York: Springer-Verlag.

Butcher, C., Davies, C. and Highton, M. (2006) *Designing Learning from Module Outline to Effective Teaching,* Abingdon: Routledge.

Cazden, C. B. (2001) *Classroom Discourse: The Language of Teaching and Learning* (2nd edition), Portsmouth, NH: Heinemann.

Chambers, P. (2008) *Teaching Mathematics: Developing as a Reflective Secondary Teacher,* London: Sage.

Clarke, S. (2005) *Formative Assessment in the Secondary Classroom,* London: Hodder Murray.

Clarke, S. (2008) *Active Learning through Formative Assessment,* London: Hodder.

Claxton, G. L. (1995) What kind of learning does self-assessment drive? Developing a 'nose' for quality, *Assessment in Education,* 2(3), 339–343.

Claxton, G. (2008) *What's the Point of School?* Oxford: Oneworld Publications.

Claxton, G., Chambers, M., Powell, G. and Lucas, B. (2011) *The Learning Powered School,* Bristol: TLO Ltd.

Coffield, F., Moseley, D., Hall, E. and Ecclestone, K. (2004) *Learning Styles and Pedagogy in post-16 Learning: a Systematic and Critical Review,* London: Learning and Skills Research Centre.

Concept to Classroom (undated) How does this theory differ from traditional ideas about teaching and learning? Available online at: www.thirteen.org/edonline/concept2class/constructivism/index_sub1.html (accessed 13 May 2014).

Connelly, E. M. and Clandinin, D. J. (1988) *Teachers as Curriculum Planners: Narratives of Experience,* New York: Teachers College Press.

Coultas, V. (2007) *Constructive Talk in Challenging Classrooms,* London: Routledge.

Dennison, B. and Kirk, R. (1990) *Do, Review, Learn, Apply: A Simple Guide to Experiential Learning,* Oxford: Basil Blackwell.

DfE (2014) *National Curriculum,* London: Department for Education. Available online at: www.gov.uk/government/collections/nation (accessed 27 July 2014).

Dunn, R. (1990) Understanding the Dunn and Dunn learning styles model and the need for individual diagnosis and prescription, *Journal of Reading, Writing, and Learning Disabilities International,* 6(3), 223–247.

Dweck, C. (2006) *Mindset: The New Psychology of Success,* London: Random House.

Earl, L. (2003) *Assessment as Learning: Using Classroom Assessment to Maximize Student Learning,* Thousand Oaks, CA: Corwin.

Edexcel (2013) *Specification: GCE Government and Politics. Issues 4,* Harlow: Pearson Education Ltd.

Ellis, V. (2007) *Subject Knowledge and Teacher Education: The Development of Beginning Teachers' Thinking*, London: Continuum.

Entwistle, N. (1988) *Styles of Learning and Teaching: An Integrated Outline of Educational Psychology for Students, Teachers and Lecturers*, London: David Fulton.

Fullan, M. (1993) Why teachers must become change agents, *Educational Leadership*, 50(6): 12–17.

Gagné, R. and Briggs, L. (1974) *Principles of Instructional Design*, New York: Holt, Rinehart & Winston.

Gardner, H. (2011) *Frames of Mind: The Theory of Multiple Intelligences*, New York: Basic Books.

Gillborn, D. and Youdell, D. (2000) *Rationing Education: Policy, Practice, Reform and Equity*, Maidenhead: Open University Press.

Ginnis, P. (2002) *The Teacher's Toolkit: Raise Classroom Achievement with Strategies for Every Learner*, Carmarthen: Crown House Publishing Ltd.

Glaser, R. (1966) Variables in discovery learning, in L. S. Shulman and E. R. Keislar (eds) *Learning by Discovery: A Critical Appraisal*, Chicago: Rand McNally & Co., 13–26.

Glevey, K. E. (2006) *Thinking and Education*, Leicester: Matador.

Goodson, I. (2000) Educational change and the crisis of professionalism (with Andy Hargreaves) in *Professional Knowledge, Professional Lives: Studies in Education and Change*, Maidenhead: Open University Press.

Gove, M. (2013) 'The Progressive Betrayal' Speech by Michael Gove to the Social Market Foundation, 5 March 2013. Available online at: www.smf.co.uk/media/news/michael-gove-speaks-smf/ (accessed 1/7/13).

Green, D. (2013) Michael Gove's planned national curriculum is designed to renew teaching as a vocation, *Spectator* blog article, 2 April 2013. Available online at: http://blogs.spectator.co.uk/coffeehouse/2013/04/michael-goves-planned-national-curriculum-is-designed-to-renew-teaching-as-a-vocation/ (accessed 13/05/14).

Grenfell, M. and Harris, V. (1999) *Modern Languages and Learning Strategies in Theory and Practice*, London: Routledge.

Gurlitt, J., Dummel, S., Schuster, S. and Nückles, M. (2012) Differently structured advance organizers lead to different initial schemata and learning outcomes, *Instructional Science*, 40(2), 351–369.

Hadjilouca, R., Constaninou, C. and Papadouris, N. (2011) The rationale for a teaching innovation about the interrelationship between science and technology, *Science and Education*, 20(10), 981–1005.

Harlen, W. (2006) On the relationship between assessment for formative and summative assessment, in J. Gardner (ed.) *Assessment and Learning*, London: Sage.

Hattie, J. (2009) *Visible Learning: a Synthesis of over 800 Meta-analyses relating to Achievement*, Abingdon: Routledge.

Hattie, J. (2012) *Visible Learning for Teachers*, Abingdon: Routledge.

Hattie, J. and Timperley, H. (2007) The power of feedback, *Review of Educational Research* 77(1), 81–112.

Hillocks, G. Jr. (1999) *Ways of Thinking, Ways of Teaching*, New York: Teachers College Press.

Hirsch, E. D (1987) *Cultural Literacy: What Every American Needs to Know*, Boston, MA: Houghton Mifflin.

Hurd, S. (1998). Too carefully led or too carelessly left alone? *Language Learning Journal*, 17, 70–74.

Husbands, C. (1996) *What Is History Teaching? Language, Ideas and Meaning in Learning about the Past*, Buckingham: Open University Press.

Hussey, T. and Smith, P. (2003) The uses of learning outcomes, *Teaching in Higher Education*, 8(3), 357–368.

Illeris, K. (2007) *How We Learn: Learning and Non-Learning in School and Beyond*, Abingdon: Routledge.

Ivie, S. D (1998) Ausubel's learning theory: an approach to teaching higher order thinking skills, *High School Journal*, 82(1). Available online at: http://imet.csus.edu/imet9/281/docs/ivie_1998.pdf (accessed 4 July 2013).

Jervis, K and Tobier, A. (eds) (1988) *Education for Democracy: Proceedings from the Cambridge School Conference on Progressive Education*, Weston, MA: Cambridge School.

Kamin, L. (1974) *The Science and Politics of IQ*, Potomac, MD: Lawrence Erlbaum Associates.

Kohl, H. (1971) *36 Children*, Harmondsworth: Penguin Books Ltd.

Kolb, D. A. and Fry, R. (1975) Toward an applied theory of experiential learning, in C. Cooper (ed.) *Theories of Group Process*, London: John Wiley.

Kranch, D. A. (2012) Teaching the novice programmer: a study of instructional sequences and perception, *Education and Information Technologies*, 17(3), 291–313.

Lamott, A. (1995) *Bird by Bird: Some Instructions on Writing and Life*, New York: Anchor Books.

Laurillard, D. (2012) *Teaching as a Design Science: Building Pedagogical Patterns for Learning and Technology*, Abingdon: Routledge.

Leach, J. and Scott, P. (2002) Designing and evaluating science teaching sequences: an approach drawing upon the concept of learning demand and a social constructivist perspective on learning, *Studies in Science Education*, 38, 115–142.

Leahy, S. and William, D. (2009) *Embedding Assessment for Learning: a Professional Development Pack*, London: Specialist Schools and Academies Trust.

Leahy, S., Lyon, C., Thompson, M. and Wiliam, D. (2005) Classroom assessment: minute by minute, day by day, *Educational Leadership*, 63(3), 19–24.

Lee, P., Dickson, A. and Ashby, R. (2001) Children's ideas about historical explanation, in A. Dickinson, P. Gordon and P. Lee (eds) *International Review of History Education (Volume 3) Raising Standards in History Education*, Portland OR: Woburn Press.

Leithwood, K., McAdie, P., Bacia, N. and Rodrigue, A. (eds) (2006) *Teaching for Deep Understanding: What Every Educator Should Know*, Thousand Oaks, CA: Corwin Press.

Meiring, L. and Norman, N. (1999a) Planning a programme of work, in N. Pachler (ed.) *Teaching Modern Foreign Languages at Advanced Level*, London: Routledge, 119–138.

Meiring, L. and Norman, N. (1999b) Planning an integrated topic, in N. Pachler (ed.) *Teaching Modern Foreign Languages at Advanced Level*, London: Routledge, 139–159.

Morgan, C. and Neil, P. (2001) *Teaching Modern Foreign Languages: A Handbook for Teachers*, London: Kogan Page.

Morrison, G. R., Ross, S. M., Kemp, J. E. with Kalman, H. K. (2007) *Designing Effective Instruction* (5th edition), Hoboken, NJ: John Wiley & Sons.

Novak, J. D. (1998) *Learning, Creating and Using Knowledge: Concept Maps as Facilitative Tools in Schools and Corporations*, Mahwah, NJ: Lawrence Erlbaum Associates.

Ollerton, M. (2006) *Getting the Buggers to Add Up*, London: Continuum.

Pachler, N., Barnes, A. and Field, K. (2009) *Learning to Teach Modern Foreign Languages in the Secondary School* (3rd edition), Abingdon: Routledge.

Papadouris, N. and Constantinou, C. (2011) A philosophically informed teaching proposal on the topic of energy for students aged 11–14, *Science and Education*, 20(10), 961–976.

Patton, A. (2012) Work that matters: the teacher's guide to project-based learning, London: Paul Hamlyn Foundation. Available online at: www.innovationunit.org/sites/default/files/Teacher%27s%20Guide%20to%20Project-based%20Learning.pdf (accessed 13 May 2014).

Paul, R. and Elder, L. (2006) *The Thinker's Guide to the Art of Socratic Questioning*, Tomales, CA: The Foundation for Critical Thinking.

Phillips, R. (2002) *Reflective Teaching of History 11–18*, London: Continuum.

QCA (2007) *English Programme of Study for Key Stage 3 and Attainment Targets*, London: QCA.

Raths, J. D. (1971) Teaching without specific objectives, *Educational Leadership*, April, 714–720.

Reigeluth, C. (1981) *An Investigation on the Effects of Alternative Strategies for Sequencing Instruction on Basic Skills, Final Report*. New York: Syracuse University.

Reigeluth, C. M. (1999) What is instructional-design theory and how is it changing? In C. M. Reigeluth (ed.) *Instructional-design Theories and Models (Volume II): A New Paradigm of Instructional Theory*, Mahwah, NJ: Lawrence Erlbaum Associates.

Rubin, J. (1990). How learner strategies can inform language teaching, in V. Bickley (ed.) *Language Use, Language Teaching and the Curriculum*, Hong Kong: Institute of Language in Education.

Ryle, G. (1949) *The Concept of Mind*, London: Hutchinson.

Sadler, D. R. (1989) Formative assessment and the design of instructional systems, *Instructional Science*, 18(2), 119–144.

Sadler D. R. (1998) Formative assessment: revisiting the territory, *Assessment in Education*, 5(1), 77–84.

Schön, D. A. (1983) *The Reflective Practitioner*, Aldershot: Ashgate.

Scott Douglas, A. (2014) *Student Teachers in School Practice: An Analysis of Learning Opportunities*, London: Palgrave Macmillan.

Seels, B. (ed.) (1995) *Instructional Design Fundamentals: A Reconsideration*, Englewood Cliffs, NJ: Educational Technology Publications.

Shayer, M. (2003) Not just Piaget; not just Vygotsky, and certainly not Vygotsky as *alternative* to Piaget, *Learning and Instruction*, 13(5), 465–485.

Shuell, T. (1986) Cognitive conceptions of learning, *Review of Educational Research*, 56(4), 411–436.

Shulman, L. S. (1986) Those who understand: knowledge growth in teaching, *Educational Researcher*, 15(2), 4–14.

Sipress, J. M. and Voelker, D. J. (2011) The end of the history survey course: the rise and fall of the coverage model, *Journal of American History*, 97(4), 1050–1066.

Smith, A. (1996) *Accelerated Learning in the Classroom*, Stafford: Network Educational Press.

Smith, P. L. and Ragan, T. J. (1999) *Instructional Design* (2nd edition), New York: Wiley.

Stenhouse, Lawrence (1975) *An Introduction to Curriculum Research and Development*, Oxford: Heinemann.

Sternberg, R. J. (1998) Abilities are forms of developing expertise, *Educational Researcher*, 27(3), 11–20.

Story, C. M. (1998) What instructional designers need to know about advance organizers, *International Journal of Instructional Media*, 25(3), 253–261.

Sweller, J., van Merrionboer, J. J. G. and Paas, F. G. W. C. (1998) Cognitive architecture and instructional design, *Educational Psychology Review*, 10(3), 251–296.

Tanner, H. and Jones, S. (2000) *Becoming a Successful Teacher of Mathematics*, Abingdon: RoutledgeFalmer.

Torrance, H. (2007) Assessment *as* learning? How the use of explicit learning objectives, assessment criteria and feedback in post-secondary education and training can come to dominate learning, *Assessment in Education*, 14(3), 281–294.

Training and Development Agency for Schools (TDA) (2007) *Developing Trainees' Subject Knowledge for Teaching*, London: TDA.

Trebell, D. (2013) Studying the effectiveness of conceptual design in secondary design and technology in England, *International Journal of Technology and Design Education*, 23(1), 23–50.

Tyler, R. (1950) *Basic Principles of Curriculum Instruction*, Chicago, University of Chicago Press.

Vygotsky, L. S. (1978) *Mind in Society: The Development of Higher Psychological Processes*, Cambridge, MA: Harvard University Press.

White, J. (1998) *Do Howard Gardner's Multiple Intelligences Add Up?* London: Institute of Education, University of London.

White, J. (2008) Illusory Intelligences? *Journal of Philosophy of Education*, 42(3-4), 611-630.

Wilhelm, J. D., Baker, T. N. and Dube, J. (2001) *Strategic Reading: Guiding Students to Lifelong Literacy, 6–12*, Portsmouth, NH: Boynton/Cook Publishers.

Wiliam, D. (2011) *Embedded Formative Assessment*, Bloomington, IN: Solution Tree.

Wineburg, S. (1997) Beyond 'breadth and depth': subject matter knowledge and assessment, *Theory into Practice*, 36(4), 255–261.

Wineburg, S. (2008) The role of subject-matter knowledge in teacher assessment, in L. Ingvarson and J. Hattie (eds) *Assessing Teachers for Professional Certification: The First Decade of the National Board for Professional Teaching Standards*, Oxford: Elsevier/JAI Press.

Wrenn, A. (2004) Making learning drive assessment: Joan of Arc – saint, witch or warrior?, *Teaching History*, 115, 44–51.

INDEX